ENVIRONMENTAL MOVEMENTS IN MINORITY AND MAJORITY WORLDS

A Global Perspective

TIMOTHY DOYLE

Rutgers University Press
New Brunswick, New Jersey, and London

Library of Congress Cataloging-in-Publication Data

Doyle, Timothy, 1960–
  Environmental movements in minority and majority worlds / Timothy Doyle.
     p.   cm.
  Includes bibliographical references and index.
  Contents: Introduction to environmental movements — Forest movements: environmental movements in the United States of America — Movements against mining: environmental movements in
the Philippines — Wilderness movements: environmental movements in Australia — Anti-roads
movements: environmental movements in Britain — River movements: environmental movements
in India — Anti-nuclear movements: environmental movements in the Germany — Conclusions to
environmental movements.
  ISBN 0-8135-3494-1 (hardcover : alk. paper) — ISBN 0-8135-3495-X (pbk. : alk. paper)
  1. Environmentalism.   I. Title.
    GE195.D76 2005
    33.72 — dc22

                                                                                    2004007529

A British Cataloging-in-Pu'blication record for this book is available from the British Library

Manufactured in the United States of America

Design by John Romer

CONTENTS

PREFACE

The rooster crows early in the majority world.

In November 1998 I woke to this familiar sound in the parish compound in Tampakan, a small town in trouble-torn Mindanao, a southern island in the massive Philippines archipelago. I was in Tampakan as part of an International Fact-Finding Mission (IFFM) into the operations of transnational mining companies in the Philippines. Over the past week we had held an intensive series of meetings with every possible sector of Philippine society to ascertain the impact of open-pit mining on Filipino people, as practiced by predominantly foreign companies. Today, we would visit a proposed mine site and interview company officials as to aspects of their environmental management regimes.

No sooner had I arisen and fulfilled my basic ablutions when I heard the bell of the church, beckoning people to the dawn service. I was not a regular church-goer in my own country, but following the ring of the bell seemed the most natural thing in the world to do. I entered the church. Despite the fact that it was a weekday and the sun had barely risen, the church was jam-packed. The priest saw me enter and publicly welcomed me. He began to talk of the impact of open-pit mining on the agriculture of Mindanao: the rice bowl of the Philippines. He spoke of the necessity of local people having control over their own resources, their own land. At the end of the service, countless people came up to me and gave me their blessing, pledging their solidarity with the IFFM's purpose.

It was a remarkably moving experience. In my own country the church had become removed from its people. But here in the outlying regions of the Philippines it still had purpose, defending people from the most recent form of colonialism: that imposed on the local people by transnational corporations from the affluent minority world. Sitting on a pew in Mindanao, I truly realized, for the first time, the enormous gulf between environmental movements in places like the Philippines and other countries in the less affluent world, when compared to those green movements which have emerged in advanced industrial nations. In the case of the latter, post-material or "higher order" concerns, such as wilderness values, have dominated agendas. In the majority world—where most people live—environmental movements fight for basic human *survival*. Indeed, this dichotomy between two worlds has framed this book.

This book is a celebration of the diverse experiences of environmental movements across the globe. It is based largely on my primary research as both an academic and an environmentalist across six countries. It is primarily written for all people who are interested in the dynamics and organics of green movements.

This book is dedicated to my youngest daughter, Matilda, my "mighty battle maiden."

Tim Doyle
University of Adelaide
September 2003

ACKNOWLEDGMENTS

As this book is largely written on my own experiences of environmental movements around the globe, there are many intellectuals and activists in these places who deserve enormous thanks—too many to list here. I have decided to bite the bullet (a more peaceful metaphor would be better!) and only nominate one person in each country from which my detailed case studies come. In the United States, much appreciation goes to Professor Tom Roy, Director of the Environmental Studies Program at the University of Montana. His humanity, enthusiasm, ability to cross-country sky over long distances without water, his cabin in the Great Bear Wilderness, and his jump-shot are truly valued. In the Philippines, Pastor Avel Sichon is simply an inspiration to many, though, I know, he shuns accolades directed at individuals. He taught me those simple political lessons that are life's most precious. In Australia, special thanks to Professor Len Webb, the son of a shearer's cook, who showed me the beauty and majesty of the tropical forests of North Queensland for the first time. In Britain, I particularly want to thank Dr. Brian Doherty of the University of Keele for his detailed and valued suggestions for this book's completion and for his passion for protest movements in the United Kingdom. In India, deepest and most heartfelt best wishes are accorded to Dr. Sanjay Chaturvedi, Director for the Study of Geopolitics at the University of Panjab, who first invited me to that wondrous and sacred place—India. Finally, thanks to Professor Dieter Rucht, Chair of Sociology at the Wissenschaftszentrum in Berlin, who I first met in Mannheim, Germany, in 1998, and who provided detailed comments on a paper central to this larger work's theme, and then edited a piece of my work with enormous thoroughness and clarity, making a rough diamond shine far brighter than it should be.

Thanks to Marcus Lane and Geoff McDonald for allowing me to publish a reworked version of the chapter "The Campaign to Save the Wet Tropics," which I contributed to their anthology, *Securing the Wet Tropics?* published by the Federation Press (2000). Similar thanks are accorded to John Elliot, my editor at University of New South Wales Press, for his permission to utilize sections of text found in chapter 4, which were previously written by myself and published in a book-length treatment: *Green Power: The Environment Movement in Australia* (2000). Finally, thanks are recorded to Hank Johnston, editor of *Mobilization: The International Journal of Research in Social Movements, Protests, and Contentious Politics,* for permission to develop some of my material now appearing in chapter 3, originally published as an article entitled "Environmental Campaigns against Mining in Australia and the Philippines" (vol. 7, no. 1, 29–42).

I would also like to take the opportunity to thank my friends, students, and colleagues in Politics and Environmental Studies at the University of Adelaide. Also, I wish to record the support of the Australian Research Council, which provided me with a small grant through the auspices of the University of Adelaide, in 1998, to formulate this work.

Finally, thanks to my family, most particularly my partner, Fiona, who continues to share her life with me, the most precious thing one person can give another.

ENVIRONMENTAL MOVEMENTS IN MINORITY AND MAJORITY WORLDS

INTRODUCTION TO ENVIRONMENTAL MOVEMENTS

Lobbyists in Washington raising campaign funds from large companies for United States congressmen in a deal to save the spotted owl from extinction in the Pacific Northwest of the country;

Direct Action activists in the forests of Idaho pouring sand into the gas tank of a bulldozer to prevent it from knocking any more old-growth forest down;

A priest preaching from the pulpit in Tampakan in the Philippines, pleading with his congregation to oppose the transnational mining company which has come into their midst;

"Green warriors," having taken an oath (*dyandi*) to fight "to the last drop of blood," moving silently through the forests of Mindanao before engaging in guerrilla conflict with the government military which is "clearing the way" for the company;

Australian aboriginal people in association with green activists from mainstream green NGOs (non-governmental organizations) attempting to get the Kakadu region of the Northern Territory listed as a World Heritage Area by lobbying international politicians and diplomats in Paris;

One hundred thousand people marching through the streets of Melbourne as part of a mass nationwide protest against uranium mining;

A band of young activists burying themselves beneath the ground in Hampshire, England, to impede the progress of road-building machinery which threatens to build a road through the mythical land of Camelot;

Catholics and Protestants meeting in a "safe house" provided by Friends of the Earth in Belfast, Northern Ireland, planning a campaign against the building of a motorway through shared communal space;

Small landholders and indigenous peoples linking hands, vowing to die by meeting the waters of the mighty Narmada River in India as it rises due to its damming, engulfing the villages and homes of a million people;

An international environmental non-governmental organization working with local Indian environmentalists in a desperate bid to save the last Bengali tigers which roam the earth;

"Hippies" entering the German Parliament dressed without suits and ties, attempting to change the ways in which Western parliaments operate and administrate;

Massive numbers of German anti-nuclear protestors dismantling railway tracks in their efforts to halt the transport of high-level nuclear waste from France to an "interim" waste repository at Gorleben.

Question: What on earth do these people have in common?

Answer: They call themselves environmentalists. They are part of environmental movements.

■ ■ ■

Environmental movements are amongst the most vibrant, diverse, and powerful social movements occurring today, across all corners of the globe. Their global distribution allows the researcher of these movements to range widely, to experience the multitude of ways in which different cultures engage in their political lives. This book is based on the premise that there is no one global environmental movement, but that there are many, and that the differences between these movements far outweigh their similarities despite the fact that most share the symbolic nomenclature of "environmental movement."

It was within environmental movements that a modern environmental sensibility was born in most countries. In the nations of the minority North, this generally began in the late 1960s and early 1970s; whilst in the majority South, the environmental agenda emerged forcefully in the late 1970s and throughout the 1980s. Without environmental movements there would be no "green" businesses or bureaucracies, no high-level United Nations conferences on global warming and population control, no governments which have created "greener" legislative frameworks relating to quotas on industrial pollution or limits on genetically modified foodstuffs.

To research and write a book on environmental movements is a bit like producing a work on "life, the universe, and everything." First of all, there are so many issues which fall under the symbolic rubric of "the environment":

air, water, earth, fire, and all the others in between. All of nature is often perceived and portrayed as part of the environment and, depending on where you come from, humans can also be understood to be part of nature. If this book began with a list of environmental issues, the book would finish before the list making was complete.

Secondly, environmental movements are types of social movements. There is a wealth of conflicting and fascinating theories on the emergence and reality of social movements. I have discussed some of these theories elsewhere (Doyle and McEachern 2001; also see Doherty 2002a) and do not have the space or the inclination to repeat this task here. For the purposes of this work, I have chosen to view environmental movements through the theoretical frame of *new social movements* (NSMs). It is tempting, on some occasions, to argue that NSM theory is more appropriate to describing the post-materialist movements of the minority world; whilst more homogenous, often class-based theories outlining earlier, more traditional social movements may be more suited for analyzing the green movements of the less-affluent majority world. There is some merit in this argument; but to adopt such polarized theoretical tools for analysis at the outset of this book would be too simplistic, and not particularly rewarding in a comparative studies sense. Instead, I have decided to persist with the NSM model, for, despite its imperfections, its general applicability to the phenomena I have experienced, both in the minority and majority worlds, is excellent.

Box 1.1 lists the key characteristics of NSMs. The new social movements, which champion environmental issues, are extremely diverse and multitudinous in the ways in which they pursue their politics. Social movements, by their very definition, are amorphous political forms, often undergoing rapid changes in their polity. They are living political collective identities, unable to be captured exclusively within the terms and conditions of formal and institutionalized political histories. Social movements usually include many non-institutionalized networks, groups, and communities and the more formal non-governmental organizations (NGOs), as well as dabbling in the worlds of party politics. Of course, social movement activities can also take place within institutionalized and corporate realms, such as churches, governments, and corporations. Although some people are doing their part by "greening" bureaucracies and corporations, it is not the purpose of this work to investigate these forms of politics. They have been addressed adequately elsewhere (Doyle and McEachern 1998; Connelly and Smith 1999). Also, apart from the German case, there has been a strong inclination to avoid the formal politics of political parties from within the movements themselves.

What is fascinating about researching and participating in the noninstitutional politics of social movements is that it allows one to see politics in the

Box 1.1

Characteristics of New Social Movements

NSMs do not bear a clear relation to the structural roles of the participants. There is a tendency in NSMs to transcend class structure. More important are the different social strata provided by youth, gender, sexual orientation, and professions.

Ideologically, NSMs are profoundly different from the Marxist perception of ideology as a unifying and totalizing element for collective action, though this can differ markedly from minority to majority worlds. Marxist frames still inform much environmental action in certain third world cultures (see chapter 3 on the Philippines). NSMs exhibit a multitude of ideas and values.

NSMs often involve the emergence of new dimensions of identity. The grievances are based on a set of beliefs, symbols, values, and meanings, rather than just on the economic grievances that characterized the working-class movements. Again, this characteristic is more applicable to minority-world movements, though environmental movements do cross class divisions and other social boundaries in majority worlds regularly.

The relationship between the individual and the collective is blurred. Many contemporary movements are "acted out" in individual actions rather than through or among mobilized groups. The movement becomes the focus for the individual's definition of himself or herself, and action within the movement is a complex mix of the collective and individual confirmations of identity.

NSMs often involve personal and intimate aspects of human life, e.g., what we eat, wear, and enjoy.

NSMs use the radical mobilization tactics of resistance, which differ from those practiced in working-class movements, characterized by civil disobedience and nonviolence.

There is a disdain on behalf of NSMs for conventional politics. Consequently, NSMs maintain elements of autonomy from traditional mass parties.

NSMs seem to be segmented, diffuse, and decentralized. There is a tendency toward considerable local autonomy of local sections.

SOURCES: *Adapted from Johnston, Larana, and Gusfield 1995, 6–7; Doyle and McEachern 2001.*

raw; to see the power relations, the decision-making, and the ideas of people often at the beginning of issue cycles, before these human relationships are obfuscated by the formalization of constitutions and the overarching control of law.

Studying the noninstitutional politics of networks, informal groups, and fluid, living movements demands quite separate methodological techniques than those for studying constitutionalized institutions and corporate bodies. There is no standard "repository of record" where one visits to analyze the documents. Of course, there are secondary sources and some archival, primary material, such as organizational correspondence; but much of the political field exists outside of the realm of the more vitrified, formal histories.

One way to overcome this sparseness of official material is to engage more fully with the research subject. On many occasions, to visit and understand, even if only partially, the politics of dynamic networks, both at the macro and micro levels, demands a willingness to research "at ground level." Accordingly, much of the research which is presented in this book is rooted in the author's fieldwork. As well as ethnographic and interview-based material, this book also relies on both official and informal correspondence which provides extra and more verifiable primary information. By cross-referencing this material, this study provides a clear and rich picture of the actual mechanics and organics of the policy-making processes of environmental movements.

Obviously, there is also much of this book which utilizes secondary evidence, but in all cases the empirical detail is supplemented by face-to-face, primary encounters with movement academics/participants predominantly throughout six countries: England, Germany, the United States, India, the Philippines, and Australia. So, this perspective of such vast and quickly changing phenomena is based, ultimately, on the author's own subjective, but informed experience. Despite the attempts to be representative of movements across the globe, there are gaps in the overall coverage of the case studies. Where these gaps occur, such as in Africa, China, and South America, there has been some attempt to incorporate these movement experiences in boxes which are spread throughout the text.

With so much based on the author's experiential knowledge, the only way to truly ground this vast topic is to admit to the place of the author in the research; to understand the author as a subject as well as an object. This placing of the author provides a fixed point from which to view the cascade of movements, shooting in all directions, in different dimensions, at alternate times across the political firmament. Without constructing this viewpoint, analysis of amorphous phenomena becomes quite meaningless. As one outcome of this epistemological/methodological approach to this book, each major chapter begins with a first-person piece, which places the author within the context of the country in question.

First of all, the author is an Australian, a culture which shares much of its recent white ancestry with European and North American cultures, whilst its traditional indigenous culture more readily explains its geographical location in the South. Also, the author is an environmental advocate as well as an academic. He has been an environmental and human rights activist for over two decades, in his own country as well as others. The author's interest in environmental movements is always premised on the need to find better ways in which to engage in environmental politics, to understand and ascertain better pathways in which to hopefully resolve, even partly, environmental issues/problems. In this vein, this work takes on the cloak of positive criticism.

In the modern tradition of environmental studies, the cool separation between objective political analysis and subjective environmental engagement is questioned. Without the author being an activist, many elements of the knowledge presented in this book would not have been accessed. There is a deep suspicion amongst many noninstitutional, social-movement actors in relation to "official" recorders of their activities. As well as this, there is a richness and color which is gained through engaged action research. Obviously, there are trade-offs to these added strengths. Such research cannot ascertain the same levels of repeatability and objectivity as can be attained through more positivist detachment. On the other hand, disengaged research exclusively embarked upon from "the other side of the fence" would simply not gain enough access to the predominantly fluid and informal environmental movement politics to gain any more than the most basic understandings.

Diversity is the most important trait of environmental movements. Due to their amoeba-like NSM forms, many of their constituent parts are undergoing constant change, reconfiguring their boundaries on a whole range of criteria. Sometimes it is useful to talk of national traits and differences, but green movements also differ dramatically within countries. In addition, many environmental movements simply bypass nation/state borders, playing politics within more globalized or, at least, regionalized boundaries. Consequently, there is a kaleidoscope of frameworks and themes through which these movements can be viewed and compared. The decision to choose any one of these will dramatically alter this snapshot of movement activity, as it will alter the very definition and constitution of the movement.

I have adopted a simple rule about which movements and networks to include in this book on environmental movements. Quite simply, I have chosen to adopt an emic perspective; that is, I have included in my purview all movements which the activists themselves regard as environmental movements. This avoids the unnecessary clutter of academic debate and scholastic boundary-drawing around who should be included and who should not. I am willing to abide by the definitional understandings of the environmentalists.

THREE FRAMEWORKS FOR ANALYSIS

In this work I have chosen just three different ways to regard these movements, and, in turn, these order the book and its component parts (see box 1.2). In each chapter, apart from the first and the last, the comparative analysis will be three-tiered: (1) at the national level, (2) at the movement *issue banner* level, and (3) at the microlevel of specific campaigns. Furthermore, in chapter 8, I will regard movements as phenomena which transcend nation-states whilst acting in transnational arenas.

Box 1.2

Three Frameworks for Environmental Movement Analysis

Chapter	Nation	Movement "Issue Banner"	Campaign
2	U.S.A.	Forest	Cove/Mallard
3	Philippines	Anti-mining	Tampakan
4	Australia	Wilderness	Wet Tropics
5	England	Anti-roads	Twyford Down
6	India	River/anti-dam	Narmada
7	Germany	Anti-nuclear	Gorleben

National Experiences of Environmental Movements as a Framework for Analysis

From chapters 2 to 7, first, some broad-brush description of the general traits of environmental movements in each country is provided. Apart from focusing on my own primary fieldwork, there are other, strong reasons for the selection of each country and, indeed, these informed to a large extent my selection as sites of primary research. All chosen countries simply have fascinating environmental movements and, to some extent, pick themselves. Australia and the United States have been at the vanguard of wilderness movements; India and the Philippines have forged new and exciting environmental justice movements; and England and Germany have created movements based on political ecology and, in the case of the latter, have actually made the transition from social movement politics to the politics of ruling a nation-state.

There is also a certain amount of geopolitical sense behind the selection of these case studies. Later in this chapter and, indeed, the book itself, quite a deal is made of the division between movements which have evolved in minority (more affluent) and majority (less affluent) worlds. England, Germany, and the United States have been chosen as largely representative of the former category; whilst the majority-world case studies concentrate on research experience gathered in the Philippines and India. Australia, of course, is not so easily slotted. It comprises a strange mixture of first and third world cultures and economies.

Movement "Issue Banner" as a Framework for Analysis

These broad national (and sometimes regional) pictures prove quite useless if not coupled with the next level of refined focus aimed at a particular style, element, issue, or theme falling within the broad rubric of environmentalism.

All of these movements will understand themselves to be involved with politics under the broad sign of green or environmental movement. Many of these movements, however, will have subtitles which subcategorize them from other types of environmental movements operating in their own country as well as others, providing additional parameters around which their identities cluster and coalesce. The most common flag of identity at this level is based on the specific issue to which these movements have dedicated themselves.

For example, in this book we will concentrate on six major issues which define and inform environmental movements: forest movements; movements against mining; wilderness movements; anti-roads movements; movements against mega-dams (or pro-river movements); and anti-nuclear (or alternative energy) movements.

These movement issues have been chosen for their diversity, but also for their importance in their country of origin and their impact across the globe. The anti-dam movement in India is the most iconoclastic environmental movement within that country. Forests and wilderness issues have dominated United States and Australian ecopolitics. The anti-roads movement, without doubt, is the most vibrant part of green movements in the United Kingdom; whilst in Germany, the anti-nuclear movement was the hallmark issue which gave birth to the powerful German Greens as well as the topic which fuels continuing protest movements today. Finally, in the Philippines, the issue of mining dominates the environmental agenda like no other. As aforesaid, these movement issue banners are the names which the activists themselves use to frame their movement, to identify with other activists involved in similar struggles, and, most importantly, to define enemies.

Having said this, and further muddying the amazingly complex waters of NSM analysis and understanding, it is paramount to comprehend that whilst many people within, for example, the anti-mining movement in the Philippines understand their political activism to be part of the environmental movement; others within the anti-mining movement may see their own political allegiances as lying elsewhere; for example, with the labor movement or movements for indigenous rights to ancestral domain. Probably a better example of this point is the anti-globalization protests which occurred across the globe at the turn of the millennium, beginning with "the Battle for Seattle" in the United States. Many of these activists classified this protest as an environmental campaign, as part of the green movement; whilst others involved saw it as part of a different movement, under separate banners: be they anarchist, socialist, feminist, anti-capitalist, etc. Still others understood these protests to be part of an emerging new NSM: the anti-globalization movement. The point here is that NSMs do not have perfect external boundaries. Just as their component parts are always changing, their outer boundaries are also fuzzy, interacting and harmonizing with other NSMs on occasions, and on others, coming into direct and sometimes rugged opposition. This point, with particular reference to the anti-globalization protests, is tackled in more detail in chapter 8.

These green movements which coalesce around a particular issue often have very different characteristics from other types of environmental movement operating within their own country. Sometimes they share certain traits and not others. These similarities and differences may be ideological. Other defining characteristics may be cultural, determining that some types of movements possess activists who dress, behave, eat, or live in certain ways. Other differences may relate to the distribution of power and the forms of decision-making which are pursued within certain movements. Still others will possess different arsenals of strategies and tactics and may organize themselves alternatively. Other types of environmental movements, though often sharing some networks of activists, may be largely made up of a clearly distinct group of people, whether these distinctions are based on class, gender, race, religion, education, age, etc. In fact, different types of environmental movements are as diverse as societies as a whole, and their politics cross the full gamut.

For example, in India, the movement against mega-dams like the Narmada is distant from the nature movements which mobilize in an attempt to save the Bengal tiger. In Australia, the anti-nuclear movement has quite a distinct membership from those participating in the wilderness movements (Holloway 1990); that is, very different sets of people are involved within either subcategory of movement. In Germany, the movement which involves itself in electoral politics—the Greens—is poles apart from the movement which primarily involves itself in direct-action protests against the transport of nuclear waste. In the United States, deep ecology movements which use militant activities in the forests of the Northwest are dramatically different from the environmental justice movements which have emerged more recently in poorer, urban American communities of color.

Consequently, subcategorization based on the issue base of environmental movements is essential. To simply place the green movement experience in a "national basket" is not enough. Why then review movements' activities along national lines at all? Why not just investigate anti-roads or anti-dams movements worldwide? The fact remains that a national context is useful in that it provides a common political-cultural context within which these disparate phenomena can be understood. Many activities of green NSMs occur as a direct result of what occurs in a national political context. This leads onto the next point. There are obvious similarities between subcategories of movements or issue types of movements across the globe. At the very least, they share their defining symbol, for example, "forest movements." Despite this shared nomenclature and, on occasions, mutual activities, again, the differences between particular issue-based movements operating in separate national political contexts far outweigh their similarities.

For example, one issue banner of green NSMs—anti-nuclear movements—is markedly dissimilar in the six countries which get major treatment in this work. The Indian movement has really just begun due to the fact that the Indian nuclear weapons program has only just recently increased in size, albeit dramatically. In the United States the movement has progressed only incrementally since the 1970s, when it was confronted by such catastrophes as the meltdown at the Three Mile Island nuclear plant. The current Bush administration is accelerating the nuclear industry, and opposition may become more vocal in the near future, partially as a result. England, although possessing a wealth of environmental movement experiences, has traditionally lagged behind on the anti-nuclear front. Issues of nuclear energy and uranium exploitation have barely touched the Philippines' political canvas, and this obviously relates to its status as a third world country. Both Australia and Germany currently possess vibrant anti-nuclear movements gathering beneath their broader environmental movement banners; but both movements possess very divergent foci: in Germany, most activities within the movement occur either within the institutions of the state or amidst quite militant direct confrontation against the transport of nuclear waste; whilst much ecoactivism in the Australian movement is aimed at preventing uranium mining itself and has been almost always strictly and passively nonviolent. These cross-national comparisons between issue-based movements will be made in the specific chapters.

One final point needs to be made about this second level of movement classification. As green NSMs move beneath, between, or above the political borders of nation-states (although more rarely than commonplace), blurring and sometimes overcoming national distinctions, movement issue banners also describe fuzzy identities, despite the legitimation which ensues due to their emic nature and usage. They sometimes share characteristics with other movement banners. For example, the English anti-roads movement derived and then adapted a good number of its direct-action tactics from the Australian and U.S. forest movements. In turn, the German anti-nuclear movement used similar tactics borrowed and then enhanced from the English anti-roads movement (Wall 1999). Apart from tactics, some issue-based movements have certain clusters of issues/interests in common with other types of movements. For example, the anti-mining movement in the Philippines, the Indian movement against mega-dams, the wilderness movement in Australia, the forest movement in the United States, and even the anti-roads movement in the United Kingdom all champion, on occasions, indigenous people's causes. In short, although there are massive differences, there are also substantial crossovers between movements which rally beneath different issue-based banners. These crossovers validate the notion that there is a broader identity referred to as "environmental movements." This important concept is revisited in the final chapter.

The "Campaign" as a Framework for Analysis

The third and final attempt to provide a working framework to create some order of understanding to this amorphous "madness" which is the noninstitutional politics of environmental movements is to focus at the microlevel of individual campaigns. "Campaign" is a word derived from the language of warfare. It is commonly used by environmentalists to describe a series of "battles" waged within the field of one particular environmental issue. Commonly, an environmental campaign is defined by a shared sense of time and place. Also, whereas it would be impossible to define a shared goal between all participants within broader environmental movements,[1] campaigns bring activists together with a specific or closely aligned set of goals. In a special edition of *Mobilization* (an international journal on social movements), dedicated to environmental campaigns, Della Porta and Rucht define a "campaign" as a "thematically, socially, and temporally interconnected series of interactions that, from the viewpoint of the carriers of the campaign, are geared towards a specific goal" (2002, 3). They go on to describe the attributes of environmental campaigns and their usefulness as a unit of analysis as follows: "Campaigns are situated on a middle ground below the level of movement but above the level of individual activities. . . . A campaign focus captures the dynamics of a conflict with a particular emphasis on interactions. . . . [It] reveals a movement or parts of it in the complexity and variety of actions, but with regard only to those groups that are relevant . . . [and] it can tell us much about the movement in action" (Della Porta and Rucht 2002, 3).

The last point is the most illuminating. Studies at the campaign level illustrate for us the color and richness of environmental movements, often obscured by processes of formalization in institutionalized politics. By rummaging through the minutiae of environmental movement campaigns, we truly confront the organics and dynamics of environmental movements. It is here that power relations are forged, that decisions are made, that resources are allocated and distributed, that ideas are shared and/or clash violently; and here the culture and identity of movements, organizations, and informal groups and networks are created. Campaigns are the coal-face of movement politics.

Within any type of issue-focused environmental movement there are usually many different campaigns. Within one specific country's experience of one issue-based movement, campaigns can be so different as they flex, change, evolve, and transmute over time. Each campaign may have completely different participants and some will have people who cross over between campaigns. Apart from dissimilar personnel, each campaign may operate on very separate political philosophies, with very different strategies and goals. Some may involve themselves in militant direct actions, some may concentrate on media campaigns to pressure elected representatives, and others may pursue reform in the courts of the United Nations in The Hague in the Netherlands. Of course, in certain campaigns, all variants of these strategies will be pursued at different times, along with many other forms of political activity.

As evidence of this cacophony of disparate voices at the microlevel, let us take a snapshot of the anti-nuclear movement in Australia. At this time of writing, there are at least five major anti-nuclear campaigns unfolding concurrently.

1. Jabiluka: The most world renowned Australian anti-nuclear campaign is the Jabiluka campaign, fought at Kakadu in the Northern Territory. It arguments are three-pronged, interchanging between the rights of indigenous peoples (which is the most dominant voice), the values of Kakadu wilderness in its national park, and its anti-nuclear stance against uranium mining. In chapter 4 we will look at this campaign in some detail.

2. Roxby Downs: The campaign against Western Mining Corporation's (WMCs) Roxby Downs is aimed at curtailing the expansion of one of the biggest uranium mines in the world. Mostly, this campaign is run out of South Australia. Environmentalists opposing the mine primarily utilize anti-mining and anti-nuclear arguments, though there are some subservient indigenous arguments and a very small number oriented around wilderness values.

3. In situ leach mines: Also in South Australia are campaigns leveled at halting the development of two "in situ leach" mines which are currently under production. The mines are owned by two transnational corporations, General Atomics (primarily a U.S. corporation) and Southern Cross (a Canadian-based company). Most of the movement's arguments in these cases are leveled at inappropriate third world technology being utilized by these companies, which pump a uranium-depleted, acid-based solution back into the aquifer when the mining process has been completed. This process is illegal in the corporations' "home" countries.

4. Lucas Heights Reactor: In New South Wales, another Australian state, there is a key anti-nuclear campaign which focuses on shutting down the existing Lucas Heights Reactor in Sydney and preventing the building of a new reactor facility to replace it. Also in Sydney is a campaign which focuses on matters of nuclear war. Most particularly, strategic arguments

have emerged which contest the United States' proposed missile defense strategy championed by U.S. president George W. Bush.

5. International and national waste dumps: In Western Australia and South Australia large campaigns based on mass mobilization techniques are aimed at stopping Australia, and those specific states within Australia, from becoming an international and/or national nuclear waste dump.

In all of these campaigns there are enormous differences and some similarities which go far beyond the form and content of argumentation. The most blatant similarity is that most participants see themselves as part of the anti-nuclear movement, and many also see the anti-nuclear movement as a subset of environmental movement, though not all. The differences are more obvious, more numerous, and more profound. In most cases, different networks of activists dominate. Partly as a consequence and partly as a causational factor, each network possesses different goals and advocates different strategies for ascertaining those goals.

This is caused by and results in very separate demographic profiles for activists involved for each campaign.

1. Jabiluka: The actors in Jabiluka are largely generation Xers and local aboriginal communities. The Gen Xers were recruited by mainstream green organizations, such as the Australian Conservation Foundation, mainly from large capital cities on the eastern seaboard.

2. Roxby Downs: The aforementioned campaigns focusing on Roxby Downs in South Australia are largely confined to that state. Most eco-action takes place in the capital city, Adelaide, with some direct actions occurring at the mine sites themselves and within local aboriginal communities. These activists are usually older and have been fighting these campaigns, specifically the expansion of Roxby, for fifteen years. They have a sound knowledge of the complete nuclear cycle, beginning with mining and finishing with nuclear waste. They have little support from mainstream non-governmental organizations (NGOs) based along the eastern seaboard of Australia, in cities such as Sydney, Melbourne, and Canberra.

3. In situ leach mines: This campaign is being fought by a close association of green activists from the South Australian office of a national NGO, the Australian Conservation Foundation, alongside aboriginal communities living near these mines.

4. Lucas Heights Reactor: This campaign has been waged by local residents living next to the reactor in Sydney. Due to the fact that most Australians live in Sydney and Melbourne, this campaign gets support from large international NGOs like Greenpeace and Friends of the Earth.

5. International and national waste dumps: On the other hand, campaigns against nuclear waste in Australia (reminiscent of movements against the transport of nuclear waste in Germany, see chapter 7) involve the full gamut of people from schoolchildren to elderly pensioners, bureaucrats, businesspeople, and farmers. There is little campaign rhetoric emanating from these networks relating to the danger of the nuclear fuel cycle; rather, it concentrates on concerns of dumping wastes in activists' localities. As is often the case with campaigns which partly appeal to NIMBY concerns, the manner in which they play politics is far more conservative than those previously discussed. There are within this campaign, however, more radical (but powerful) minority factions which link waste issues to the generation of nuclear power and which connect this issue with opposition to the building of the new reactor at Lucas Heights.

Again, this is further confirmation of complexity and the fact that campaigns often have crossovers of personnel and/or focus. David Noonan, of the national green NGO, the Australian Conservation Foundation, writes: "The national radioactive dump is driven by the plan for a new Sydney reactor. To gain the public and political credibility to be allowed to build the proposed $500 million reactor the Australian Nuclear Science and Technology Organization (ANSTO) needs to clear this site of radioactive wastes. This is planned to occur by transport of lower level wastes to the repository in central South Australia, and transporting the high level spent fuel rods across the oceans to France and Argentina for reprocessing. With resultant reprocessed nuclear waste to later be returned to Australia through some as yet unnamed port and then transported onto the store" (1999, 7).

Campaign case studies provide this level of complexity which is a central and defining characteristic of environmental movements. Campaigns, although indicative of the properties of a particular movement, are not necessarily representative of all campaigns within that movement sector. As such, a single campaign focus is not enough, it must be housed within the two previous frameworks/levels of analysis: within the aforementioned frames of the national experience and the issue banner of the movement. Consequently, this three-pronged framework for analysis structures each chapter.

INTRODUCTION OF THEMES

In looking at environmental movements at the national, issue banner, and campaign levels, certain dominant themes emerge which further focus this work. These themes are also other ways of viewing and ordering movements, placing additional sets of analytical boundaries around them. The mega-theme which informs this work is to understand the comparative experiences of environmental movements across the globe with special reference to similarities and differences between movements operating in the North versus those operating in the South, the minority world versus the majority world. In their aforementioned work on environmental movements and campaigns, Della Porta and Rucht note that the topic of environmental campaigns that cross the North-South divide are "understudied." This work seeks to redress this gap in the literature (Della Porta and Rucht 2002, 10). Also, this work will obviously be viewing North-North comparisons as well as those oriented around a South-South axis; but the North-South comparative dimension provides the most fascinating and informative angle of focus.

During this work I will be using North/South, first world/third world, developed world/developing world, and minority world/majority world interchangeably; but I acknowledge that all these terms are imperfect categories. It is important to note, however, that I have a stronger attachment to the latter category—minority world versus majority world—and, consequently, I will use this terminology more frequently. At the outset of this work, therefore, it is imperative that the reader understand what I mean when I refer to the terms "minority world" and "majority world." It is true that many nations existing in the Northern Hemisphere are wealthier than those existing to the south of the equator, hence the North-South terminology. There are some countries, however, which frustrate this more traditional model borrowed from the subdisciplines of international relations and geopolitics. More importantly, however, in any study of social movements, terminology must be employed which is not wholly based on a discourse relating to nation-states as social movements often traverse nation-state boundaries.

What are the other definitional options here? "First world versus third world" still has some validity, though the status of the "second world" has always been ambiguous. "Developed world versus developing world" is still used by some writers for purposes similar to mine. Unfortunately, often these terms are loaded in favor of the more developed first world; as if the less developed third world must automatically make the "natural journey" along the unilinear path of progress, ultimately aspiring to be like those already developed, existing in the realm of the numero uno. There are numerous other attempts to portray, in classical, dualistic styles, two worlds opposing each other. Though unlike some elements of postmodern analysis, I still find the mega division a useful one to perpetuate, as it usefully continues to match and describe the "empirical reality" as I have encountered it; but I argue that these great divisions are neither necessarily geographically oriented, nor nation-state specific. Rather, there is an immense gulf in the context of comparative environmental movements between the experiences of the majority of the earth's people (the majority world), when contrasted with those encountered by a small minority (the minority world).

A rather simple, often quoted equation needs to be spelled out here. Approximately 80 percent of the Earth's resources are either consumed or owned by approximately 15 percent of the Earth's people. On the other hand, 85 percent of the Earth's people have access to only 20 percent of the Earth's resources (Doyle and McEachern 1998). It is obvious that the typology of environmental issues fuelling the politics of environmental movements which emerge amongst those societies with access to most of the Earth's wealth—the minority world—are going to be very different from those movements which come to light in circumstances of much greater poverty—the majority world. It is obvious, therefore, that movements which surface in countries like India, China, and Chile—in the majority world—will be more oriented around issues of human health, shelter, food security, and survival. In the minority world, in nations such as the United States and Australia, environmental movements are seen more often fighting for post-materialist wilderness issues and the rights of other nature. Similarly, majority world countries like the Philippines and Cameroon are not likely to witness strong anti-nuclear or post-industrialist movements; whereas in Germany and England the anti-nuclear and anti-roads movements have emerged with gusto.

Moreover, the majority versus minority world dichotomy is equally useful within the confines of the nation-state. The forest preservation movements of the Northwest of the United States most obviously comprise a minority world environmental movement; whilst the U.S. environmental justice movement, born in communities of color, originally in deliberate juxtaposition to what was perceived as the "white elite" environmental movement, can be usefully designated as a majority world experience.

Apart from the minority or majority world focus, there are other themes which flow through and emerge from discussions. Most national environmental movements wrestle with issues associated with these themes at some time or another. Having said this, some themes dominate movement activities in certain national movements. Let me now discuss the basic threads of these themes.

Several of the themes relate to ideology or component parts of overarching ideologies. Green ideologies are remarkably diverse. There are often dominant ideologies owned and sold by the powerful, but all people have their own worldview. Ideas shape actions and actions reshape ideas. Over the past twenty years discussions revolving around green political thought have been remarkably fecund (see Doyle and McEachern 2001, chapter 2; Doherty 2002a). In certain national experiences different green ideologies have been more dominant than others. In the New World, the more post-materialist ideology of deep ecology has been a powerful idea structure informing many networks within forest and wilderness movements, and this is investigated in chapters 2 and 4. These ideas impact upon the types of strategies used within campaigns and upon how structures for decision-making are set up. Nearly every aspect of one movement's experience with environmentalism is shaped by dominant green ideologies.

In the forest movements of the South, activists have little time or comprehension of deep ecology, and it is usually considered as a green elitist worldview. Likewise in the movements of Europe, where wilderness issues do not dominate green agendas, there is far more emphasis on human, social, or political ecology. This green ideology and its impacts upon ecoactivity are discussed in some detail in chapters 5 and 7.

Other ideological differences might appear under another specific label of environmentalism, like ecofeminism; but others may not. The second dominant ideological theme in this book explores the dominant definition of "environment" in certain countries, with a strong emphasis on the relationship of human beings to the rest of nature. As touched upon, most countries in the majority world focus on human survival issues. They do so not only from necessity, but also from the fact that in many majority world cultures the separation between humanity and nature, as is evidenced in both Western and Christian cosmologies, is not so complete. In fact, in many parts of the majority world humans understand themselves to be part of nature, rather than distinct from it. Obviously, this has huge ramifications on the very definition of what constitutes the environment and, indeed, on what issues are addressed by environmental movements in different cultures. There are also important distinctions on this issue that can be made within minority world movements: green movements in Europe, for example, do include many more human-oriented issues into their environmental agendas than are apparent in those New World cultures such as found in North America and Australasia.

The third theme concentrates on a discussion of violence versus nonviolence. Some movements remain committed to the concept of nonviolence as a strategic tool in their struggles against a usually more powerful foe. Indeed, in the United States and Australia, green movements evolved in close association with peace movements. In the latter case, in many early campaigns the Society of Friends (the Quakers) were key players consistently advocating nonviolent means for achieving nonviolent ends. Within these movements debates have raged between interpretations of nonviolence: from the more passive to the more active, and in recent times, there has been growing evidence of the emergence of more militant tactics which sometimes result in violence toward property, but rarely violence toward people.

The minority world–majority world dichotomy is only partially useful here. The Indian environmental movement, also, has been forged by the

Gandhian traditions of non-cooperation and nonviolence. Although sharing some similarities with the North American forest movements and the Australian wilderness movement, in their idea of nonviolence, the Indian definition of nonviolence is far more than just passive resistance; rather it is a way of life which affects everything from what a person eats through to how they relate to the world around them. In chapter 6 this deeper understanding of nonviolence is explored in relation to the campaign to stop the building of the Narmada Dam.

In the Philippines, nonviolence is considered a luxury position which activists feel they cannot attain. Many Filipinos within the anti-mining movement, for example, see themselves in a fight to the "last drop of blood" with government forces from their national military supported by large transnational interests. Consequently, in chapter 3, we discover that in the Philippines green activists are sometimes involved in guerilla warfare in the forests in a bid to check the advances of their enemy.

Obviously religious differences are huge drivers in determining the levels of violence/nonviolence which are apparent in different countries' green movements. In the Philippines, Christianity dominates the religious canvas, though there are also many who follow the teachings of Islam, particularly in the southern islands of the archipelago. Within Christianity there are always tensions between Christian traditionalists and liberation theologists: the latter advocating more militant and violent resistance, and the former preaching peace and nonviolence. It is safe to say, however, that Christian societies have historically been more tolerant of violent solutions than, for example, those societies dominated by Buddhism. The ecoactivists against the Yadana Gas Pipeline Project in Thailand (see box 3.2) only consider peaceful protest, even though, often, they are hopelessly outnumbered by proponents of the pipeline. Regardless of whether you are talking about a national movement, a movement coalescing around a specific issue, or a particular campaign, the debate between nonviolent and more militant strategies is a constant theme manifesting itself in the everyday language and operations of environmentalists.

Another powerful theme shaping tensions within green movements is the issue of institutionalism. At a conference in April 2000, Chris Rootes, the co-ordinator of the TEA project and renowned environmental movement commentator in Britain, argued that "the strongest story line in recent discussions of the environmental movement in Britain is that of institutionalization" (Rootes, Seel, and Adams 2000, 2).

Indeed, in many parts of the more powerful minority world debates rage about the appropriateness of environmentalists engaging in the more formalized politics of the nation-state and big business. All environmental movements began outside these institutions, whether in the North or the South; and now, increasingly, many networks of green activists are being incorporated into the very political structures which many believe have been the cause of much environmental degradation. Some greens maintain their adversarial style of politics by remaining in antagonistic opposition to these institutions of state and corporate power; whilst many others have made the move inside these structures and are attempting to change environmental agendas from within. In all minority world national cases investigated in this book, this is a major point of contention, and, as such, it will be addressed in chapters 2, 4, 5, and 7.

In the majority world, however, "levels of institutionalization" is not such a hot topic. Green movements in the South reached critical mass at least a decade later than their northern counterparts. Their shorter histories mean that less of their politics have become institutionalized. Moreover, due to the levels of powerlessness held by many green activists in the majority world, engagement with the more formal structures of power is not seen as a viable strategy. As can be seen in chapter 3 in the case of the Philippines, the only source of power which activists believe they possess is their own solidarity, and by "dancing" with their adversaries, they believe they will lose their only source of power.

As such, there is far less time spent in the majority world playing institutional politics, though this is changing. Many in the third world are increasingly dealing with both government bureaucracies and global institutions such as the World Bank, the United Nations Development Project (UNDP), large transnational NGOs—such as the Worldwide Fund for Nature (WWF)—and international aid agencies. Regardless of these increases, it is fair to say that in the less affluent world more time is spent on developing methodologies of mass mobilization than on appeals to elites.

In the minority world these appeals-to-elites tactics are more numerous and more apparent. Two of these avenues for change are treated in this book as separate themes, though obviously they are tied closely to issues of institutionalization. Although social movements are predominantly noninstitutional, there are some elements which have engaged in party politics more than others. When this has occurred, again, it has occurred in the minority world. Green parties, as such, have been rarely sighted on the electoral ballots of the South. Also, within minority world countries there are important differences in playing environmental politics through electoral systems. The most famous and successful environmental movement to engage in this style of politics is the German Green party, which currently shares power with the Socialist Democrats in Germany's federal government. This is investigated in chapter 7. Other minority world countries have had more limited success in the electoral arena and, as well as the German case, this is touched upon in each of the other minority world case studies: chapters 2, 4, and 5.

Electoral gains for environmentalists in a country like the United States have been extremely limited, though green lobbyists are very visible in their more indirect ways of assuring a certain candidate wins a specific office. Moreover, the green movement in the United States leads the world in its involvement with big business in free-market "environmental solutions." There is intense debate in many countries as to how much environmental change can be achieved within structures chiefly created for profit making: corporations. This private-sector movement response is very powerful in the United States and is reviewed closely in chapter 2.

It is important to note that such is the diversity of experience in environmental movements that for every dominant theme which describes the key struggles and contestations of power in a certain country or type of movement, there are numerous subservient traditions, subgroupings, and networks within each movement which operate counter to these more powerful groups. For example, although there is much time spent on the green business response in the United States, there are many other groups, though perhaps less visible and less powerful, which are directly opposed to these free-market processes. In short, there are many exceptions to the thematic rule.

In the final chapter these themes are revisited and one other theme is introduced: the issue of the globalization of environmental movements.

CONCLUSION

It is the sheer diversity of political experience which will be the ultimate reading of this work. This myriad of meaning and activity which shines and refracts through the green prism of environmentalism includes, no doubt, some of the most dramatic and exciting forms of local, national, and transnational politics which straddle the second and third millennia. Let us now look into this fascinating political kaleidoscope.

FOREST MOVEMENTS

Environmental Movements in the United States of America

Walking through the forests in the Great Bear Wilderness, on the border between northern Montana and the southern reaches of Canada, I felt there a very intense quiet, amplified (if quiet can be) by feet of snow. It seems almost blasphemous, then, to start singing or whistling within this enormous "cone of silence." But that is exactly what I did, watching the reverberations knock chunks of snow off huge tree bows with as much impact as a sledgehammer. I felt like a vandal. On bush walks in my own country I would never have knowingly disturbed the natural peace; but here it was different.

Earlier that morning I had left the car some miles back, as I tracked my way to my friend Tom's cabin. Before I left Missoula, I had asked Tom about the chances of coming across grizzly bears in the wilderness, expecting to be reassured about remote possibilities with matching platitudes such as, "You'd have more chance of being struck by lightening." Instead, Tom disappeared into his cellar and reappeared with a can of "bear mace" to spray in the face of an angry grizzly if I got unlucky. He wasn't joking, and then he proceeded to tell me of several previous episodes he and others had experienced with grizzlies in the exact area into which I was walking. As he pushed me into the car he just said, "Remember to sing a lot, or make lots of noise, when you're walking. It scares the bears off and any other critters you don't want to see."

So, here I was, exhausting my repertoire of ballads or whistling nervously. Occasionally the beauty of the place was just so devastating that I forgot my fear: mountainous glaciers rising from the forest canopy. Just before nightfall I reached the cabin, which was three-quarters covered in snow. I was so relieved to enter its solid timber sanctum, to crank up the old woodstove, to eat a simple meal. The sky was black before evening could even get established, and there was nothing more to do than to crawl into my sleeping bag and listen to the sounds of the nighttime world outside these log walls. Amongst the scurrying of small squirrels and other unknowns, I heard the bellowing of a moose break the night clean in two. And then, in what seemed like the hour before dawn, I heard the movements of a large animal scratching around the perimeter of the cabin.

I have never felt so overwhelmed by a sense of "other nature" as I was on that night. For the first time I truly understood the North American environmental movement's fascination with wilderness and mega fauna. Many of the animals which once infested Europe's forests still existed here, at least in sacred pockets. Other nature had a heaviness to it here: there were predators which were not human. And there was a profound respect for these predators. In Australia, whenever a crocodile or dingo attacked (which is extremely rare) large numbers are "culled," the silent subscript reading, "How dare you take human life!" How different, then, are the conservation practices in the high Rockies of Idaho, Montana, and Wyoming, where entire packs of wolves are being reintroduced into "the wild."

The North American environmental movement's obsession with other nature occurs due to the fact that such a nature still exists. This archetypal nature forms an essential core of the American imagination as to what constitutes the "true America," or what William Kittridge refers to as "the Last, Best Place." The continued existence of such a magnificent example of other nature, however, is only part of the answer. Other issues have been actively excluded from the green agenda. This imagination is very much a white, American imagination, often denying issues of equitable resource distribution and overconsumption, understanding "true nature" as a wild place within which humans are tenuous visitors.[1]

■ ■ ■

INTRODUCTION

It is evident from the discussion in the previous chapter that there are major differences between environmental movements functioning in the minority and the majority worlds. Indeed, this division between North and South, the more affluent versus the less affluent, the developed versus the developing, the first world versus the third world is the most important form of categorization which takes place in this book. This is not to say, however, that there

FIG. 2.1. Tom and Sue Roy's cabin, Great Bear Wilderness, Montana, U.S.A., 1996. *Author's private collection.*

are not significant differences between and within national experiences in both the minority and majority worlds. This chapter concentrates on very different forest movements operating within one minority world country: the United States of America (USA).

The campaign case study, which completes this chapter, is the long-term struggle for the forests in a place known as Cove/Mallard in the United States' Northwest. Before we enter into the specifics of this on-the-ground campaign, it necessary to review, briefly, the outstanding characteristics of the U.S. environmental movement and to introduce the logic which informs forest struggles across the globe, but predominantly within the minority world.

The Environmental Movement in the United States

The United States is currently the most powerful nation on the planet.[2] As a nation of approximately 270 million people, it publicly champions pluralist styles of democratic systems and radical libertarian, free market economics.

Its power is often utilized in a global manner and its cultural influences are immense, backed up by the most technologically sophisticated armed forces in the world. The U.S. environmental movement operates with this rubric.

Due to the largely noninstitutional nature of social movements, agreements on points of history are more difficult to find than in the *monumental* histories of formal institutions. Exact dates of origin, seminal figures, and divisions into epochs are more hotly contested than usual. This is hardly surprising when one considers the amorphous nature of environmental movements and their subjective definitional boundaries. Despite this, most American writers date the emergence of the movement late in the nineteenth century. This early movement shares certain traits with similar *nature conservation* movements which emerged in Europe, Australia, and most parts of the minority world at roughly the same time.

The reading of more recent events which characterize modern environmental movements is more heavily debated. For example, Lester sees two major periods emerge within the modern American movement: 1960–1990 and then from 1990 until the present. The thirty years after 1960 are characterized as a time which integrated the conservation and preservationist concerns of earlier movements "with a broader set of ecosystem concerns—such as air and water quality, threatened and endangered species, pesticides, and protection of prime farmland" (Lester 1998, 3). Since 1990, Lester argues that the environmental movement has broadened its constituency even more. New sets of issues have been added to the environmental agenda: global warming, biological diversity, and sustainable development.

In a more detailed exposition of the movement in the United States, Mark Dowie divides this modern period into the same number of categories or "waves," but they begin at different times and the categorization is based on different factors (1995a). The "second wave" (the first being in the late nineteenth century until the early twentieth century) began with Earth Day, which was celebrated all over the United States in 1970, and this wave "ushered in the era of protective legislation in the early 1970s and was abruptly ended by Ronald Reagan in the 1980s" (Dowie 1995a, 35–36). It was at this time that mainstream environmental NGOs began their move from being outsiders to insiders, but this transition most truly occurred during the third wave, under President Bill Clinton.

Both writers also refer to a current/future wave: in Lester's case a "fifth" wave, and in Dowie's, a "fourth." This recent wave is far more grass-roots oriented, is intensely democratic in its decision-making, is less middle-class, is more militant, and operates outside of established bureaucracies. Importantly, this wave reconnects with radical elements of past American environmental movements; but it also challenges the elitism. This most recent collec-

Box 2.1

The Environmental Justice Movement in the United States

The environmental justice movement has redefined environment to include where people live, work, play, go to school, as well as how these things interact with the physical and natural world. The environmental justice movement is led by a loose alliance of grassroots and national environmental and civil rights leaders who question the foundation of the current environmental protection paradigm. The environmental justice movement was born in Warren County, North Carolina, on land that has been predominately black since the time of slavery. The movement began when Warren County was selected to be the final burial site for over 32,000 cubic yards of soil contaminated with PCBs (polychlorinated biphenyls). This area was selected not because it was the most environmentally suitable (it was not) but because it was a poor, black, powerless community.

The 1991 First National People of Color Environmental Leadership Summit was probably the most important single event in the movement's history. The summit broadened the environmental justice movement beyond its early anti-toxics focus to include issues of public health, worker safety, land use, transportation, housing, resource allocation, and community empowerment. The meeting also demonstrated that it is possible to build a multi-racial grassroots movement around environmental and economic justice

SOURCE: *Alston 1992, 30–31. Cited at http://www.ejrc.cau.edu/ejinthe21century.htm.*

1. The environmental justice framework incorporates the principle of the "right" of all individuals to be protected from environmental degradation.

2. The environmental justice framework adopts a public health model of prevention (elimination of the threat before harm occurs) as the preferred strategy. Impacted communities should not have to wait until causation or conclusive "proof" is established before preventive action is taken.

3. The environmental justice framework shifts the burden of proof to polluters/dischargers which do harm, discriminate, or do not give equal protection to racial and ethnic minorities and other "protected" classes. Under the current system, individuals who challenge polluters must "prove" that they have been harmed, discriminated against, or disproportionately impacted. Few impacted communities have the resources to hire lawyers, expert witnesses, and doctors needed to sustain such a challenge. The environmental justice framework would require the parties that are applying for operating permits (landfills, incinerators, smelters, refineries, chemical plants, etc.) to prove that their operations are not harmful to human health, will not disproportionately impact racial and ethnic minorities and other protected groups, and are nondiscriminatory.

SOURCE: *Adapted from Bullard 1993a, 319–335; 1993b, 23–26, 55–56.*

tion of networks is often referred to as the *environmental justice movement* (see box 2.1 for attributes).

The issue of race in the United States is intense. Such a divide in American society also manifests itself in the environmental movement. Until very recently, the movement has been almost exclusively a white one. In an extensive interview process with over five hundred prominent professional and volunteer environmentalists in the United States in the early 1990s, 95 percent agreed with the following statement: "Many, perhaps most, minority and poor rural Americans see little in the conservation message that speaks to them" (Snow 1992, 71).

X For the first time, the "new wave" of environmentalism seems to be picking up on issues of resource overconsumption and maldistribution, which were the hallmark of much earlier political ecology movements which emerged in Western Europe in the 1970s (see chapter 5). For example, in a groundbreaking work, Robert Bullard contends that American people of color are more likely to live next to toxic waste dumps than white Americans (1990). By beginning to pursue such arguments, the recent movement has become more politicized, but this is still a very recent, minority tradition in the X story of American environmentalism. In fact, it is the *apolitical* nature of the movement in the United States—when compared to most other green movements across the globe—which is its most ardent characteristic.

⟿ I use the term "apolitical" here in a manner which must be explained. I do not use it in the narrow sense of being related to party politics. Indeed, as will be discussed later, U.S. green politics is dominated by the indirect lobbying of major political parties, combined with a sophisticated tradition of corporate strategies. I use the concept of politics here, as I do elsewhere in the book, in a far broader, more inclusive manner, to include the politics of the *everyday,* that place where noninstitutional policy-making is born (Doyle 2000). First and foremost, the North American movement is apolitical in its perception of what constitutes the environment. The recent phenomenon of the environmental justice movement aside, the U.S. experience has been dominated by issues of *other nature.* In this manner, people are not seen as part of nature; rather, nature is seen as either something which should be managed more effectively or something which needs protection *from* humans. Unlike the examples in the Philippines in the next chapter, or in India and Germany in later chapters, the "environment" in the United States is treated fixedly as an *externality.* Obviously, this stance is similar to that experienced in Australia (see chapter 4), which is not surprising, as the latter increasingly shares cultural norms and values with the United States.

With issues such as human health, shelter, and food security traditionally absent from the American green agenda, it is not surprising that the movement is largely apolitical. With the environment seen as peripheral to humans, it does not necessitate a serious challenge to existing political systems. Again, unlike what has unraveled in both the third world and the minority green movement's of western Europe, there has been sparse critique of existing political systems in the United States. Usually, environmental problems are seen as being able to be solved by incremental changes to politics and business-as-usual. Often these forms of politics are referred to as *appeal-to-elites* tactics. These are very different from the mass mobilization tactics of the aforementioned anti-mining movements in the Philippines or the anti-dam protests in India, featured in the later chapters.

Furthermore, whereas movements in the South are involved in the actual provision of life-giving infrastructure which helps alleviate environmental suffering and degradation (Doyle and McEachern 1998), environmental movements in the North, such as evidenced in the United States, are customarily more distanced from the people/nonpeople they seek to represent. Although on-the-ground service provision programs and/or mass mobilization strategies do occur in some parts of North American movements, they are very much marginal practices, both in mainstream and in the more radical, peripheral networks.

As touched upon, appeals-to-elites tactics in the United States usually take on two major forms: (1) environmentalists attempt to indirectly influence elected policy-makers whilst acting in their capacities as *lobbyists* and (2) environmentalists involve themselves as players in the market. Let us now view these two sets of strategies separately, whilst acknowledging that, on occasions, these strategies intersect.

Pluralism: Movement as Lobbyists

This acceptance of existing political systems in the United States is not a movement-specific phenomenon, but rather saturates much of the American polity. Its *pluralist* system is so dominant that most of its citizens do not perceive it as a political model at all, but rather understand it as *reality*. In pluralist political systems, of course, citizens are seen in their *natural state* as apolitical. It is only when something minor goes wrong and a tear appears in the fabric of "democracy" that these apolitical individuals coalesce into interest groups and *lobby* the state (usually perceived as an independent arbiter), which ultimately patches up the "apparition," and the citizens return to their individualized, apolitical *true nature*. This version of pluralism is often referred to as *civil society*. Regardless of its merits, or lack thereof, it is a political system based on ideology.[3]

This dominant and rarely questioned ideology partly explains, with its concomitant reliance on more formal lobby groups, the earlier comments made by Dowie in relation to the vast and powerful environmental NGOs which dominate the movement from Washington. No other green movement on the planet includes such a powerful nexus of formal organizations. Three defining features of these organizations are their exclusionist tendencies; their close association with mainstream political parties and the machinations of central government; and, finally, their level of association with big business. When taken in comparative perspective with what will be investigated in subsequent chapters, these features are striking.

The most powerful of these organizations are sometimes collectively known as the "Big Ten." In a major book on the decline of American environmentalism, Dowie writes of the manner in which the Big Ten first emerged in 1981, in the early days of the Reagan administration, and how the groups' self-selecting criteria revolved around access to Washington decision-making: "Robert Allen, executive director of the Kendall Foundation, convened a discreet meeting . . . over dinner at Washington's Iron Grill Inn, a block or two from the White House. . . . Allen invited to this soiree only those officers of organizations that were 'active,' that is, that regularly met with members of Congress and corporate representatives. . . . Allen clearly sought to exclude groups conducting, supporting, or advocating direct action against polluters, whalers, the military, and, even more troubling, against corporations" (Dowie 1995b, 68–69).

Whereas in many parts of the world environmental movements involve themselves in mass mobilization tactics outside of the corridors of governmental and corporate power, mainstream U.S. green NGOs operate classically as lobby groups, *indirectly* influencing the policies of governments, administrators, diplomats, major parties, and corporations through guaranteeing electoral support and by generating funds for party political campaigns. Ultimately, legislation and changes to administrative practices are sought to protect or ensure good management of the environment. Furthermore, any environmental networks which attempt to operate outside of accepted status quo practices are actively excluded from decision-making, financial resources, and media access.

Unlike the German parliament, visited in chapter 7, the first-past-the-post system in the United States (also shared in Britain) ensures that either one or the other of the major political parties—the Republicans or the Democrats—gains power. As a consequence, green activists who wish to play electoral politics in the United States can do so only indirectly. They cannot hope, in the foreseeable future, to actually gain direct representation. This explains, to an extent, the reliance on lobbying for those activists who wish to play as close as possible to the electoral game. In short, in the U.S. scene, this is as close to governmental power as it gets. To non-Americans, what is somewhat startling about interest group politics in the United States is the overt use of money in directly buying support from, for example, a particular congressperson. Most special interest lobby groups possess political action committees (PACs) which specialize in raising monies for these purposes. The environmental lobby is no different. Each year the mainstream NGOs invest tens of millions of dollars in their lobby. Dan Becker, a Sierra Club lobbyist, explains how it works and what the limitations are when he says, "We do have a small PAC, about $500,000 a year. . . . But when I call on congresspersons, they know the absolute maximum contribution they can get from me is $10,000. A Chemical Manufacturers Association lobbyist is backed up by hundreds of companies, each of which can give that candidate $10,000" (Becker quoted in Dowie 1994, 18).

Despite the lack of funds when compared to big business, the U.S. movement has been very good at playing these lobbying games, although different analysts write of very different outcomes from this process. Sean Paige gives a very positive spin on the access to decision-making which environmentalists won in the past through pursuing this type of political strategy under the Clinton-Gore administration. He contends, "The environmental lobby has infiltrated the federal land-management establishment with a cadre of budding ecobureaucrats intent on ecologically correct policymaking. . . . Without ever having elected a Green Party candidate to major public office or putting major components of their agenda on a ballot, environmentalists have succeeded—through agitation, litigation, indoctrination and cajoling friends in high places—in seizing the levers of power and bending the machinery of government to their will, turning the movement outside in" (Paige 1998, 16).

Other analysts are not so sure of the advantages of these appeal-to-elites tactics. Dowie writes:

> The Clinton election occurred at the pinnacle of the third wave of environmentalism. Mainstream greens had tears in their eyes at the Environmental Ball before the inaugural. The environmental presidency, they believed, had arrived . . . salt[ing] the government with professionals raided from almost every mainstream environmental group. All the money and talent that their leaders had invested in Washington politics seemed to pay off. . . . A year later, Beltway environmentalists were weeping again. But this time, their tears were bitter. In decision after decision Clinton, Gore, and the greenest Cabinet in American history betrayed the environmental promise, buckling to industries and special interests. . . . One by one, bills dealing with mining, grazing, and pesticide reform, reauthorization of the clean water and Superfunds acts, and the protection of ancient forests, endangered species, and fisheries were squashed in committee—without effective protest from the White House. (1995a, 36)

Although green lobbyists have continued to operate in the Washington *beltway* since the election of George W. Bush to the White House in 2001, it is true to say that ever since the emergence of the modern environmental movement in North America, the overriding aim of the majority of green lobbyists has been gaining ultimate power for the Democrats. This is a similar situation within the Australian party political experience, where overly close bonds have been forged between the Australian Labor Party (ALP) and the movement. This close affiliation with the Democrats has had dire consequences for environmental policy-making in the United States, with the current regime clearly seeing no favors having to be repaid to the environmental lobby. As will be seen later in this chapter in relation to Cove/Mallard, administrative orders and minor legislative wins can be reversed by incoming, hostile governments. This is the dilemma of investing enormous amounts of energy into mainstream party politics.

Playing Corporate Games

No other green movement on earth is so closely connected to business or so advanced in their development of market-based strategies. It is within the United States that market-based strategies first evolved and then spread to Europe and beyond. There is a strong tradition of corporate philanthropy in American culture, which is largely missing in many other cultures. This partly explains the myriad of corporate games employed by environmental movements in the United States. This chapter will only be able to convey the experience of a handful of these. Also, before this discussion proceeds, it must be said that many environmental networks in the United States work in direct opposition to big business, positioning themselves in rugged opposition to free market ideologies. As far as the U.S. green movement experience is concerned, however, these anti-corporate voices remain a minority tradition.

Powerful networks in the American green movement have been broadcasters of global, free market capitalism as much as any other group operating within U.S. society. An excellent example of this was the endorsement of the North American Free Trade Agreement (NAFTA) by many of the Washington Big Ten organizations in the mid-1990s. Conservation International, the Audubon Society, the Environmental Defense Fund, the Natural Resources Defense Council, the National Wildlife Federation, and the World Wildlife Fund (now the Worldwide Fund for Nature) formed the Environmental Coalition for NAFTA in 1994, pushing for the green movement to accept NAFTA and to actively support it through Congress (Dowie 1994, 16). This endorsement occurred at the very same time when green movements in the South and many other parts of the North worked assiduously against free market rhetoric and practices, as it was feared that global free markets would result in lowering standards of environmental and labor practices. Moreover, critics of NAFTA and other trade agreements such as the Multilateral Agreement on Investment (MAI)—which effectively do away with national regulative boundaries—argued that such a trading equation would further exacerbate the growing disparities in wealth between the minority and majority worlds.

The Worldwide Fund for Nature (WWF) is synonymous with environmental movement corporate practices, trading its panda logo widely. It has worked closely with conservative governments, international agencies such as the World Bank and the International Monetary Fund, as well as some of the richest transnational mining, nuclear, forestry and chemical companies on earth. Its support for NAFTA, though hardly surprising, was wholehearted. In a document it produced in support of NAFTA, its free market, pro–big business position is never far from the surface. It reads: "The NAFTA package will effectively protect the North American environment by fostering cooperation between the parties . . . [and] by mandating transparency both within NAFTA institutions and the countries themselves" (WWF 1994).

WWF's support of NAFTA is just one example in a long list of practices that have won the organization an ambiguous reputation amongst human and indigenous peoples' rights and environmental movements across the globe. Chatterjee and Finger write about the close relationship that WWF and other U.S.-based NGOs have forged between themselves and big business in recent times: "WWF, for example, received $50,000 each from oil companies Chevron and Exxon in 1991. The National Wildlife Federation conducts enviro-seminars for corporate executives from such chemical giants as Du Pont and Monsanto for a $10,000 membership fee in their Corporate Conservation Program. The Audubon Society meanwhile sold Mobil Oil rights to drill for oil under its Baker bird sanctuary in Michigan, garnering US$400,000 a year from this venture" (1994, 70).

There are so many examples of corporate strategies deployed by the U.S. movement that it would take a book-length treatment to do justice to them. Just one more example can be given here. In many ways the example chosen is archetypal as it defines all such alliances between green movements and big businesses: the alliance between McDonalds, the global, fast-food chain, and the Environmental Defense Fund (EDF).

In the early 1990s, culminating in the Rio Earth Summit in 1992, sustainable development (SD) became a dominant catch cry within mainstream northern environmental movements, governments and big business alike. At the heart of SD is the assumption that the pursuit of environmental goals is not necessarily at odds with the profit motives of corporations. This was a fairly dramatic mind shift when it first occurred, as, previously, large corporations, in their quest for profits and shareholder satisfaction, were almost unilaterally seen as the biggest environmental offender. Now *enemy* had become *friend*. Consequently, the limits-to-growth arguments of the 1960s and '70s were ousted and replaced with this mantra: "Business is good for the environment, and environment is good for business." Indeed, the guiding principle behind the alliance between EDF and McDonalds reads, "Business can thrive without damaging the environment" (Prince and Denison 1992, 1). McDonalds is known throughout the world as a quintessential transnational corporation. Its symbolism is rarely lost on anti-globalization protesters who continually target McDonalds' outlets in direct, symbolic actions.

McDonalds sells American fast food in every market, from New Delhi, where its "Maharaja Mac" is made of mutton instead of beef, to Paris, where a meal of fries and a hamburger has been sold under the nomenclature of *un grand repas.* Despite these subtle nods to cultural differences, McDonalds sells a uniform product the world over, and underlying this product is a philosophy at the heart of disposable, consumerist culture. The product is more than just hamburgers, it is "a way of life." As such, the company's image is everything. Understanding this dynamic, in 1992, the EDF approached McDonalds to form a partnership with the articulated goal of reducing waste. Despite the validity of this goal, a more important transaction was being made here. EDF was trading on the integrity of its name, as a mainstream environmental organization, in a bid to green the image of the fast-food giant. McDonalds has long had a questionable reputation in relation to its environmental record. Apart from supplying mass-produced food, with its reliance of large-scale monocultures, it has been roundly criticized for its utilization of cheap, youth labor; its disposable waste practices (despite the best intentions of the EDF-McDonalds accord); and its reputed destruction of tropical forests to make space for cattle ranches which, its critics argue, have supplied the beef for their hamburgers. In addition, it has further damaged its reputation by suing environmentalists who publicly speak out against its practices. The McLibel case is a very widely quoted defamation case, where McDonalds sued two penniless activists in Britain (see *www.mcspotlight.org*).

In making the public alliance with McDonalds, the company's product was effectively *greened.* The silent script reads, "If EDF is working with McDonalds, then McDonalds cannot be that bad; they must have sound environmental practices." This is the same strategy which led McDonalds to fund the construction of the McDonalds Orangutan Rainforest in Sydney's Taronga Zoo in Australia. McDonalds is now seen not as a destructor of rainforest habitat, but as a savior of the creatures who dwell within it.

What do green organizations such as EDF get out of this? Money, and large amounts of it. But even more than this, the image transfer is mutual. EDF is now seen by other companies, funding agencies, and governments alike as accepting of the free market economy. The organization is seen as *realistic* in its goals and practices. This strategy is understandable. Those organizations accepting the new world economic order, and the place of the environment within it, have gained enormous wealth in order to achieve their limited goals. These environmentalists understand the earth itself as a massive corporation which, if run on correct *best-practice* business strategies, will survive the current environmental hiccups. These greens see no fundamental crisis at all. Rather, with efficient and effective utilization of the earth's resources, everyone will be in a win/win situation. This is the ideology of the powerful, an ideology which is consistently challenged by green movements in the majority world, an ideology which protects the minority world from claims that it has an inequitable share of the earth's resources and habitats.

Of course, it is simplistic to suggest that these environmentalists merely work closely with big business to achieve their goals: on many occasions, they constitute big businesses in their own right. Concurrently, it must be strongly rearticulated, there are also parts of the environmental movement in the United States, though less visible, which are vehemently opposed to global free markets.

As aforesaid, the movement in the United States is dominated by an apolitical agenda. Added to its removal of humans from environmental equations and its rarely questioned and widespread acceptance of established political and business practices are other elements which emphasize the movement's apolitical nature. First of all, there is no other more litigious movement on the planet. Again reflecting its culture, movement professionals place a heavy emphasis on environmental action pursued through the legal system. Between 1990 and 1996, Justice Department statistics list 262 separate environmental lawsuits being filed. Even more dramatic are the figures since June 1997, with 184 cases filed (Paige 1998, 16). This reliance on the legal system is partly based on the fact that the U.S. legal system is sophisticated enough to handle often complex, ecological disputes. Less positively, this cacophony of litigation has seen the development of a plethora of one-off victories. As such, the United States is not a society where we have seen the emergence of a permanent parliamentary or administrative environmental response. For example, as aforesaid, the success of green parties in the United States is virtually nonexistent, and there is no long-standing cabinet-level portfolio in national government. This reliance on the legal system is partly responsible for the lack of development of a really lasting administrative infrastructure built to deal with environmental issues on a daily basis. This situation also accounts for the ease with which incoming governments can reverse or displace past environmental practices (as is now the case with reversal over Cove/Mallard since the election of the Bush administration in 2001).

Another consequence of this apolitical individualism is an attraction to New Age environmentalism. This form of environmentalism seeks to change values from within the individual. Often these changes are psychological and spiritual: individuals must change their inner selves and their inner relationships with nature. Whilst some of these points are attractive, they often further divorce the movement from the political realm, which requires an interplay between social groupings, not just within the individual (Doyle and McEachern 1998).

Penultimately, the U.S. movement is apolitical in the sense that it remains transfixed by domestic issues despite operating within a nation which increasingly involves itself in transnational issues. When the green movement does attempt to widen its gaze to include the world outside its national boundaries, it does so in a manner which yet again depoliticizes the environmental agenda. The agenda relating to *global ecology* is a perfect example of this point. When it does have to acknowledge that it shares the planet with the majority world, the American movement sells the major issues, again, as having little to do with people, but rather *natural forces.* The minority world now portrays the major problems of the majority world as species extinction, global climate change, desertification, the international shortage of freshwater, and over population. Needless to say, these are not issues high on the environmental agenda as defined by most people living in the third world. Other issues of more immediate survival dominate. In a provocative book entitled *Tears of the Crocodile,* Moyo et al. argue that the developed world has managed to divest itself of its responsibility to the global environment by moving the arena "away from people and onto things, forces." They write: "In short the developing world, for the first time, is being asked to be an equal partner in a world-wide endeavor precisely because the emphasis has shifted away from the needs of the poor. By advancing an environmental agenda the North has once more concentrated on its own interests and has called them globalism" (Moyo, O'Keefe, and Middleton 1993, 5).

The final point which must be made here is one that was made at the outset of this book and must litter its subsequent pages. Because movements are so fluid, there are so many ways in which one can depict component parts of it. So far, this chapter has concentrated on the American movement as largely played out by its mainstream, big-end-of-town NGOs. There are many other depictions of the movement which can be recorded by focusing on less dominant, less quasi-institutionalized networks, as is definitely the case in the struggle for the forests of Cove/Mallard, reviewed in the final pages of this chapter. But by focusing on the more elite, mainstream part of the movement, it is apparent that, to date, it can be characterized as the domain of a white, well-connected elite who are more intent on preserving mega fauna in wilderness parks than on fighting for the basic living needs of under-privileged human beings, as is largely the focus of majority-world green movements.

In recent times, with the aforementioned emergence of the environmental justice movement (deciding to strategically co-opt the mainstream American symbol of environmentalism for its own purposes), new hopes have emerged. As we move further into the third millennium, the U.S. environmental movement will increasingly be confronted with a political space where the social and political ramifications of being green have to be embraced.

FOREST MOVEMENTS

Forest movements today are most powerful in the majority world as well as in those parts of the minority world which were most recently invaded by Europeans: the New World continents of North America and Australia. Forest movements in Europe still exist; they are a not dominant on the environmental agenda. There are, of course, several exceptions to this rule, including the forest movements of Scandinavia, Russia, and Estonia. Also, within certain countries, there are still regional environmental networks which fight vigorously to protect remaining stands of old-growth forest. The German movement to protect the Black Forest is an excellent example of this type of activity. An obvious explanation for this is that much of Europe, most particularly western/central Europe, is highly industrialized; and most of the ancient forests, such as those which once existed in the intensely degraded land of Ireland, have disappeared long ago.

The forest movements of the South, in Mexico, Chile, Brazil, Malaysia, Indonesia, continental Africa, and India—just to list a small number of examples—are faced with enormous pressures. Forest clearing in the third world continues at an astonishing rate, despite thirty years of intense local (and, more recently, transnational)[4] environmental activism. This decimation of the world's last remaining grand stands of forest has actually increased in the last decade due to such global trading mechanisms as the previously discussed NAFTA and broad agendas introduced by the World Trade Organization. Despite the *green stamping* of NAFTA and other free trade programs by the likes of WWF and other Big Ten NGOs, according to the U.S. Department of Labor's Trade Adjustment Assistance Program, over 5,500 U.S forest workers have lost their jobs since NAFTA's implementation in the mid 1990s. From 1996 until 1998, $4.5 billion was invested in low-cost countries such as Brazil and Indonesia. Menotti writes of the future costs of these free trade regimes: "Thus, the result of this process will be that most of the new jobs created will be in lower-cost nations, where environmental regulations barely exist. Workers will be pitted against workers in an international struggle to remain competitive, and national stands will fall dramatically in a spiral race to the bottom. We will witness the near-complete destruction of the world's few remaining forests, the globalisation of suicidal stands, a loss of jobs in the North, and further exploitation of jobs in the South" (Menotti 1999, 181).

The Indian Chipko movement is an excellent example of a majority-world forest movement (see chapter 6). In the early 1970s, women in northern Indian villages in the foothills of the Himalayas formed networks and organizations to stop the felling of ancient trees in and around their villages. The women became famous for their tree-hugging tactics (*chipko* literally means "to embrace"). The writings of Vandana Shiva are full of inspirational accounts of people's forest movements which have emerged across the majority world. On nearly all occasions, they are dominated by women activists, and this is a clear trend for much environmental activism which is sustained at the community level throughout the South.

Due to the thematic focus of this chapter, the forest movements of the South will not be fairly represented here. Instead, the chapter, as from its outset, will remain focused on the more affluent New World forest movements of the United States. Before the discussion moves on, however, it must be fully understood that in no other kind of environmental movement is the gap between first and third world movements so profound. First and foremost, what separates the forest movements of the majority world from those of the minority world is that the forests of the former are still peopled, whilst the forests of the latter are largely devoid of human habitats or, at least, they are perceived as thus. This point partly explains the construction and habitual utilization of the prevailing concept of *wilderness* in the minority world as a wild place where people do not dwell. This concept of wilderness is further developed in chapter 4. As with all movements in the South, most environmental issues are based on the assumption that local people should have more control over their lives, rather than on nonhuman nature's rights to exist beyond humanity's perception.

This European vision of wilderness has driven the northern forest movements since the first Western nature conservation movements began over a century ago. As a consequence, most minority-world forest movements have concentrated their efforts on wilderness preservation through the creation of parks and reserves which either dramatically limit human *intrusion* or carefully manage nature in a bid to make its utilization more efficient and more *sustainable.* There are some differences between these two schools: the former can be referred to as the *deep ecology* or *preservationist* approach (though, again, there are large differences between this subcategory), whilst the latter is known as the *resource conservation approach.* The resource conservationists see forests as places which can fulfill a multitude of uses, from timber cutting to recreation and tourism. This position is popular with the mainstream NGOs in Washington which were reviewed earlier in this chapter. The deep ecology position is more dramatic in its view of nature, according it value beyond human perception. This latter position is often held by those direct-action ecoactivists involved with the Cove/Mallard issue, to be examined in the next section.

Whatever the approach, most of these models of interaction/management see humans as *outside* of the forest. Despite the mythology of humans evolving from these fecund DNA hot-beds, the forest habitat is largely perceived in the minority world as *other nature.*

Succinctly, deep ecologists, or *ecocentrists,* see nature as having *intrinsic worth,* regardless of its value in terms of human utilization. Hay and Haward explain the radical nature of this position as follows: "The impulse to defend the existential rights of wilderness in precedence over human-use rights has led to a spirited challenge to the most fundamental tenet of western civiliza-

FIG. 2.2. Wild Horse Island, Montana, U.S.A., 1996. *Author's private collection.*

tion, the belief that rights are strictly human categories, and that no counter-veiling *principle* exists to bar humanity from behaving in any way it deems fit towards the non-human world" (1988, 437–438).

Another major assumption of the ecocentrists is that all nature is inter-connected and that no particular species, including humans, is more central to existence than any other. This position is usually interpreted in a positive vein for all species, although it has been used, at times, in rather misanthropic ways. Although these instances have been greatly over-inflated, it is fruitful to mention them here, as much of the "anti-humanity debate" has emerged from the forest movements of North America. The most commonly quoted statements are attributed to Earth First!s Dave Foreman, who has supported aids and starvation in the third world, amongst other things, as natural *overflow valves* (Doyle and McEachern 1998, 43). Most of the deep ecology position is not anti-human at all, but simply values nature from a perspective which has little to do with humans.

Still, positions like Foreman's (who more recently has served on the board of the U.S. Wilderness Society, a mainstream environmental organization) led to a split in Earth First! between the Holies and the Wilders. Wilders are more militant, understanding their role as "defending Mother Earth" from the human *scourge,* whilst Holies attempt to incorporate social ecological arguments into Earth First!s position, arguing that not all humans can be lumped to-gether as environmental vandals, that some sections of society are bigger con-

Box 2.2

The Wise Use Movement

The wise use movement advocates a range of instrumental attacks on environment movements. They include the creation of right-wing think-tanks that produce propaganda challenging dominant myths of green movements, the use of "dirty-tricks" campaigns (designed to "smear" the reputations of its opponents), and the formation of anti-green front groups (masquerading as environment groups to confuse the general public).

The wise use movement emerged in the late 1980s in the U.S.A., but did not emerge in Australia until the mid 1990s. One of the founders . . . argued that business could not survive the attacks made on it by environmentalists unless it, too, took on the attributes of a social movement. This movement is largely rural-based, "anti-environmentalist," "localist," and populist. The wise use movement may also be considered as "radical libertarian in its economic focus, and pathologically conservative in its morality."

The wise use movement is backed by large extraction corporations, including Exxon, . . . and Boise Cascade. The key movers on the ground, however, are right-wing lobby groups . . . and thousands of "populist, small-town, and rural citizens' groups."

Source: *Doyle 2000b, 178–179.*

tributors to ecological destruction than others. Bron Taylor describes this split when he states, "Wilders . . . focus exclusively on wilderness, and thereby, in their minds, on biodiversity and biocentrism. . . . They consider themselves true patriots, trying to preserve the sacred landscape of America (and don't rule out militant forms of protest). . . . Opposite the Wilders, . . . the Holies . . . insist that a 'holistic' perspective is needed; one has to examine how threats to biodiversity are related to other issues (they rule out militant strategies)" (1991, 263).

There can be no doubt that the many indigenous peoples also possess meaning systems which understand nature (or a similar concept) to possess intrinsic worth. The meaning systems of Native Americans are often referred to in this light. Whatever the subtleties of the deep ecological position, forged by such green philosophers as Naess, Sessions, and Fox, in its current form it is very much a Northern, New World environmental movement phenomenon. Even if the minority-world-crafted deep ecological position philosophically accepts humanity's place as being *part* of nature, strategically, much of the emphasis has been less holistic, focused on *other nature:* wilderness areas, and not the cities, towns, rural communities, and even forests where the majority of the earth's people dwell. It is obvious that in the South these Northern models, through their human exclusionist vision, are regarded with deep suspicion.[5]

The deep ecological position is particularly pertinent here as it informs, in varying degrees, much of the radical activism which takes place in the fight to protect Cove/Mallard. Furthermore, it is this position which has inspired a counter forest movement—the wise use movement—to materialize. In no other part of the world have such vehement pro-business counter movements emerged (see box 2.2 for wise use movement).

COVE/MALLARD

The Cove/Mallard region consists of two roadless areas of coniferous forest (seventy-six thousand acres) found in Idaho's "Big Wild." This is the largest intact forest ecosystem—the Greater Salmon-Selway—in the United States. This last great wilderness in the United States is home to eagles, lynx, wolves, wolverine, moose, mountain lion, and many types of fish, including the bull trout, which are on endangered lists. In the late 1980s the U.S. Forest Service created a plan to move into the Cove Roadless Area and the Mallard Roadless Area: hence the name Cove/Mallard. They dedicated $6 million for this task. After the roads had been established, it was envisaged that this would open the area up for nine massive timber sales, with a projected volume of 81 million board feet (Kreilick correspondence with author 2001).

It was Earth Day 1992 which saw the beginning of an eight-year campaign against this road building and these timber sales: an Earth First! activist climbed atop a forest supervisor's office in Grangeville, Idaho, with a banner reading, "Save Cove/Mallard—Abolish the Forest Service!" Jake Kreilick, a long-time forest activist with the Native Forest Network and the Missoula Maggots, describes the early days of the campaign: "That summer, about 20 activists from Wild Rockies Earth First! and the Ancient Forest Bus Brigade set up base camp near the Noble Road. . . . Despite the low numbers and the fact that the area was closed to the public, the activists were successful in blockading road building activities with twenty-foot-tall tripods (three poles lashed together teepee style with a person standing in the crux) and by locking themselves to logging equipment with Kryptonite bicycle locks" (Hemstreet and Kreilick 1995).

Over the next few years, direct-action campaigns occurred each summer, and the Cove/Mallard Coalition was born, bringing together a diverse network of activist organizations. The forms of direct action were many and varied, ranging from *ecomilitia* tactics to more passive forms of resistance. Many of the more nonviolent actions are remarkably similar to direct actions occurring in other first world countries. There can be no doubt that the Australian wilderness movements' direct-action campaigns (chapter 4) and those within forest movements in the United States freely traded strategies and tactics during the past fifteen to twenty years. Also, the British anti-roads (chapter 5) and the German anti-nuclear (chapter 7) movements used—and then upgraded—such direct-action tactics developed in New World forest and

Fɪɢ. 2.3. Environmental Rangers compound and the Northwest Rockies, U.S.A., 1996.
Author's private collection.

wilderness movements. The extent of this globalization of the ecoactivists' direct-action *armory* is touched upon in the final chapter.

The Environmental Rangers, involved in the campaign, was one peripheral group which did not necessarily advocate nonviolence. It argued for the use of arms against the forest service "to turn the tide of environmental destruction." Rick Valois of the Rangers, an ex-Vietnam combat veteran, argues the following: "This war to save the planet isn't a metaphoric war. . . . It is the gun that is actually sweeping the world clean, and that's a reality that environmentalists have not taken into account" (Valois quoted in Oko 1996, 11).

This militant wing of the movement has ideological connections with the "Freemen" movement of the Northern Rockies, which argues that the "gumment back east" (national government) has become corrupt and seeks to control too many aspects of American lives, including interfering in the forestry industry by controlling public lands. This right-wing movement is radical libertarian in its support of free markets and, as such, is strongly in favor of the rights of the individual—this forms the original basis of what it perceives as a rapidly eroding American democracy. The wise use movement shares this ideological base (see box 2.2). Its affiliates are closely associated with the gun lobby, as the right to bear arms is regarded as an inalienable right of all Americans. It is through gun ownership and the threat of its use that Freemen and other such political groups believe their salvation from the "gumment" lies.

Following the arrest of Theodore Kaczynski—the Unabomber—much was made about the links between ultra-right-wing extremists and direct-action environmental groups such as Earth First! by the national media. Citing the 1995 bombing of a Sacramento timber lobbyist, *USA Today*'s opinion page read, "The Unabomber may well have taken his inspiration from the writings of Earth First!'s radical fringe" (Chavez quoted in Oko 1996, 11). Also, much was made on ABC television of the fact that Kaczynski had attended an activist conference at the University of Montana. There can be no doubt that Dave Foreman of Earth First! had advocated the use of bombs against property in the early 1980s, and that the tree-spiking antics of Earth First!'s Mike Roselle (now director of the Cove/Mallard Coalition) in the mid 1980s have resonances here. But the mainstream media's calling for green blood here has more to do with the Federal Bureau of Investigation's (FBI) desire to justify their heavy presence in Montana in the mid-1990s and their close monitoring of direct-action environmentalists. In fact, earlier in the decade, the FBI had raided the records of the Environmental Studies Department at the University of Montana for information which would lead it to "uncover ecoradicals."

Too much has been made of the ultra-right-wing networks of the green movement. They are very much a minority tradition; but they are there. What makes them interesting in this book is the fact that they appear in few green movements outside of the United States. But this is where the interest must end, as the over-riding tactics of the Cove/Mallard Coalition, Earth First! and the Native Forest Network in the decade-long campaign to save the last roadless areas of the Big Wild have largely extended from strictly passive to more active forms of *nonviolent* actions.

In fact, to break the law in the forests of Idaho has become increasingly easy since 1994, when the Idaho state legislature passed what has effectively become known as the "Earth First! Act," which made it a felony to "solicit any person, or conspire with any other person to commit any crime against property or person with the specific intent to halt, impede, obstruct or interfere with the lawful management, cultivation or harvesting of trees or timber" (quoted in Hemstreet and Kreilick 1995). This law was largely written by the Intermountain Forest Industries Association, a lobby group for the timber industry, and basically outlawed Earth First! and the direct-action antics of the Cove/Mallard Coalition. This did little to deter activists as the very point of most of the direct actions was to deliberately ignore or break laws which they regarded as serving the interests of the industry. As the coalition argues, "Civil disobedience becomes necessary when injustices have hardened into institutionalized practices" (Cove/Mallard Coalition 1994).

All this law did was increase the number of acts of resistance in the area. In 1995, piecemeal actions became more coordinated when Earth First! decided to hold its "national rendezvous" in the Nez Perce National Forest, part of the broader Cove/Mallard region. The editorial from the Spokane-based *Spokesman Review* wrote of the upcoming "invasion": "Idaho's timber industry is bracing itself for an invasion of 500 Earth First! radicals hell-bent on 'fun' in the woods this summer. . . . A plague of locusts would be preferable. In Earth First! speak 'fun' means groups of screwballs chaining themselves to gates, trucks, equipment and even a buffet table; pouring sand in gas tanks; draining oil from police cars, burying themselves in a logging road; trespassing; sitting in trees—anything that will hamper legal logging on public land. . . . Earth First! and its allies are the abortion-clinic bombers of the environmental movement" (3 March 1996, 6).

Abortion-clinic comments aside, this editorial does get the flavor of many of the types of civil disobedience employed. Most of these acts are attempts at delaying logging, for however short a period, and gaining coverage by national media outlets about the plight of these remote forests. Billy Stern, a Native Forest Network activist out of Missoula, describes just one more inventive action with gleeful pride:

> On September 17, after 74 days, the second longest timber sale blockade in US history was busted. This was no simple tree-sit. The Forest Service had to bring in a 50 foot high "cherry picker" over seventy miles to take down activists sitting on platforms suspended from four huge wooden tripods and bipods. But before they could even get to the sitters, they had to deal with the "Dragon." The Dragon consist of a metal pipe large enough to put your arms through, with a metal pin welded in the center. The pin is positioned for you to clip or lock a small chain to it, with the other end locked around your wrist. This set up is then encased in a pear shaped concrete slab, and buried in the ground. Above the dragon sat a carefully constructed huge pile of slash timber (left over from roadbuilding). It took authorities over seven hours to cut and chisel out the blockader locked into it. (Stern 1997, 1)

Most of these actions include placing the body of the activist in some potential danger. Ceramic tree spiking (ceramic spikes cannot be found through metal detection) are mostly a thing of the past. Most of the more militant actions are aimed at property, not people. In 1993, twelve members of Earth First! were fined over one million dollars for damaging the property of roadbuilding company Highland Enterprises in the Cove/Mallard area. Most of the activists escaped the fines due to lack of definable income (*Anchorage Daily News*, 18 November 1996, 5).

It would be unidimensional just to focus on direct-action tactics in the case of Cove/Mallard. In January of 1995, the Forest Service began poling Noble Road, facilitating future access for loggers. The Bennett Lumber Company began taking 11 million board feet from the Noble sale in Cove (Hemstreet and Kreilick 1995). After only two days a new injunction from the U.S. Ninth Circuit Court of Appeals stopped all logging, mining, and grazing in six of Idaho's national forests. This action was brought to court by two Big Ten organizations, the Wilderness Society and the Sierra Club. Incredibly, however, the decision was reversed when Craig Gehrke, the Idaho representative of the Wilderness Society, instructed his lawyers to stay the action and allow the loggers to proceed (Cockburn 1995a, 228). Cockburn, a journalist with the *Nation*, writes of the overly close connections which the Big Ten have with the industry in their pursuit of corporate games, which may have explained this dramatic volte-face:

> The bizarre somersault allowed logging to commence on the Cove/Mallard area in the Nez Perce National Forest: the largest roadless area remaining in the Lower 48. Ron Mitchell of the Idaho Sporting Congress said, "The Wilderness Society betrayal is devastating." There are three Wilderness Society board members from Idaho, and the most influential of them is Walter Minnick. He is C.E.O. of the multinational timber company called TJ International. . . . As a manufacturer of doors and windows, TJ International has a big appetite for pondersoa pine. . . . So much for corporate environmentalism. Tear up your Wilderness Society membership card and ask for a refund. Send the money to Roselle, Fullum and the Earth First!ers in Idaho. (Cockburn 1995b, 300)

The Wilderness Society's legal withdrawal revealed something about their unwillingness to offend their funding base; but for the direct-action environmentalists of the Cove/Mallard Coalition, it reaffirmed their stance that by continuing to deal with the legal system and mainstream green NGOs they would only achieve limited gains in this instance. In the years after the failed legal attempt, direct actions continued and the plight of the last Big Wild became national news. In the summer of 1999, President Clinton, concerned over the conditions of remaining roadless forest areas in the Northwest, instructed the Forest Service to create an administrative rule which would protect these areas. This was a welcome end-of-presidency gesture for environmentalists, though not reflective of Clinton's relatively poor environmental record, which failed to live up to its hype. In correspondence with the author, Kreilick partly rejoices, but also reflects on the short-term nature of victories reliant on presidential decrees and administrative orders and not based sufficiently in legislation: "In the end, they cut three of the sales amounting close to a quarter of the projected volume of 81 million board feet. We saved the best and, in so doing, this campaign catalyzed the needed attention around the plight of roadless forested areas. . . . It is as I write that this administrative rule is in the process of being scrapped by the Bush Administration and the new Forest Service chief Dale Bosworth who came from Missoula where he was the Regional Forester" (Kreilick to author 2001, 1).

Much of this chapter has asserted the apolitical nature of the environmental movement in the United States. It is tempting to argue that those actions of Earth First!ers, the Cove/Mallard Coalition, and the Native Forest Network are more political in that they explicitly regard the current political system as contributing to environmental degradation and, consequently, actively involve themselves in civil disobedience against that system. Only part of this conclusion, however, rings true. Many of the acts of disobedience are relatively uncoordinated exploits of individuals, with little counter-ideology or systemic critique forming part of their baggage. The ideology of American pluralism is so often all-consuming that it is impossible to imagine different systems of human organization. People who challenge the system are in a small minority, acting deep in forests, mostly outside of *normal* political arenas. They are regarded as mutants and, as the *Spokane Review* records, "screwballs." Ultimately, much of the focus of these ecoactivists is gaining mainstream media coverage for their forms of *ecotheater*. Far from being mass mobilization politics, this is classic pluralist appeals-to-elites strategy. Having said this, it is reasonable to conclude that without the direct-action politics of the forest activists within the U.S. Northwest, logging would have continued unabated.

The campaign for Cove/Mallard continues.

CONCLUSIONS

The environmental movement in the United States is sophisticated in its lobbying techniques and corporate strategies. No other green movement is wealthier. Much of the movement concentrates on issues of either efficient management or the intrinsic rights of *other nature,* though the more recent advent of the environmental justice movement is challenging this dominant ideology. As well as these more professional strategies, more radical environmentalists, such as those found at Cove/Mallard, operate largely outside the mainstream U.S. movement. They are best characterized by their more militant, direct-action techniques and strategies. Despite their *outsider* status, they rarely vocalize systemic opposition or alternatives, focusing on individual acts of *ecotage*. In this sense, they also reflect the *apolitical* nature of the mainstream environmental movement. This point will become more apparent as diverse national experiences are revealed in the following chapters.

As is the case of most green movements in the minority world, it is normal to experience powerful networks within national movements which have become largely *institutionalized* existing at the same time with other networks which deliberately abstain from institutionalization and formalization. Obviously these *two wings* are often in dynamic interplay/opposition, feeding off the strengths and weaknesses of each other. Social movements are remarkably diverse phenomena, with many different faces of political activity. Environmental movements are no exception to this rule. The major theme of institutionalization and its impact on minority-world green movements appears again and again throughout this work (see, particularly, chapters 4, 5, and 7).

It is apparent from the material presented in this chapter that environmental transnationalism is not a recurrent feature of mainstream American ecoactivism, which, apart from the symbolism of *global ecology*, remains transfixed by domestic concerns. Within new social movements, different political forms are better at playing transnational politics. It is obvious that the Washington beltway environmentalists find it extremely difficult to see the woods for the trees outside the parameters of American executive politics. On the other hand, it seems that environmentalists who are more adroit at crossing nation/state boundaries do so at the grassroots level, playing politics which is more informal and anarchistic in style. The Native Forest Network (NFN) is an outstanding example of these informal linkages operating at the global forest-campaign level. Also, Earth First! has managed to cross many nation/state boundaries, though usually these are restricted to Northern border crossings, whereas the NFN is truly transnational. In the final chapter we revisit this phenomenon.

The case of Cove/Mallard was chosen to balance out the earlier section I have written on the American movement, which, at times, overly concentrates on the mainstream U.S. environmental movements which operate their lobbying and corporate campaigns from national and state capitals. The campaign to save Cove/Mallard is important, also, as it provides evidence of its more militant tactics, though often overplayed by the mainstream media. Whilst environmental activism in most parts of the minority world is almost always nonviolent (at least by its own definition), the more radical wings of the forest movement in the United States are renowned for more militant tactics. The militancy of Cove/Mallard is very different, also, from the militancy of the Philippines movements witnessed in the next chapter. In the Philippines, violent environmental actions occur almost always in concert with other environmentalists, activists, indigenous peoples, and peasant farmers; whilst the militancy of American direct-action participants is ordinarily more off-beat and more individualistic. This is understandable, as in the case of the Philippines, or in many other third world forest campaigns, as direct action most often occurs when there is a corporate and/or governmental assault on the forests where people live. In this vein, people are simply protecting their habitat, their place on earth: there is often nowhere else to go. In the case of minority-world forest activists, direct actions occur in forests when activists usually enter the forest from "the outside" to directly interfere with logging procedures.

Let us now turn to the case of Philippines, to a very different set of green ideologies, themes, and issues which characterize green movements in the majority world.

MOVEMENTS AGAINST MINING

Environmental Movements in the Philippines

At Manila airport, customs officials quizzed us as to our purpose in Mindanao, which was regarded as extremely "unsafe" for tourists. Local newspapers were full of stories of anarchy and a society run by bandits in this southernmost island of the archipelago. Other official reports focused on the formation of large armies in the mountains, like the Moro Islamic Liberation Front (MILF); the New People's Army; the National Defense Front; the BHP (the soldiers of the people); the indigenous tribal warriors, such as the Bagani (the warriors of B'laan tribes); and convergences of other militant people's organizations (POs), such as the Alliance for Genuine Development.

From General Santos City, on the southern edge of Mindanao, we began to travel by road into the interior of the large and mountainous island. I was member of an International Fact-Finding Mission (IFFM) hosted by the Uniting Church of the Philippines and BAYAN, a Philippine nationalist umbrella organization (including environmental, labor, church, and human rights groups).[1] The IFFM was investigating the operations of an Australian-based transnational mining company, Western Mining Corporation (WMC), which had reputedly discovered the second biggest copper deposit in Asia in the mountains of Mindanao, the "rice-bowl" of the Philippines.

In November 1998, we conducted extensive interviews with different individuals and groups, including church leaders (both Christian and Muslim), municipal mayors, Filipino "settler" farming groups, environmental and human rights organizations, teachers in WMC-funded schools, WMC-funded "community organizers," and WMC employees at the Tampakan base camp.

One attempt at seeking this community input will live with me always. The IFFM was camping in the parish compound of a small town at the foot of the "Mossy Mountain" called Columbo in the Province of Sultan Kumarat. Early in the morning we set off on foot to speak to a community of B'laan people living at approximately two thousand feet above sea level. This particular community had refused to sign WMC's Memorandum of Agreement (MoA), which basically entailed handing over all legal and commercial rights of their ancestral domain to the company. When we finally arrived in this tiny village set on the edge of the forest, at the farthest point of assault by global markets, it appeared no one was there. Pastor Avel, the B'laan priest, told us to sit down, whilst he moved quietly into the village to investigate and, as we found out later, to negotiate. After a substantial wait, a cry or whistle rent the air, with warriors and other local people appearing from the forest into the clearing, flooding the village, welcoming us with food and water.

Soon we were sitting in the central hut talking to the elders and warriors of the community. After some significant time of negotiation, we learned that the people had hidden in the forest when they had seen the color of both my own and my countrywoman's skin. Also, with traditional communication, they had heard that Australians were amongst the party, and Australians could not be trusted as they were the oppressor. I explained that not all Australians supported WMC and other transnational companies mining the Philippines, and how many Australians, both indigenous and from the predominantly white environment movement, fought a similar campaign against the company in Australia. I explained that I was here to share these experiences and to pledge my own organization's solidarity with their struggle. I told them that they were not alone.

After this initial period, through the translations of our indigenous priest, the IFFM learned, firsthand, of the tribe's dealings with WMC. We learned of the specifics of the company's divide-and-rule tactic, the tensions it had created in the community, and the deaths and injuries that had ensued. We learned of the story of one particular B'laan chief, Afnelu-Timon, of Buluf Salo, Kiblanan. The Seventy-fifth Infantry Regiment had recently burnt all the houses in his village and killed his people's caribou. The chief believed that this was an act of retribution delivered due to his tribal group's unwillingness to sign agreements with WMC. This story reinforced the Australian Broadcasting Corporation's reports that WMC had condoned the use of the military to resolve land conflicts delaying its mining operations.

We discussed strategy. The B'laan explained that they had no place to go, that over recent generations, due to different pressures of invasion and resettlement, they had been driven from the lowlands into the highlands. First came the Spaniards; then came the Americans; and now the Australians (or more accurately transnational capital). If they lost this place, then they were dead. They argued against dealing further with the company, as any dealings had always led to trouble and grief. The Bagani warriors sitting quietly in the room (who are arrested by the military on sight) explained that they had performed a secret pact known as "Dyandi." This ritual relates to the defense of the land "to the last drop of blood": there was nothing post-materialist or post-modern about this conflict. It was not about such Northern concepts as biodiversity or greenhouse gas emissions: it was about immediate life or death.

The rain fell in the afternoon, and we were forced to say our good-byes to this particular community in a hurry. The clearance of the forest by a Japanese logging company had been so intense and so rapid on Mossy Mountain that any significant downpour became a flash flood, and rivers which we had traversed at ankle depth on the way up would become walls of water on the way down within hours. On leaving, one old B'laan man said good-bye to me through a translator and asked me, in song, a parting question: "Why has God made you so powerful and the B'laan so powerless?"

One other image stands out in my mind here. I was with a Catholic parish priest just out of Tampakan, and we were attempting to cross a river at a time of a flash flood. A WMC four-wheel-drive vehicle appeared, and an employee offered us a lift through the raging waters. Coming from a society and social movement which were used to dealing with the company, I was about to gladly accept the kind offer, when the priest bluntly answered in the negative for both of us. After waving the vehicle on, we plunged into the murky, fast-flowing waters. On the way back to the parish housing, the priest explained, "Tim, when battling against an adversary of equal strength, engagement and negotiation is a useful tool. But when the adversary is far more powerful than you, usually to engage is to lose. The only power the people of Mindanao have against WMC is their own solidarity. Once some of us deal, then trust is broken within our own ranks, and we lose our key source of power."

Many minority-world environmental movements increasingly perceive themselves in recent times using a misconstrued notion of post-modern space where all possible avenues are to be pursued simultaneously. Unfortunately, the strategic weapon of traditional adversarial politics, of disengagement and dissent, has been increasingly forgotten. My trip to Mindanao reinforced the point that "nice negotiations" with an adversary may not always be appropriate.[2]

■ ■ ■

INTRODUCTION

If the United States is an *apolitical* culture in the way which I have described it, then in the Philippines the experience is the polar opposite. *People power*

FIG. 3.1. The clergy at Tampakan, site of a proposed open-pit mine, the Philippines, 1998. *Author's private collection.*

dominates political arenas, as most Filipinos actively engage and celebrate in their political lives. This cultural difference has huge repercussions on social movement phenomena: from the strategies which are pursued to the ways in which movement decisions are made and implemented.

There are some commonalities which have emerged amongst environmental movements, between those just reviewed in the United States and those existing in the Philippines. Large "green" coalitions of seemingly disparate groups have formed in both countries as part of many protests/campaigns. It is the profound difference, however, between the two movements' operational styles which is more apparent. These differences are echoed time and time again in any work which seeks a comparative understanding of environmental movements from a North/South perspective (see box 3.1 for a discussion of African environmental movements). Although sharing elements of environmental discourse and identification, the movements reviewed in this and the previous chapters pursue vastly different forms of environmental protest, using the rhetoric of different ideologies to justify their actions and strategies.

In part, this reflects the cultural and political milieus of the two countries. As aforesaid, the U.S. movement is post-materialist in its ideology; is dominated by appeals-to-elites tactics; is usually reformist; and is dedicated to ultimately producing individual *value-change*, rather than envisioning and pro-

Box 3.1

African Environmental Movements: The Ogoni People versus Shell

Ogoni is a land of half a million people in the Niger Delta region of Nigeria. Since 1958, oil companies such as Shell, in conjunction with Nigerian elites, have exploited Ogoni's oil wealth, while the Ogoni people have suffered economic deprivation, the environmental devastation of the land, and the discriminatory policies of successive Nigerian governments (http:/www.oneworld.org/mosop/, 26 August 2001).

To date, 900 million barrels of oil worth some 30 billion U.S. dollars have been taken from the land in Ogoni. The Ogoni have seen few of the financial benefits of the oil, having no running water, no electricity, and improper government health services. However, their land has been ruined by oil blowouts, gas flaring, and other oil operations.

MOSOP and the Ogoni people's first massive peaceful protest was the 4 January 1993 demonstration. More than 300,000 Ogoni took to the streets and not a soul was injured. Disturbed by the effectiveness of MOSOP's organization, Shell officials began to meet with Nigerian representatives to find a way to stop MOSOP. It was clear in these meetings that Shell was passing on information to the Nigerian military that could potentially threaten the safety of Ogoni activists. In the same year, a number of raids against Ogoni communities were played up by the Nigerian dictatorship as being ethnic clashes between Ogoni and Andoni peoples.

Shell has long denied that it financially supports the military forces in Nigeria. However, in leaked memos, the Nigerian military has made it clear that it expects Shell to pay for its military operations in Ogoni. In late 1995, it also emerged that Shell had been buying weapons for the Nigerian police who operate around oil facilities.

"As a result of this state-orchestrated violence, more than 2,000 innocent Ogoni have died. Approximately 30,000 have been forced to leave their homes and are internally displaced in Ogoni. Approximately 2,000 have escaped to neighboring states, or have been forced into exile as refugees" (http://www.oneworld.org/mosop/).

Shell has been working hard behind the scenes, trying to convince the Ogoni people so that they can start their operations once more. The Ogoni people still refuse to let Shell into Ogoni until they properly compensate the Ogoni people for decades of pollution and pay the Ogoni a fair share of oil revenue (http://www.mosopcanda.org/shell.html).

SOURCE: *Adapted from Wiwa,* Obsanjo and Transnational Oil Companies: Rightsizing Shell in Nigeria, *http//:www.mosopcanada.org/review.html#rightsizing.*

moting structural societal change. It promotes the pursuit of all possible strategic pathways, both working within and against the state, big business, and other sectoral communities.

In the Philippines, although still predominantly a neo-feudal state, more traditional, structuralist, and oppositional understandings of power are usefully deployed to describe this nation's politics and its forms of environmental protests. In turn, social and environmental protests are more revolutionary and more readily definable, with clear lines of conflict drawn in the sand. "Enemies" are visible (despite transnational capital's "no-fixed address"); the "other" is discernible; there is usually lucid difference between the boundaries of the powerful and the powerless. The language of Marxism and derivations thereof is never far away. Consequently, these battles are not particularly metaphorical, nor is power unduly dispersed or hidden. Its most visible manifestation occurs in direct, violent conflict between two armed forces: the state's military, police, and multinational security forces versus a *green army*.

THE ENVIRONMENTAL MOVEMENT IN THE PHILIPPINES

The Philippines is geographically situated in the South, more particularly in the Asia-Pacific region.[3] True to the nomenclature of the South, economically the Philippines, a vast archipelago of islands, is commonly referred to as being part of the third, developing, emerging, or majority world. The Philippines' economy, as touched upon, is still semi-feudal by definition; it is largely preindustrial and neocolonial. It continues to have few local industries which produce basic metals, chemicals, and capital goods. It remains largely agrarian (Sison and De Lima 1998, 9). The Philippines chiefly comprises a peasant population, with approximately 70 percent of its people living in rural areas; 15 percent are regarded as working class, with approximately another 12 percent judged to be middle class. The society is largely governed, however, by an extremely small elite (1 to 2 percent) which controls the military and most of the country's financial resources. This elite includes the landlord class as well as urban elites, and its power remains relatively intact, despite the fall of the Marcos regime in the late 1980s. The power of these elite networks is further supported by large, predominantly northern-based transnational corporations and, in certain instances, their governments.

Environmentalism is not particularly fashionable in the middle class in the Philippines. Broad and Cavanagh, in an excellent travelogue detailing the devastation of the Philippines' environment and the activism which seeks to restore it, explain that the environmental movement is largely a movement of poor people, working alongside the political left, development NGOs, and church-based organizations, which have been on the "wrong end" of decades of environmental plunder carried out by both national and transnational elites (Broad and Cavanaugh 1993).

There is nothing post-materialistic about the Filipino environmental movement: its green agenda is not centered on luxury and higher-order ideals relating to those wilderness values mentioned in the previous and the subsequent chapters (although there are some nature conservation issues included); but rather, as with most other majority-world green movements, activists involve themselves in the struggle to *survive*—a fight for social and environmental justice.

Moreover, the dichotomy between humans and *other nature* is not so marked, as is the case in first world forest and wilderness movements, loosely informed as they are by the philosophies of Western science and philosophy. In an edited work which focuses on Asian environmental movements, Kalland and Persoon contend, "At best, the distinction between anthropocentrism and ecocentrism . . . is irrelevant to the Asian context and might distract attention away from more pressing problems. Worse, it distorts and conceals the subtlety of much Asian thought" (Kalland and Persoon 1997, 5). This comparative difference between the minority and majority worlds over the issue of the human/nature divide is a most important one and is taken up again in chapter 5 on the Indian environmental movement.

Since the fall of Marcos, "civil society" in the Philippines is regarded as one of the most active and inspirational in the world. In the Philippines a vast and vibrant environmental movement is fighting environmental degradation head-on across a range of fronts (Broad 1994, 813). Whilst many minority-world green NGO organizational numbers are decreasing, in the last decade there has been a veritable explosion of environment and development NGOs in the Philippines (Doyle and McEachern 1998, 82). In 1994, Princen and Finger counted eighteen thousand NGOs which could be labeled green (1994, 1–2). There is, no doubt, ten to a hundred times this number of networks and community groups which also exist, though not formalizing their operations to the extent where they could be considered fully fledged, constitutionalized organizations. Mittleman describes the movement in the Philippines and elsewhere in the majority world as follows: "Environmentalists are playing a prominent role in the rapidly growing resistance to globalization. . . . Their resistance can be best understood as a deep-rooted process, and may be likened to a broad tree whose branches and shoots consist of several institutions—churches, trade unions, the business sector, peasant associations, and student groups—that have participated, and often joined together, in rallying around environmental issues" (2000, 383).

Although transnational green NGOs, such as Greenpeace, Worldwide Fund for Nature (WWF), and Friends of the Earth (FoE), are involved in the Filipino movement, it is both the national and community-based organizations which dominate the scene. Probably the largest umbrella organization is the Caucus of Development NGO Networks (itself a network of networks), including approximately three thousand individual organizations (Mittelman 2000, 383).

One of these national organizations (itself another network) is KALIKASAN (People's Network for the Environment). Much of the emphasis of such organizations is not to end environmentally degrading development per se, but rather to take control of such development from the auspices of large transnational corporations (usually with head offices in other countries) and place it in the hands of local people, who, it is hoped, will pursue appropriate and "genuine" development, with fewer negative environmental consequences. In a presentation at the International Conference against Mining Transnational Corporations in the Philippines, Carol Almeda, chairperson of KALIKASAN makes this very point, a message which is repeated again and again in the environment/development responses of green NGOs in the majority world:

> Thus, globalization keeps impoverished Third World countries in the orbit of the moribund monopoly capital: a global system of exploitation for the sake of accumulation of profit. It is the chain that binds the people to poverty, deprivation and repression. To break free from this bondage, there is no other recourse but to collectively tread the path of self-reliant development which instills an orientation that sets as priority the needs of the people. It is never an attempt to romanticize underdevelopment and shun modernization and progress. Rather, it aims to establish an order more responsive to the needs of the people as they propel society to a higher and better quality of life. (Almeda 1998, 3)

Apart from these larger NGOs at national level, there are grassroots organizations sometimes referred to by the activists as people's organizations (POs). These have disparate purposes: some provide yet another layer of networks at the regional level. The Alliance for Genuine Development (AGD), based in General Santos City in Mindanao, is a political convergence of militant people's organizations. Such organizations actively oppose the militarization of their environments imposed by government forces which, they argue, use their "executive, legislative, judiciary and military might to promote foreign monopoly control" (AGD 1997). One task of POs affiliated to the AGD is to challenge what they perceive as the *dominant propaganda* of these development interests with their own propaganda. One group, itself called the Armed Propaganda Team, Section 03, Front 72, CPP/NPA/NDF, writes, "Defending our ecology from a giant multi-national firm's aggression to the lands of the lumads is a very noble cause. We are one with you in protecting our environment and defending the welfare of the lumads in particular and the Filipino people in general. Down with U.S. imperialism, Feudalism and Fascism. Mabuhay!" (Armed Propoganda Team 1998).

Other POs are employed in the actual implementation of environment/development projects. Unlike the Australian, United States, English, and German movements, many of these POs are not involved in lobbying governments, working with "green" corporations, or involving people in mass demonstrations. Instead, they are on-the-ground service providers for communities whose interests have not been served by government or corporate programs. Again, this is a common characteristic of majority-world environ-

FIG. 3.2. Muslim and Christian groups working together in Colombo, the Philippines, 1998. *Author's private collection.*

mental movements. One example in the Philippines is HASIK. Formed by a group of women (as so often is the case in the context of majority-world POs and grassroots groups) in the mid-1980s, HASIK provides assistance to the urban poor through a "community-based approach that includes organizing, livelihood, and other social services" (Hrichak 2001, 208). Hrichak describes some of the programs of service provision as follows: "Addressing basic needs first, the group builds alternative housing technologies and designs known as eco-shelters. It also promotes the use of secondhand container vans and other alternative building materials to provide economical and environment-friendly housing for the poor. Early childhood care and development programs are another important focus. Members created a curriculum adapted to the urban poor and trained teachers from the communities to handle the classes" (2001, 209).

One other feature of environmental movements in the Philippines is the role of religious institutions, and this point was singled out for treatment in the preface of this book. Their role is contrasted starkly with the decimation of organized religion as moral leader in many parts of the minority world. In the Catholic Church, which is the largest in the Philippines, all levels of the church are opposed to WMC, from the bishops down to the lay clergy.

In the Uniting Church of the Philippines and the Methodist Church, on the other hand, there are informal networks of "liberation theologists" (not usually referred to as such) who join the struggle, though their own hierarchies are largely pro-mining. One NGO, the Philippines Churches for People's Resistance (PCPR), provides organizational support for these liberation theologists of all persuasions in the absence of support from their own institutions. Both Muslim and Christian religious organizations often work together, hand in hand, in these networks of POs.

Chief characteristics, therefore, of Filipino environmental movements include their anti-institutional nature, their militancy, their heightened use of networking as a political form, their broadness (even more diverse than their minority-world counterparts), and their often revolutionary nature. The last point is most crucial of all. As elucidated in the opening to this chapter, the lines of opposition in the Philippines' movement are clearly drawn. This leads to structuralist language and ideology as well as adversarial politics. On few occasions are the *appeals-to-elites* strategies—utilized so often in the North— employed.

ANTI-MINING MOVEMENTS

The minerals industry is one of the most powerful forms of industry on the planet. Its extraction of earth, its use of chemicals, its pollution of waterways and land, its clearance of native vegetation, its displacement of people, amongst other factors, also make the industry one of the earth's largest environmental offenders. The capacity for the industry's social and environmental devastation has increased in the past five to ten years in the Asia-Pacific region due to the unfettering of the global marketplace, with the concomitant weakening of national legislation. Roger Moody, a key transnational anti-mining activist, contends:

> The economies of the South are now being reopened to mining TNCs through structural adjustment and the liberalization of the global economy. Under pressure from the IMF and the World Bank, more than 70 countries have changed their mining laws to make themselves more attractive to foreign investment; foreign ownership restrictions have been watered down or abolished; and mining TNCs are being invited to bid for state-owned mining assets, as huge sections of industry—from Brazil's national flagship CVRD, the world's biggest iron ore producer, to Zambia's copper industry—are being offered for sale under "free market" privatization programmes. (1996, 46)

The anti-mining movement includes Northern NGOs such as Moody's Partizans, which follows the exploits of the world's largest mining company— Rio Tinto Zinc—across the globe. Due to the fact that these huge transnational companies operate largely outside the legislative boundaries of nation-states, it is imperative that their movements are tracked by social movements which are, in theory at least, equally as capable of making these cross-country traverses. Transnational information-sharing becomes even more important than usual. In this information-sharing, there is no doubt that, at the cyber level at least, these movements are becoming increasingly transnational, despite the abiding existence of very different ideological frameworks informing most activism in the North and the South. Demonstrating this global reach of the anti-mining movement, one particular "mines and communities" Web site is sponsored by JATAM (Mining Advocacy Network, Indonesia; Mines, Minerals, and Peoples, India; Minewatch Asia Pacific Project, Philippines; Partizans, People against Rio Tinto Zinc and Its Subsidiaries, U.K.; Philippines Indigenous Peoples Links, U.K.; the Society of St. Colomban, U.K.; and Third World Network, Ghana).

Minority-world NGOs include those which support a more radical stance, such as Partizans, as well as those which decide to *work with* the big companies. Again, Worldwide Fund for Nature (WWF) presents itself as the quintessential example of the latter approach, attracting wide criticism by many Southern green NGOs for what they perceive as WWF's mercenary character and its lack of solidarity with their needs. One excellent example of this strategic approach was the deal struck between the Rio Tinto Zinc (RTZ) and WWF in April/May 2000. The world's biggest miner paid WWF, now one of the world's richest environment NGOs, $1.2 million over four years for its "frogs" project in Indonesia. Some environmentalists described these actions by WWF as the *"greenwashing"* of RTZ and pointed out that it occurred at the same time that the company actively lobbied against greenhouse protocols and promoted mining in national parks in the North. In WWF's partial defense, some NGOs defend their engagement with the corporate sector in this manner as a means of gaining information, due to the fact that there are few other avenues of effective involvement, now that the state is increasingly devolving its environmental management role in many nations of the earth.

The local Filipino movement does not usually embark upon such strategies of embracing the companies in order to "change their ways from the inside." As already asserted, the movement usually maintains a separate and aggressive opposition to the transnationals.

There has been no substantial history of medium- or large-scale mining in the Philippines initiated either by the state or local companies. In just a short span of time, however, multinational mining companies have already produced dramatic devastation. For example, in both the Cordillera (Benguet Mines) and Marinduque (Marcopper-Placerdome), open-pit mining operations have led to massive erosion and siltation of agricultural areas; water resources have been contaminated or depleted; communities—both settler and indigenous—have been violated and impoverished; and, in Marinduque, fishing areas have vastly been reduced and poisoned. Despite these environmental disasters occurring with such rapidity, the doors to foreign mining investment have been opened fully since the adoption of the New Mining Act of 1995, set up by then President Fidel V. Ramos.

The act and its implementing mechanism, the Financial and Technical Assistance Agreement (FTAA), have proved particularly attractive to Australian, U.S., and Canadian mining companies due to numerous unprecedented incentives offered to them. These include a five- to ten-year tax break, a twenty-five- to fifty-year tenure over one hundred thousand hectares of land per mining contract, exclusive water and timber rights, and absolute authority over mining areas. There are now 100 FTAA and 1,502 Mineral Production Sharing Agreement (MPSA) contracts pending approval. These applications cover almost half of the Philippines' land area. What is additionally interesting in relation to the following case study is that Australian governments, at both the state and federal levels, have been intimately involved in the drawing up of Filipino bureaucratic regimes which allow for "best practice management" of Australian mining companies (Corpez 1966, 1). Let us now look at the specifics of one transnational mining company, Western Mining Corporation, and the environmental campaign which has grown around its discovery of what has been claimed to be the second largest copper deposit in Asia.

THE CAMPAIGN FOR TAMPAKAN

Western Mining Corporation (WMC) is an Australian-based multinational company. In Australia, it is currently expanding its copper-uranium mine to become one of the largest uranium mines in the world. Much opposition to the company in its own country is based on anti-nuclear sentiments and advocacy for the basic rights of Australian indigenous peoples. In the Philippines, WMC has discovered its copper deposit on the southern island of Mindanao. The company is nearing the end of a decade-long "exploratory" phase.

Although Western Mining has received an award from its own industry relating to the quality of its environmental reporting, and regardless of the fact that it portrays itself as a socially and environmentally sound citizen, it can be safely said that few mining companies evoke the ire of environmental movements to the same extent in both countries. In its country of origin, Australia, and in the Philippines, WMC has succeeded in pressuring governments (and working directly with them) into producing legislation which favors its long-term operations and limits the powers of those who wish to regulate or oppose it. The Philippines 1995 New Mining Act has already been mentioned in this context. In Australia, the Roxby Downs (Indenture Ratification) Act of

1982 prohibits the public disclosure of any material passed between the state government and WMC without both parties' mutual consent. The implications of confidentiality arrangements are significant, to say the least. Shared secrets lead to further shared arrangements.

In their efforts to ascertain "public acceptance" from the indigenous chiefs, the company has consultants to initiate Western-style elections to form a "Tribal Council" which has produced "representatives" of the indigenous communities. Obviously, this process has offended many of the chieftains, who are culturally selected by other means, but it has ensured that Western Mining has been able to put a framework into place which undermines those tribes which do not sign the Memorandum of Agreement, whilst empowering B'laan people who are willing to work with the company.

WMC Philippines is diligent in selling the concept that it is a company which operates on "best environmental practice." One example of rhetoric ruling over reality is the company's creation of a community committee (CBEMP) which oversees the environmental monitoring of the company's exploration phase. There are no scientists on the CBEMP. Members are trained briefly at a local high school in basic data collation techniques, and then this data is sent off to the multinational Dole Chemicals for "independent analysis." As it does at Roxby Downs, in Central Australia, effectively, the company "self-monitors."

When asked by the IFFM if WMC Philippines would release the results of its own corporate, scientific analysis on its projected options for tailings management, the IFFM was informed that this information was not "public" despite WMC's constant claims that it is a "transparent" organization. What was ascertained from a meeting which the author attended with WMC staff at the Tampakan base camp in November 1998 was that the company was seriously considering dumping its tailings directly into the sea. "Marine disposal," an operation which is illegal in Australia, would bring unknown hazards to the thousands of fisher folk who pursue a subsistence living along the coastal area.

In the Philippines, proof has emerged which supports the case that WMC has condoned the use of the military to resolve land conflicts delaying its mining operations (Williams 1998). The IFFM received evidence from one particular B'laan chief, Afnelu-Timon, of Buluf Salo, Kiblanan. The chief described the operations of the Seventy-fifth Infantry Regiment, which had burnt all the houses in his village and killed their livestock.

The network of groups and organizations fighting the campaign against WMC in the Philippines is vast. In addition, this network perceives the problem to be more than just WMC, but often places the issue within the broader context of other transnational mining companies. The network is impossible to list here: it is simply too long. Some of the groups included are BAYAN (New Peoples Alliance); CPA (Cordillera People's Alliance); INNABUYOG

Fig. 3.3. Village of resistance to the Western Mining Corporation mine, Mindanao, the Philippines, 1998. *Author's private collection.*

(Alliance of Indigenous Women's Organizations in the Cordillera); KAMP (Alliance of Indigenous Peoples in the Philippines); KALIKASAN (People's Network for the Environment); the Alliance for Genuine Development; UMALPAS (People's Network against Mining and Land Conversion); KMP (Peasant Movement of the Philippines); PAMALAKAYA (National Fisher Folk Organization); KMU (First May Movement); HEAD (Health Alliance for Democracy); KARAPATAN (Alliance for the Advancement of People's Rights); COURAGE (National Organization for Government Employees/ Workers); MORO (Muslim Liberation Front); and the list goes on.

For reasons already alluded to, Filipino green activists rarely pursue appeals-to-elites politics. Nearly all of their strategies revolve around mass mobilizations, informed by structuralist/Marxist ideologies. Obviously, in this light, the movement does not deal with corporate- and state-dominated roundtables. The separation of the movement from WMC and the state is even more dramatic than this example can provide. In this vein, to enter into negotiations is nearly always seen as positioning into a situation which will favor the company. Maintaining absolute separation from one's adversary is seen as the only way and, as such, to work on a company-inspired roundtable would be regarded as foolishness and with profound suspicion. The structural divisions are profound. To suggest that structuralist/Marxist models, framing all issues as *masses versus elites,* are the only ways in which environmental movements perceive and play their politics in the Philippines would be a gross simplification. There are green NGOs which do lobby government, which do work with corporations, which do work within the established systems of politics and business-as-usual. Majid Cooke writes, "The path of resistance has not been unilinear; it is replete with stories of accommodation. . . . Some groups suffered from the effects of the Aquino regime's 'total war' counter-insurgency policy, the subsequent amnesty offered to resisting groups, and the split in the Left that ensued" (1999, 184).

In partial agreement with Cooke, there can be no doubt that there are many subtleties to be understood in the story of Filipino resistance to various programs of "development." But when compared to green movements in the minority world, for example, this strategy of *non-engagement* with an adversary (apart from militant engagement) must be regarded as a general and defining trend, *indicative* of the broader green movement in the Philippines and a primary characteristic of so much environmental activism in the majority world.

There are a range of different mass mobilization strategies that demand attention here. First, and most importantly, is *community organizing*. Activists from the green coalitions place themselves within communities. Due to the predominantly peasant demography, activists move into villages and seek to become full-time, trusted members of the communities. In this manner they educate the community about the negative aspects of WMC, whilst learning from the community what their needs are. This is the politics of insurgency which was well-practiced in the Philippines during the long Marcos dictatorship. Again I refer to Cooke, in her work on forest politics in the Asia/Pacific region, as she writes about community organizing in the Philippines:

> In the 1970s, in relation to Martial law by Marcos, community orga-nisers, which began with the initiatives of church groups, influenced by liberation theology and the violent student protest movement of the late 1960s, spread beyond urban centres to rural areas. Community organis-ers worked with cultural communities exposing them to local issues and general political education. Such exposure strengthened their resolve and helped make sense of their resistance to a range of development projects (for example the Chico hydroelectric dam and the Cellophil Resource Corporation) that, in the long run, were seen as having an effect of deny-ing them access to their sources of subsistence. (1999, 184)

Interestingly, WMC is mimicking this style of grassroots organizing. During the IFFM, several company community organizers were interviewed, and they explained their counter-insurgency role within these villages. These company-employed community organizers are placed in the village to secure signatures on the Principal Agreements. Other community organizers attempt to sabotage the signing of such agreements. In any one village, it is usual to have several different community organizers advocating conflictual interests and promising different things to the people. One may be from the Peace and Justice Desk of the Catholic Church; another will be from the "Maoist-style" KMU; whilst the third will be the company's man. According to Pastor Avel Sichon of the Uniting Church of the Philippines, "This is ideological warfare." Obviously, this form of politics relies on the existence of "communities" in the first place.

Mass mobilization also includes mass information programs. Bayan reports, "Massive information campaigns were launched by the affected residents, support groups, religious, local government, united peoples organizations in the affected provinces, and other multi-sectoral groups advocating for the Lumad's (broad term for indigenous people in the Philippines) rights to self-determination and ancestral domain. The local populace are getting more aware and apprehensive about the effects of mining laws, agreements, policies and projects" (IFFM 1999, 10).

The church is also involved in these education programs. In this light, anti-WMC seminars are delivered from the pulpit in, for example, the township of Tampakan, and comprehensive anti-mining campaigns are being waged in church-run schools. These mass education programs also extend to the indigenous peoples. For example, Sister Susan Bolanio, of the Justice and Peace Group of the Catholic Church in the Diocese of Marbel, utilizes the concept of *exposure tours* to educate indigenous communities of the dangers of open-pit mining. She has arranged five different tours to the disastrous BENGUET open-pit mine, which resulted in several tribal chiefs withdrawing their support for WMC and refusing to sign the Memorandum of Agreement.

Loosely related to these education programs and exposure tours are the International Fact-Finding Missions (IFFMs). IFFMs are far more, however, than just forms of education. They have several other raison d'être:

1. They promote the concept of international solidarity and build networks with groups outside of the country, thus recognizing the transnational character of global capital and the necessity of establishing different types of networks across nation-states. These networks allow and encourage actions back in the international participants' home states. Actions are then initiated which strike at the source of the WMC shareholder's cultural context.

2. Northern exposure is provided for international members of IFFMs. Experience is the only way to educate non-Filipinos of the nature of the struggle. The reality is so shocking and confronting to Northern participants that it galvanizes their support, as well as that of the Northern NGOs which they are representing.

3. They provide protection on the ground for local activists who are involved in community organizing at the grassroots level. This is based on the belief that the military is far less likely to involve itself in open hostility when international citizens of "a certain standing" are involved. In this manner, the internationals play the role of shield.

4. The presence of international "visitors" also promotes curiosity and resultant media coverage.

5. Insights and information relating to the company's activities and maneuvers are shared by both international and local participants. In the case of WMC, valuable information was traded relating to the company's tactics for confusing ancestral domain issues. As the treatment of Australian aboriginal people was so similar to the unfolding scenario in the Philippines, including the employment of the same personnel, the B'laan people were empowered to the extent that they could fine-tune their tactics for resistance. In addition, after learning of the appalling treatment of indigenous people in Central Australia, this further strengthened the conviction to resist.

6. They raise much needed campaign funds.

Protests also occur in the form of mass rallies, marches, and "caravan" processions. Mass rallies have been held in both Manila and Mindanao against WMC and other transnational corporations. Forms of protest are varied. Mass protests, which are usually illegal, often involve direct physical confrontations between protesters and the military, police, and security forces. The caravan rally or procession is an interesting protest phenomenon. Activists are gathered and ferried to and from base communities to the place of protest in "jeepnies" (substantially modified Second World War U.S. Army jeeps). These movements through the streets are physical manifestations of mechanical mobilization, which is necessary in any ultimate conflict between two armed, opposing forces. These caravan rallies constantly attract attention from the broader community; but they also advertise the fact to potential supporters and their adversaries that their oppositional force is sophisticated, well-organized, and capable of striking with precision.

Environmental protest in the Philippines is violent at both the individual and collective levels. Acts of coercion and force are normal. Whereas in most parts of the minority world concepts of nonviolent action are central to all forms of protest, this is regarded by Filipino green activists as a luxury response. Of course, as the culture is dominated by Christian and Muslim traditions, the nonviolent strategies of, for example, engaged Buddhism, used so effectively in green protests in Sri Lanka and Thailand, are not as evident in the activists' menu here (see box 3.2 for reference to environmental movements in Thailand).

Box 3.2

Thai Environmental Movements and Buddhism

Thailand made a definite move towards westernization with its progression from an absolute monarchy to constitutional monarchy in 1932. Since then Thailand has followed Japan and the "Asian Tigers" to become the model developing capitalist economy of Asia. The resultant change in the structure of Thai society has included a demographic transition towards urbanization and an increase in the "afflictions of affluence."

Since 1989 Thailand has instituted a ban on logging, however it is still involved in projects which clear old growth forests. In particular, the gas pipeline from the Yadana gas field off the Burmese coast to the Ratchaburi power plant in Thailand has required the felling of forests in national parks and, for many, symbolises the nation's abandonment of its Buddhist heritage in favour of western-style development.

The Yadana Gas Project was formally initiated in 1992. Once construction is completed gas sales to Thailand are estimated at between 200–400 million USD annually. The completed pipeline is to be approximately 700 km long. The construction of the pipeline has had numerous impacts on the surrounding environment.

Many groups, both inside and outside Thailand, have been concerned with the linking of the Thai Government with Burmese military junta through the Yadana project. . . . numerous international reports have documented the environmental and human rights abuses occurring on the Burmese side of the border. . . . these issues were also linked to the Buddhist protests over environmental concern in Thailand and beyond.

Buddhism has often been seen as a reclusive spiritual pursuit in the west, and as an inhibitor to development in the east. There is, however, another side to Buddhism . . . "Engaged Buddhism" . . . socially active Buddhists who promote peace and social and environmental awareness. By 1989 this activity had turned into a worldwide social movement and the International Network of Engaged Buddhists was formed in Bangkok . . . to help co-ordinate socially active Buddhist groups across the globe. In this vein, a coalition of new and extant activist groups was formed to try and prevent the Yadana pipeline from being built, on the grounds of wilderness destruction, environmental degradation, inappropriate development, and collaboration of the Thai Government with the Burmese military junta.

Violence, in the forms of individual cases of murder and threats of murder, is also relatively common in Northern terms, reflecting the profound violence splashed across the entire Philippines political canvas. It is the formation of large coalitions of militant people's organizations which, if anything, characterizes the most dramatic difference between movements against mining in minority worlds and those in majority worlds. These *green armies* usually engage themselves in forms of guerrilla warfare. This militant network includes the Moro-Islamic Liberation Front, the "Bandits," indigenous tribal warriors such as the Bagani (the warriors of B'laan tribes), the New People's Army, the National Defense Front, the BHB (the soldiers of the people), and convergences of other militant people's organizations, such as the Alliance for Genuine Development. It is difficult to measure this resistance, although on cur-

Box 3.2

Continued

One of the most fundamental and most visible practical results of this Buddhist activism is the principle of non-violence. Non-cooperation or peaceful protest in the face of violence, whether physical or environmental, requires greater self-discipline than violent retaliation. Nonviolent activism is not limited to Buddhism but . . . true Buddhist practitioners consider it the only way to fight injustice, whether social or environmental.

Symbolic of this Buddhist approach was the protest at the pipeline site for 72 days by the Kanchanaburi Environmental Group (KEG), culminating in the arrest of [a] renowned Buddhist scholar. . . . [Another] strategy . . . used . . . at the pipeline site is the ordaining of trees to prevent them being felled. This . . . is the Buddhist philosophy of valuing all life equally put into a political perspective. . . .

. . . . an important aspect of the protests was the press coverage gained in questioning such large scale development projects in an area where few protests had previously been seen. This coverage, together with . . . mass protests in Bangkok . . . brought the community together and raised an awareness of issues which had hitherto been unquestioned. The Buddhist influence on many of the groups . . . also the protests were held non-violently and allowed the groups to view the environmentally disruptive development in the context of their Buddhist cultural heritage.

The impact of Buddhist spirituality in, predominantly lay, activists has become more evident as responses to ecological and social issues, such as the Yadana pipeline project, have become more vociferous. These responses by Buddhists in the east are symptomatic of a growing global battle between spiritual and material concerns. In future, therefore, we are more likely to see a more activist-based Buddhist laity and sangha across the globe as the essence of Buddhism, rather than its petrified ritual and tradition, becomes the focus of Buddhist practitioners.

SOURCE: *Simpson 1998.*

---

rent estimations approximately thirty thousand counter-troops have been mobilized in Mindanao in opposition to WMC and other corporations perceived as the face of transnational capital.

CONCLUSIONS

It is critical to understand that Northern and Southern movements are largely ideologically distinct. This factor, more than any other, explains their difference and, perhaps, their inability to ultimately mesh.

There are some *descriptive* advantages of post-modern and post-structural models of power in the context of the minority world, as depicted in the previous and subsequent chapters. On the negative side, there are many weaknesses in these arguments when they are asked to *prescribe* future actions which question the power of capital as a class, most obviously manifested in the operations of large corporations. Some "new philosophers" have used Foucault's work to discount the possibility of any real change in the distribution of power amongst people (Anderson 1988). Let us not forget, as we juggle the subtle strengths and weaknesses of structural versus post-structural perceptions of the deployment of power, that most people in the North operate every day under the notion that the *pluralist* system of power is not a model at all, but simply the reality which they live under. The pluralist democratic system advocates that every citizen has equal access to power, with no additional power given to any specific interest group or section of society. It does not accept that large corporations have a privileged position toward the state (Lindblom 1977), let alone that they often dictate terms, or even that they sometimes are indistinguishable from the state.

If we partly accept, as Stephen Bell argues, that "the whole world has now become a capitalist system"—"with its capacity to terrorize and discipline national governments through currency depreciation or capital flight"—then we must not be afraid to increasingly view the interests of large corporations and business interests as very similar, if not the same(1995, 30–33). We must, at the same time, not overemphasize their unity. Their power, despite its immensity, can also be quite fragile.

Whilst these models have some limited applications as descriptive tools for explaining environmental protest in the North, they have been wrongly interpreted as prescriptive models by strategists within the many minority-world green movements. This has led to many "protests" which reinvent the concept of community only for a fleeting moment. In the South, these models are entirely inappropriate either to describe or to prescribe future mobilization of environmental movements within or across borders.

Post-modern, ambiguous, and diffuse notions of power and their resultant strategies are more effective in places where advanced industrialism/capitalism has led to most people's ideological acceptance of radical libertarianism and free-market economics, where it has reduced the capacity of local communities to exist separately (let alone to engage in dissent), where life has been largely privatized and commodified, and where local and diverse cultural meanings have been replaced with the meta-narrative of nature as global marketplace.

Less ambiguous strategies, which are more conflictual and revolutionary, seem both more popular and appropriate in neo-feudal and neocolonial societies such as the Philippines, where ruling elites—either national or transnational—are in a small minority and where the ideological struggle between advanced capitalism and other idea frameworks (those based on alternative religions, socialism, feminism, indigenous and community-based knowledge frameworks, etc.) still exists with some power to challenge.

POSTSCRIPT

Since completing the fieldwork for this chapter, against all odds, the campaign against WMC has proved successful. At the company's annual meeting in 2000, WMC management announced that the project was to be abandoned despite "insufficient work having been completed to enable a sound estimate to be made of its extent or likely commercial viability" (Mudd 2000). Reverend Avel Sichon, a remarkable man working with a remarkable band of activists in Mindanao, responded to WMC's withdrawal as follows: "Whatever the real reasons behind the marching-off of WMC, the massive protest actions and massive advocacy campaigns have definitely contributed to the slowing down of the giant mining corporation (Indigenus Pilipinas 2000).

WILDERNESS MOVEMENTS

Environmental Movements in Australia

Camp Coorong exists about an hour's drive to the east of Adelaide, which is the capital city of South Australia. It is an ecotourism venture established by the Ngarrindjeri, the indigenous people of the Coorong. The Coorong is a massive sweep of sand dunes where the Murray River, Australia's largest, meets the cold Antarctic waters of the Southern Ocean. Many who have been fortunate to see the film *Storm Boy* would be familiar with its land and seascape. Caught between these dunes and the mainland proper is a wondrous system of lakes. The Ngarrindjeri have lived here beyond time.

Increasingly, environmentalists in Australia have seen aboriginal peoples as "natural allies." Indeed, many environmental movements across the globe have sought to incorporate the rights and needs of indigenous peoples into their environmental rhetoric. Enlisting the support of indigenous peoples adds further weight to environmentalists' demands. Apart from this political reality, there are some shared interests: there is no doubt that green and black movements in Australia both have a profound respect for the natural landscape.

With this in mind I organized a group of students from my university to spend the weekend at Camp Coorong. All experienced a wonderful weekend: weaving traditional baskets and listening to the stories of the aboriginal dreamtime. In one of these stories, one of Ngurunderi's (a key figure in the creation) sons fled across the Coorong whilst being pursued by a "devil" named Mirka. Ngurunderi saw his son and the devil approaching and wounded Mirka at Red Ochre Cove. The red ochre outcrops which are along this route today were made by the dripping blood from Mirka's wounds. Most of the major natural features of the Coorong and beyond are included in song lines.

These stories of the dreaming are immensely powerful and they pervade the landscape, full of silence and stunted trees, bent backwards in the sand by the hellish winds which often confront them. One evening the students watched pelicans and black swans circle into a huge sunset over the sea and lakes and imagined a time before European invasion. This reverie was suddenly shattered by two short, sharp bursts of a shotgun, followed by the downward spiral of one of the black swans. It hurtled into the lake in front of us. We all cursed an imagined hunter as two of the students waded out into the briny waters to salvage the injured swan. We were all stopped in our tracks as one of the Ngarrindjeri men from the camp appeared in a small boat with the shotgun crooked in one arm. He waved us away from the swan and took it on board.

Back at Camp Coorong we were told that the hunting of the black swan was an integral and sacred part of Ngarrindjeri men's business. The students had enormous problems reconciling their interests in the rights of the black swan to exist (and their abhorrence of hunting indigenous fauna) with their respect for aboriginal culture. It was made clearly apparent to them that the differences between the predominantly European view of nature as wilderness (however enlightened) and the view of the indigenous people who were indistinguishable from the land were fundamental and immense. Australian environmentalists, like many of their counterparts across the globe, are leaders in their society in building networks with aboriginal peoples; but their concept of wilderness—which has dominated their environmental agenda for a generation—casts a deep shadow over their attempts at reconciliation.

■ ■ ■

INTRODUCTION

In this chapter we move back to the minority world and investigate *wilderness movements,* using the national backdrop of Australia. By moving from the Philippines to Australia, from anti-mining to wilderness movements, the juxtaposition between environmental movements found in majority worlds versus minority worlds, again, is stark. Indeed, although constituting a subservient position, wilderness networks do not dominate environmental movements in the majority world. Alternatively, wilderness advocates have been particularly powerful in the minority world, most specifically in New World countries such as those found in Australasia and North America.

First world forest movements are a subcategory of wilderness movements.

Forests are just one type of habitat (although extremely popular) which wilderness advocates fight to defend. Consequently, wilderness movements have already been introduced, alongside basic elements of the wilderness position, in chapter 2. The idea of wilderness is further developed here, with special reference to the tensions between the concept of wilderness position and the rights of indigenous peoples across the globe. Although there are direct connections between forest and wilderness movements in the minority world, forest movements in the majority world are rarely informed by the wilderness position.

There is some debate, however, as to whether Australia qualifies as a first, second, or third world country. There can be no doubt that its economic system, which is so heavily reliant on minerals exploitation and other primary industries (with little value added), is strongly reminiscent of many of the neocolonial economies which exist to its north, including the Philippines. Whatever Australia's economic status, it has a large, white middle class which is still dominated by European culture, despite the population's rapidly changing racial mix. In Australia, this sizeable middle class possesses a relatively high standard of living. Australia is one of the most urbanized countries on the globe, with nearly half of its 20 million people living in just two major cities: Sydney and Melbourne. Whatever the correct terminology denoting Australia's economy and society, most of its citizen's rate their country as first world and post-industrial. For the sake of argument, for the rest of this book it will be assumed that Australia is a post-industrialized nation.

Unlike parts of Europe where there have been some substantial adjustments made to laissez-faire economic practices over the past decade, Australia (under conservative federal government since 1996) is operating on radical libertarian market principles, experiencing Thatcherism and Reaganomics all at once, but lacking an intellectual tradition to provide any sustainable challenge or to provide any subtle edges to these hard-line, antisocial equations. In many ways, Australia is increasingly removing much of its cultural and economic association with Britain and is now more often seen in the South as the United States' *junior partner* in the Asia-Pacific theater.

THE ENVIRONMENTAL MOVEMENT IN AUSTRALIA

The environmental movement in Australia, like any social movement, has gone through distinct stages. I have found it useful to divide the last thirty years of movement activity into three periods. Similar divisions have been drafted by movement analysts in other countries. Box 4.1 illustrates the key dates and characteristics of these three periods. It must be said, however, that the majority of movement initiatives have been reactive over all three periods

Box 4.1

Three Periods of Australian Environmental Movements

Period	Date	Dominant Ideology	Models	Strategies
1	1960s to mid-1980s	Unrestrained use	Pluralism / structuralism (outsider politics)	Dissent/mass mobilization and govt. lobbying. Responding to govt.
2	Mid-1980s to mid-1990s	Sustainable and multiple use	Corporatism (insider politics)	Working with govt. to formulate and implement policy.
3	Mid-1990s until now	Wise and sequential use	Post-modernism (bypassing state)	Work directly or against business and other sectors.

SOURCE: *Adapted from Doyle 2000b.*

of its operation. It has rarely dictated terms, though there have been some bright and telling anomalies.

The first period includes the first twenty years, up to the mid-1980s. During this period, Australia was primarily governed at federal level by conservative governments, though this period also includes the important, but brief, Whitlam years in the early to mid-1970s. Period 1 saw the Australian movement playing *outsider* politics. Environmental concern was largely based on direct, oppositional dissent to unrestrained environmental use. Environmentalists, on the whole, were considered deviant folk devils, regardless of whether their demands were radical or reform oriented. Radical environmentalists demanded revolutionary changes, considering the state as incapable of bringing about sufficient social and ecological reforms. These activists concentrated on mass mobilization techniques and strategies. Their ideas and actions can best be understood utilizing conflict models of politics.

More reformist environmentalists, though still very much on the outside, demanded legislative change to enable the state to *manage* the environment more effectively. Their major strategy was one of lobbying elites. They succeeded insofar that an unprecedented range of legislation was forged during these early days, most prolifically in the 1970s. Pluralist public policy models, described in chapter 2, are useful in explaining these political initiatives.

By the mid-1980s—period 2—the accord style of politics, championed by Labor Prime Minister Hawke began to dominate environmental policy-making. This second period can be characterized using corporatist models of power. Although the radical wings of the movement have continued to play oppositional, outsider politics through all three periods, many other parts of the movement began to deal more closely with the state at this stage. Dominant and mainstream green NGOs became incorporated into the Labor Government's policy-making processes and agendas. Environmentalists became *insiders*. This is reminiscent of the mainstream United States environmental movement as it increasingly dealt with the Clinton administration after his election in 1992.

Period 3 emerged during the final days of Labor's national ascendancy under Prime Minister Paul Keating, but it is more purely characterized by the reign of the conservative coalition government led by Prime Minister John Howard. Although conservative on a range of moral issues, most of this current government's politics and economics can be understood as stridently neoliberal or radical libertarian. Due to this neoliberal stance, this period has seen the state increasingly remove itself from its role as environmental legislator, monitor, and regulator and again set itself up in active opposition to environmental concerns. In reaction, the movement has often been forced to bypass the state and deal with a whole range of sectors more directly, most specifically, the business sector. This has led to a challenging time for movement strategists. Post-modern/post-structuralist models of power sometimes become useful in comprehending these disparate strategic responses, whilst proving problematical when utilized as prescriptive models for action.

In a separate book dedicated to analyzing the politics of the Australian movement, *Green Power,* I have argued that the agenda which framed the movement right through all its periods of development is an extremely narrow one when compared with other such movement agendas across the planet: "The environment movement in Australia has been dominated by issues that do not truly include the human dimension. Social and environmental justice issues have been rarely considered, and nature continues to be regarded as something separate from people. The Australian movement most closely resembles the North American movements (with some important exceptions), as our whole society increasingly does" (Doyle 2000, xvii).

In Australia, during this third and current phase, the current attack on the environment movement by the conservative/neoliberal coalition government in close collusion with powerful business interests is without precedence in the last thirty years. The Howard government has attempted to disempower and discredit environmental concerns in four major ways. First, it has renamed its own environmental agenda as a "brown" one, with most of its "environmental" moneys derived from the partial sale of Telstra (a previously state-owned telephone company) being directed toward rural, primary industries. Second, it has removed or reduced funding for its most vociferous critics, like the Friends of the Earth and the Australian Conservation Foundation. In turn, additional moneys have been given to many of the more broad-based and, by their very nature, necessarily more conservative conservation councils. Penultimately, wherever possible, it is removing globally recognized green issues, like greenhouse and forests, from its national agenda (Doyle 2000b).

This current period now threatens the very existence of the environmental movement in Australia as a viable political force. The mainstream movement is graying and still overly focuses on post-materialist issues such as *wilderness preservation.*

WILDERNESS MOVEMENTS

"Wilderness" covers a vast range of associated subjects, approaches, and campaigns.[1] The concept largely addresses the value of the nonhuman world, or what traditional science refers to as "nature." Wilderness can be valued instrumentally or intrinsically. Instrumental value is awarded by humans (who are seen as distinct from wilderness, separate from nature). Warwick Fox refers to one of these perspectives as "resource preservation." He then lists nine separate types of argument that are used to justify the value of wilderness in human terms (Fox 1990, 154–161). These include arguments pertaining to the life support system, the early warning system, the laboratory argument,

Fɪɢ. 4.1. Iconic Australian wilderness scenes, Deep Creek Conservation Park, Australia, 2002. *Author's private collection.*

the silo argument, the gymnasium argument, the art gallery argument, the cathedral argument, the monument argument, and the psycho-genetic argument. It is crucial to understand that these types of justification for preserving wilderness pockets are still anthropocentric (human-centered). It is these resource preservation arguments which have grounded the dominant wilderness perspective in the Australian environment movement.

The other more recent, substantial but more marginal tradition—and a philosophically more radical one—accepts that nonhuman nature has intrinsic value (regardless of human value). Robyn Eckersley refers to this as ecocentrism: "According to this picture of reality, the world is an intrinsically dynamic, interconnected web of relations in which there are no absolute discrete entities and no absolute dividing lines between the living and the non living, the animate and the inanimate, or the human and the non-human" (1992, 49).

There are many subcategories of this position. Fox lists four deviations of "intrinsic value theory": ethical sentientism, biological ethics, ecosystem (Gaian) ethics, and cosmic purpose ethics (1990, 162). In this general case, however, humans become part of nature, equal component parts with other species and natural entities. In this worldview, at least theoretically, the separation between humans and the rest of nature is banished. Strategically, though, as ecocentric politics has been played out, much of the emphasis of ecocentrists (or deep ecologists) has been less holistic as it has focused on those parts of nature that have been the least disturbed by white Australians: wilderness areas.

In some forums this dominant wilderness focus—whether it be fuelled by anthropocentric resource preservation or ecocentric arguments—has been attacked by environmentalists who are not driven by wilderness arguments, but whose political aspirations lie in other green traditions such as "resource conservation," "human welfare ecology," or "social ecology" (Eckersley 1992, 33–47). By conceiving the "environment" as protecting and valuing wilderness refuges and pockets, wilderness advocates have been slighted for being, on occasions, anti-human, anti-urban, and anti-rural. Much of this criticism has portrayed the wilderness networks of the movement as composed of middle-class, wealthy professionals looking to parcel up tracts of nature.

Before we lash out at these conflicting radical environmental traditions, it is always important to remind ourselves what the dominant views of the environment/nature movement are: the *unrestrained use* ideology portrays nonhuman nature as either totally expendable or as something that can be transformed, made better, conserved, and developed simultaneously.

Forests have dominated wilderness concerns particularly in the early movement in Australia. Even in South Australia—where there are no large, native hardwood forests to speak of—the issue of native vegetation clearance has assumed some importance. Forestry issues have demanded so much attention that some environmentalists interested in other habitats have been reluctant to mention the "f" word. Despite the fact that Australia has vast coastal, arid, and semi-arid wildernesses, nearly all wilderness conflicts have occurred in temperate, subtropical, or tropical rainforests. Their profound beauty generates passion, and the fact remains that forests are just so directly under threat. They inhabit sections of the Australian continent that humans also like to inhabit: the coastal areas where there is reasonable rainfall. It is no wonder we have seen conflict on their behalf. This primacy of the wilderness agenda began early in the movement's development. When compared to movements elsewhere in the world, this is *the* defining characteristic of Australian environmentalism.

Wilderness-oriented perspectives have also dominated elsewhere, particularly in Scandinavia, North America (most specifically the western regions discussed in chapter 2), and New Zealand. This has occurred, in part, because of a dual reality. First, in these countries, there are still large tracts of relatively "undeveloped wilderness" (Eckersley 1992, 70), unlike in most European countries. Also, a large proportion of the citizens in countries where wilderness remains are wealthy enough to be able to afford to define the "environment" symbol in this way (unlike many countries in the developing world) (Doyle and McEachern 1998 and 2001).

This is not to say that wilderness ecoactivists are entirely absent from the South. In the Philippines, green organizations fight to protect eagles and other birds of prey from extinction. In India, a battle goes on to protect dangerously low numbers of Bengal tigers. In Africa, a long campaign has been waged against the ivory trade in its savage slaughter of elephants. All of these campaigns focus on individual species as well as the conservation of the wilderness habitats which support them. Of course, some of the most famous wilderness struggles have been fought in the forests of Brazil and Indonesia (see box 4.2 for reference to the Brazilian environmental movement). Many of these campaigns, however, have been initiated and resourced by Northern NGOs such as the WWF, in association with local peoples. It is predominantly a Northern agenda being pursued in the majority world.

Many of the wilderness issues have been renamed *biodiversity* issues in recent times, as the concept of wilderness has proved difficult to sell in the majority world. Probably the biggest problem relates to the fact that minority-world wilderness areas are perceived as the name suggests, as *wild* places, beyond the normal habitats of people. In the European notion of wilderness, people do not exist within it. As a consequence, in a bid to protect wilderness, human access must be severely curtailed or, at the very least, managed or controlled. Of course, in the majority world, this concept has no place. People live in the forests and, for that manner, in habitats outside cities, towns, and

Box 4. 2

South American Environment Movements: The Case of Brazil

The Brazilian movement's support base is still small, but it has a great capacity to make itself heard, despite not always managing to convey its views through the press. The movement's characteristics (spread, diversity, and local character) make it difficult to establish a national agenda and sometimes limit the activities of groups and networks. Informal mechanisms stimulate the development of common agendas between organizations.

The environmental movement is vital—all the more so because the government fails to live up to its responsibilities in relation to defending the environment. Consequently, environmental organizations are called into action by the communities themselves, which often think of them as the environmental agencies.

The Brazilian environmental movement has its origins in local activities to defend the environment against destructive development models. The Brazilian environmental movement has the capacity to mobilize public support; it has practical experience of environmental and political action; and it has technical, scientific, and legal expertise. One of the key principles for the environmental movement is the belief in a diversity of possibilities and development models—without the intention of promoting one single model for the whole planet.

The environmental movement's activities are conditioned by the following factors:

Institutional aggression against the environment.

Serious and irreversible one-off acts of destruction against the environment and/or against environmental legislation (emergencies).

Development and implementation of public policies.

The need for resources to support the consolidation of environmental organizations.

The need to attract more supporters and activists for the movement.

The need for practical action and the translation of ideas into reality.

The movement's difficulties arise from the following factors:

General lack of resources and support.

Lack of NGO infrastructure.

Lack of an environmental consciousness in the community, and the adoption of consumerist values, imposed by the dominant economic system.

Lack of commitment to the implementation of effective environmental public policies on the part of the government.

SOURCE: *Adapted from the meeting of the Brazilian Environmental Movement: Twenty-Five Years of Environmentalism in Brazil Seminar Challenges to and Perspectives on the Environmental Movement in Brazil, Brasilia, 28–30 September 1995, and from http://www.ces.iisc.ernet.in.*

fences. From an indigenous perspective, a wilderness campaign, therefore, is often seen as another form of dispossession. In this light, wilderness perspectives of environmental movements can be seen as yet another stage of Northern colonialism. Toyne and Johnston write that there is "a new wave of dispossession—the denial of aboriginal peoples' rights to land in the name of nature conservation. The creation of national parks, wilderness areas or wild life sanctuaries could be every bit as threatening and destructive to aboriginal people as were the pastoral stations or the farms of past generations" (1991, 8–10).

Although this tension over the interpretation of the concepts of wilderness and nature conservation exists in all countries between indigenous peoples and more recent invaders/settlers, it is very much apparent in the Australian context due to the manner in which aboriginal people were originally dispossessed from their land. Under British law, upon white settlement, Australia was determined as *terra nullius* (loosely defined as "land of no one"). By declaring that no one actually existed on the Australian continent, the British did not need to create a treaty or any other legal arrangement with the indigenous inhabitants. The concept of terra nullius did not see Australian aboriginal peoples even gaining citizenship until 1965. The wilderness concept is too close for comfort to the notion of terra nullius, which led Aboriginal people to the brink of annihilation. Marcia Langton, a prominent Aboriginal academic, argues that the wilderness concept is simply a new form of imperialism: "ecological imperialism" (1998, 18). She goes on to argue that the roughly equivalent Aboriginal idea of wilderness has nothing to do with uninhabited land (as does the Western concept), but rather is land "without its songs and ceremonies" (20).

These philosophical differences between the wilderness concept and ideas held by Australian indigenous peoples about their land are far more than just interesting points of theoretical difference. As the opening story to this chapter revealed, these tensions manifest themselves in *real politics,* as Australian environmentalists seek to be inclusive of issues such as Aboriginal land rights. The campaign for Jabiluka is an excellent example of this point.

Jabiluka is a world famous campaign fought in the Kakadu area of Australia's Northern Territory. This campaign is controlled by the indigenous owners of the land, the Mirrar people, but the campaign mobilizes a huge global network of indigenous and green activists. For example, in the Jabiluka networks, the activists, apart from the Mirrar people themselves, live in the eastern seaboard cities of Melbourne, Sydney, and Brisbane and many of them have not taken part in environmental activism before. In addition, this has attracted the involvement of mainstream environmental NGOs such as the Australian Conservation Foundation (ACF) and the Wilderness Society (TWS).

One of the reasons the Jabiluka campaign has been so successful in mobilizing such a huge network relates to its *tripartite* argumentation. First and most obviously, it advocates protecting parts of Kakadu National Park on the basis of indigenous land rights concerns. This position plugs into human and indigenous rights movements at the global level. It questions the rights of mining companies to dig up the Mirrar's "sacred earth" against the people's wishes. Next, the campaign mobilizes other national and transnational wilderness movements which aspire to have large portions of the territory listed as World Heritage. They argue, in wilderness preservation terms, that it possesses values which cannot simply be understood in terms of human utility. Finally, due to the fact the Jabiluka mine is a uranium mine, it invokes the support of anti-nuclear movements both in Australia and around the globe.

The all-inclusive nature (indigenous/nature/anti-nuclear) of the Jabiluka campaign appears very attractive to a lot of younger Australians who have not been involved in the stalwart anti-nuclear resistance surrounding Roxby Downs and Ranger uranium mines, in South Australia and Northern Territory, respectively. Like the German movement (reviewed in chapter 7), the Australian anti-nuclear movement had experienced a relative hiatus in the mid 1980s, but has re-emerged forcefully in the 1990s to remain as one of the most radical and extra-institutional wings of the broader environmental movement. Whilst many of the wilderness networks of the greens are *graying*, the anti-nuclear movement remains attractive to new blood.

Many of these younger activists formed Jabiluka Action Groups (JAGs) nationwide in the late 1990s . The Gundjehmi Aboriginal Corporation (GAC), an organization which represents the legal and political interests of the Mirrar people, originally endorsed these local action groups as part of a national network of support. JAG groups around Australia were largely autonomous and operated on the principles of participative democracy and consensus decision-making. They were extremely successful in the campaigns against the mining company Energy Resources Australia (ERA), placing the issue and the word—Jabiluka—under a powerful national and international spotlight. This success, however, was relatively short-lived. GAC, in late 1998, issued the "New Directions Document," which requested all JAG groups "to ensure that their activities *primarily focus* on *directly* benefiting that Mirrar fight for survival. In this way JAG groups were requested to adopt a *project-driven* Aboriginal human rights focus. 'Directly' *does not mean* activating public dissent about uranium mining and therefore benefiting all people including the Mirrar" (GAC 1999).

The impact of this document was devastating on all JAG groups across the country, as each wrestled with this "central directive" after operating autonomously from their inception. Ben Aylen, a member of JAG Adelaide, remembers the tensions:

> GACs desire for a fundamental shift from a a network of primarily anti-nuclear groups who supported the Mirrar, to a hierarchical structure of decision-making and responsive support groups was hard for many JAGs to swallow . . . [and] consensus decision-making was strained

to breaking point, and numbers dwindled . . . and anti-nuclear activism in Adelaide has never been as powerful since. . . . There were clear political lines drawn. . . . In Sydney at a particularly heated JAG meeting punches were actually thrown between a member of the Democratic Socialist Party (DSP) and an indigenous supporter of Mirrar Land Rights. There were accusations that sections of the DSP were racist and only cared about the nuclear industry, which were countered by equally damming claims that GAC had become too powerful and corrupt, bullying activists and accepting bribes. (2001, 3–4)

After the rapid depletion of the JAG networks in the late 1990s, although some activists disappeared, new constellations with new or rehashed purposes evolved. As aforesaid, watching the politics of social movements at the microlevel is witnessing the very earliest, often translucently embryonic forms of politics. It is like staring through a microscope and watching a group of particularly virulent cells expanding, breaking up, and then reforming constellations, some with older cells, and on other occasions, forming with brand new ones. This is the true fascination of studying new social movements. For example, some ex-JAG members formed Everyone for a Nuclear Free Future (ENuFF) and began to focus specifically on anti-nuclear issues. Breaking away from EnuFF were two other networks. One started to dabble with the concept of a new anti-nuclear political party: SA Nuclear Free Future Party. Another formed a loose coalition called "The Keepers of Lake Eyre," which focused on support for the Arabunna people, who are the traditional owners of the land from which Roxby Downs uranium mine draws its water. The Keepers built a camp, much in the style of England's Greenham Common, alongside Western Mining Corporation's gigantic mining enterprise in South Australia. It was this group, supporting the Arabunna people, which walked in protest from Central Australia to the Olympic Games in Sydney in September 2000.

The Jabiluka campaign is a wonderful example of differences in the ideological positions of wilderness-oriented environmentalists versus those of indigenous peoples. On a positive note, Jabiluka campaigners did at least attempt some type of reconciliation with the Mirrar people, with some successes. Most wilderness campaigns have done little to advance this agenda. The Wet Tropics campaign, fought in the tropical rainforests of the northeast of the Australian continent, incorporated indigenous concerns in piecemeal fashion, as just one other reason adding to the environmentalists' "weight of argument." It deserves mention here, however, as it constitutes a classic wilderness campaign, the longest and most prominent such campaign in Australian history. It was about forests, and it was about coral reefs. In addition, it was also an early version of an anti-roads movement, which is the focus of the next chapter.

Fig. 4.2. A remnant pocket of stringy bark, 2001. Bush walkers were some of the first Australian environmentalists to be politicized in the late 1960s.
Author's private collection.

THE CAMPAIGN FOR THE WET TROPICS

The Wet Tropics campaign in Australia illustrates a cacophony of political pathways in a long-term wilderness campaign: from direct action to governmental lobbying and from mass mobilization to corporate alliances. Even at the micro-campaign level, differences in goals and strategies emerge over time, making the comparative purpose of this book even more complex.

The Wet Tropics occupied a central position in Australian environmental politics throughout the 1980s. The environmental movement's actions during this prolonged period can be described as constituting a "campaign" in the true sense of the word. At different stages of this long campaign, different networks of environmental activists assumed dominant positions of power. The networks then determined the agenda: the political goals and strategies of the broader movement.

The power of Wet Tropics issues lay in their ability to appeal to a vast range

Box 4.3

Stages of the Wet Tropics Campaign

Date	Stage	Title
Pre-Dec. 1983	1	Critical Mass
Dec. 1983–Jan. 1984	2	The First Blockade
1984	3	Between Blockades
Aug. 1984–Mar. 1986	4	The Queensland Era
Mar. 1986–1987	5	The Professional Elites

of people. First of all, they had been foci in the debate between the conservation/preservation of native forests and traditional forestry practices, not just in Queensland (a northeastern Australian state), but in both the national and international arenas. Secondly, they were an affair upon which the issue of state versus federal rights was pinned. Thirdly, they were wilderness issues. The rights of wilderness areas to exist independently of humanity's needs and perceptions were debated. Finally, the building of the Cape Tribulation Road became a popular metaphor for what is probably the greatest issue which faces humanity and the earth: its continued, healthy existence (Doyle and Kellow 1995, 94).

Due to the long-term nature of the Wet Tropics campaign, a study of the practice of the movement must be divided into manageable segments. Particular stages can be distinguished, each disconnected from those stages previous or subsequent to it (see box 4.3).[2] Each of these stages is quite unique in its practice. A different set of players and a new political, structural, and goal-oriented form gain ascendancy over all others on the central political agenda at separate times. With these changes in time, structures, and goals, the practice of the movement is affected quite dramatically. The five stages leading up to the area's declaration as World Heritiage are represented on the matrix in box 4.3.

The First Stage: The Early Years

During stage 1 of the Wet Tropics campaign—before the first blockade—the Wet Tropics was not on the political agenda. For many years various individuals, such as renowned rainforest ecologist Professor Len Webb, had continually lobbied for the protection of these forests. At an organizational level, in 1981, the Australian Conservation Foundation (ACF) positioned a project officer—John McCabe—in Cairns to involve himself in all conservation issues pertaining to Cape York. Forest issues quickly dominated the local conservation scene. The Rainforest Conservation Society of Queensland (RCSQ) was formed in 1982: this was the first formal organization formed which concentrated its efforts wholeheartedly on the Wet Tropical Forests. During this period, also, many people resettled in northern centers like Port Douglas and Mossman.

It was during this first stage that the issue was developing a critical mass. No one individual or group was dominant, as the issue did not really exist in the eyes of the government and the general public. Consequently, arguments and strategies aimed at conserving the forests were varied and piecemeal. It is not until the second stage of the campaign that patterns of practice emerged in the movement. But this analytical difficulty must not be utilized to undermine the importance of these early days in the campaign, without which issue saturation point may never have been achieved.

Stage 2: The First Blockade, November 1983–January 1984

Critical mass was attained in November 1983 when the Douglas Shire attempted to push a road through from Cape Tribulation to Bloomfield. The Wet Tropics, through the opening of the Cape Tribulation Road at Daintree, was catapulted onto the national agenda. The first blockade—constituting a stage in itself—had begun. The media produced images of people buried to their necks in mud or occupying high-altitude perches in threatened trees (Green 1984). Due to the spontaneity of the campaign, little planned involvement was possible. The participants included locals of the Cape Tribulation area (the Cape Tribulation Community Council [CTCC] was among these), committed people from other North Queensland centers (e.g., the Wilderness Action Group [WAG] based at Port Douglas), and a group of individuals known as the Nomadic Action Group (NAG). As far as formal organizational input goes, the ACF did have its Wet Tropics project officer present, and the Cairns and Far North Queensland Environment Center (CAFNEC) was also very active. Despite the diversity of individuals at the first blockade, the more radical networks of the movement were dominant. The first blockade— stage 2—did not cost much in terms of money. Its limited financial resources were found in the participants' pockets. More importantly, its strategic resources were sought in the forest around it: trees and earth. But all of these resources would be nothing without the willingness of the protesters to use their lives as bargaining tools: a willingness to bodily defend the forest. This blockade illustrated the interrelatedness between structures of action, the goals which the environmentalists shared, and the practice with which these were expressed. All three of these facets were largely revolutionary in their nature. Arguments centered around the non-premeditated concerns of the activists: aesthetics, spirituality, wilderness, survival, and aboriginal land rights. Participants clearly expressed typical motives, and their comments illustrated several forms of radicalism.

Beauty

Cape Tribulation is a really special place to a lot of people in Queensland. It is a wild place, an incredibly beautiful place. *(Hill 1984)*

Spirituality

I, too, have learnt how special a place it is. Since arriving here nine years ago, I have come to realize that it was in a forest like this that we began. This forest has cared for me like a mother cares for her child, she has fed me and protected me, calmed and healed my physical and mental wounds, and has taught me many things, including tolerance and forgiveness. *(Hans, quoted in Wilderness Action Group 1984, 24)*

Wilderness

Where is the brotherhood we once shared with the trees? Where is the sanctity that we used to feel in the forests? Where is the respect for anything greater than ourselves? Forgotten in the plethora of images on millions of television screens. Expelled down the exhaust pipes of the swarms of motor cars that are apparently bent on colonizing this planet. Submerged by the noise, frenetic pace and confusion of the concrete jungles through which we walk as strangers. *(Grainger 1980)*

Survival

The rainforests contain fully half of the ten million species of plants and animals on earth—the very womb of life. The continued evolution of life on this planet depends on the survival of the genetic materials that these forests contain. *(Cohen and Seed 1984)*

Aboriginal Land Rights and Sacred Site Desecration

The road will violate aboriginal sacred sites. The Kuku Yalanji tribe have a number of sacred and cultural sites in the area. *(CAFNEC 1984, 2)*

The spontaneous nature of this first Daintree blockade explains why these responses were not finely honed strategic weapons designed to win over the collective minds of the Australian public. Rather, they were expressions of how participants felt about the threatened forest. Strategies were based on nonviolent direct action and consensus decision-making: "Some circle through the bush to get in front of the bulldozer. It ploughs straight ahead, into three people. Two dive out of the way at the last moment, but the third is caught and grabs a steel bar that pokes out of the front of the bulldozer. He is carried high into the air, clinging to the bar, and for long seconds his figure swings wildly against the dark green background of the silent trunks and leaves. A scream goes out as the others watch helplessly. Eventually that blockader returns safely to the ground" (Green 1984, 26). "A blockade was in place with five or more people buried up to their necks, and barricades of posts, logs, banners and signs. People chained themselves to some of the logs. . . . Then John said he had a length of high tensile chain and wanted to be assisted up a tree, situated right in the path of the 'dozers, when they started work in the morning. He was dubbed high John, for the incredible heights to which he climbed in the tree" (Wilderness Action Group 1984, 17, 47).

These strategies and tactics are strongly reminiscent of what occurred later in the forests of North America, as reviewed in chapter 2. Unlike the U.S. direct-action experience at Cove/Mallard, however, tactics were almost always *passively nonviolent.* As at Cove/Mallard, activists had exhausted legal avenues: there was no time left to lobby politicians. Moreover, blockade participants were not convinced that mainstream party politics could protect the forests. No time existed, either, for carefully managed media stunts. Yet blockaders were scrupulously nonviolent (the issue of nonviolent protest is reviewed in some detail in chapter 6, dedicated to Indian environmentalism). A "Blockade Information Sheet," hastily prepared by Cairns and Far North Queensland Environment Centre (CAFNEC), spelled out to the second wave of prospective blockaders that the action must be "totally peaceful": "Our argument is with the Douglas Shire Council and the Queensland Government, not with their agents on site, the workers and the police. We urge maintenance of peaceful and respectful relationships with these people" (CAFNEC 1984, 2).

The Wilderness Action Group wrote of the first blockade: "The blockaders' reaction to this madness has been non-violent. This assurance has been given to police, Council and National Parks Officers. . . . Rupert Russell, a well-known writer and naturalist, says that this action (bulldozing the road through the forest) is not in accordance with his principles, and is promptly arrested. He manages four steps before promptly collapsing limply to the ground. With his face in perfect repose, as though asleep, he is carried off to the paddy wagon" (quoted in CAFNEC 1984, 10).

A consensus process was used to select strategies: "As the light fades from the sky, a large tarp is spread on the damp ground, the circle for the meeting begins to form, the chairs being quick to be occupied, till all is quiet and the agenda is passed around. . . . The group is called to order by a chairman. Ideas start to flow, and pros and cons are aired, till someone says 'I'll do that!' then we are off again on another point. . . . The meeting could have been over in half an hour but for one word . . . CONSENSUS. We ran every meeting by it, an extremely tedious operation" (Wilderness Action Group 1984, 33).

Although time-consuming, this process is part of the radicalism of the resistance. Consensus represents the anti-hierarchical attitudes common in

Australian direct-action networks. For example, CAFNEC's information sheet states the desired distribution of power at these meetings: "Meetings are held each night at 6.30 P.M. All people have an equal say. The blockade may be broken into smaller groups with elected representatives if it becomes too large" (CAFNEC 1984, 2).

If an individual held office in a particular green organization, she/he received no more kudos or power than any other blockader.[3] Even mainstream environmental leaders were accorded no deference. For example, the ACF's Wet Tropics officer begged protesters to halt the blockade as an agreement with the federal Minister for Arts, Heritage, and Environment to cease logging was imminent. The protesters disregarded this plea. The first Daintree blockade was funded inexpensively. Despite the protesters' limited resources, their tactics forced observers to ask, "Who were these people risking their lives for the forest? And what motivated them?"

The Nomadic Action Group (NAG) offers an example of radical direct action in Australia during the 1980s. The media represented NAG as typical of the environment effort at Cape Tribulation: activists were buried up to their necks in mud or hanging precariously from trees (Green 1984, 26). NAG "has had a long history of direct action in eco-activity in Australia" (Doyle and Kellow 1995, 108). It has generated immense publicity for environment issues and some of its direct actions have been ultimately successful (Terania Creek and the Franklin Dam[4] are just two wilderness campaigns that achieved the desired result of all environmentalists: in the former a logging ban, in the latter the abandonment of a dam project). A brief history of the group reads thus: "The group on Errinundra Plateau which varies in numbers from 25 to 80, was based around up to a dozen 'veterans' of the Nightcap, Franklin, Roxby and Daintree actions. Initially calling themselves the 'Nomadic Action Group' they encamped on the Errinundera around Christmas, having come from the Down to Earth Confest at Wangaratta. . . . The position of the most prominent in the group was that there should be a moratorium on all logging in Australia, an immediate halt on the whole Errinundra Plateau, and that only immediate blockade action was appropriate. Others did not necessarily agree" (Harris, quoted in Doyle and Kellow 1995, 108).

The operation of the Nomadic Action Group is dominated by one overriding tactic: nonviolent action. Consensus is a principal focus, but other strands of philosophical and religious thought are also present. Since the Daintree campaigns of the 1980s have given way to other groups born of the NAG tradition, there has been a tendency to refer to this philosophy as deep ecology, particularly in the United States. While deep ecology is now directly equated with biocentrism or ecocentrism, and constitutes a potpourri of ideas and values, in the late 1970s and early 1980s it was not a common term among direct-action participants, as it was in the Cove/Mallard conflicts in the United

States in the 1990s. Apart from the dominance of nonviolent action, there was a wide variety of ideas. These more revolutionary ideologies depict the existing system as ecologically bankrupt. The revolutionaries, or radicals, advocate widespread political and/or spiritual change, while more mainstream reformists believe pragmatic changes within the system are sufficient to avert environmental problems. In the next chapter, the anti-organizational, non-hierarchical operations of Earth First! and the Dongas in relation to anti-roads campaigns share important traditions with this early band of Australian green activists.

The lessons of the first blockade at Daintree still dominate environmental direct actions in Australia. The experience further reinforced the validity of predominantly nonviolent-action tactics at both Terania Creek (New South Wales) and the Franklin Dam (Tasmania) blockades. All three campaigns were successful in the short term, with significant sections of wilderness areas being listed as World Heritage Reserves by the United Nations, thereby strengthening the claims to adequate protection.

Stage 3, 1984: Between Blockades (up to and Including the Second Blockade in August)

During the months which directly followed the agenda-setting first blockade and up to the end of 1984, the Wet Tropics issue peaked in terms of human numbers involved at any one time in the campaign's history. This third stage of the campaign would involve more diverse networks of environmentalists than any other stage. The first blockade had given all environmentalists—of whatever type—a focus toward which to work. In the early months, therefore, the spirit of representative decision-making, established at the first blockade, prevailed in the movement. This was an introspective period. All arguments, all strategies were listened to and debated voraciously: "After all, we all want the same thing," they argued. Everyone seemed intent on defining the *common goal,* and implementing suitable strategies which would lead to the achievement of these shared objectives. As a result, huge amounts of paperwork were produced and distributed throughout many different kinds of networks. In the light of later developments, it is important to note that all of this paperwork and correspondence was available to anyone who sought it.

After a honeymoon period, conflict reigned. On developing arguments and strategies, individuals and organizations became intent on enforcing their ideas. This period saw the emergence of the formal, reformist organizations as the dominant force. The radicals and revolutionaries were relegated to keeping vigil at the blockade sight. Their informal input had to be "controlled." Don Henry (then director of the Wildlife Preservation Society of Queensland, now executive director of the ACF) wrote to Aila Keto (president of the Rainforest Conservation Society) expressing this view: "However, I don't believe

FIG. 4.3. Second Valley, South Australia, 2000. The Australian environmental agenda has rarely moved away from forests and coastal environments. The continent's center is still regarded by many as "the dead heart." *Author's private collection.*

the individual groups should be left to develop their own rainforest programmes, or to do as they please with regard to rainforest conservation, albeit with the most sincere intentions" (Henry 1984).

With formal organizational takeover, dominant strategies emanated equally from three political levels: local, state, and national. Provincial conservation and environment centers based in Cairns and Townsville and key state-level organizations placed the Wet Tropics issue fairly and squarely at the top of the agenda. Involved were the Queensland Conservation Council (QCC), the Wildlife Preservation Society of Queensland (WPSQ), and Rainforest Conservation Society of Queensland (RCSQ). During 1984, an ACF Wet Tropics officer was stationed in Brisbane.

1984 was declared "the Year of the Daintree" by the ACF. The ACF was the prime mover at the national level. Also, the Tasmanian Wilderness Society, having now officially changed its name to the Wilderness Society (TWS), had chosen the Daintree issue as its new focus after the completion of the Franklin Dam campaign.

In the wake of the "successful" Franklin Dam campaign, it seemed to many organizational activists that a replica of the Franklin scenario existed in the case of the Wet Tropics. Moreover, all that had to be done was to convince the federal government to take the Queensland government to the High Court. In turn, it was sincerely hoped that the High Court would decide the future of the Wet Tropics. There was one crucial legal difference between the Franklin case and that of the Wet Tropics: the latter had not been included on the World Heritage list by the International Union for the Conservation of Nature's (IUCN) World Heritage Commission (WHC) for the duration of the *campaign proper.*

During stage 3 (1984) the federal government refused to nominate the Wet Tropical Forests, in the absence of sufficient evidence that the area was of genuine World Heritage significance. Environmentalists moved quickly to provide the federal government with the appropriate proof. RCSQ was funded by the Australian Heritage Commission (AHC) to produce a report to establish the World Heritage potential of the Wet Tropical Forests.

The mainstream green NGO dominance during *stage 3* became all-consuming. Even the direct-action strategies of the second blockade in August 1984 became more formalized. The radical networks came under severe scrutiny from the organizational activists who sought to "control" their antics for fear of an "appalling media image" (Waud 1984). The organizational activists established *rules* for the blockaders. In a "Daintree Campaign Report," Pam Waud (of TWS) listed certain criteria which would help "clean up" the blockaders image:

1. Definite rules of conduct and dress (these will be sent to the NAGs before the blockade). Those who infringe the rules will be asked (or if necessary forced) to leave the camping ground (privately owned) and be refused access to communal food.
2. Group pressure resulting from strong affiliation between local blockaders to prevent NAG "heavies" swaying or intimidating other participants (involves NVA training). They hope the NAGs will be significantly outnumbered by other participants. (Waud 1984)

Gone were the days of the first blockade, when consensus, nonviolent action, and participatory democracy were law. Now force, controlled by the formal organizations, was being utilized as a threat to "wayward" blockaders. The organizational pragmatists did not deter the more radical elements from participating in the second blockade, but the latter lost influence over proceedings.

Stage 4: The Queensland Era

After the "unsuccessful" completion of the second Daintree blockade in August 1984, the Wet Tropics campaign was referred to as a "lost" campaign by many environmentalists. At the beginning of 1985, it seemed that all movement energy had been sapped. During the first half of 1985 the campaign went through a period of hiatus at the national level: this period constituted the fourth stage of the campaign to save the Wet Tropical Forests. The ACF did not renegotiate the terms of contract for the employment of a Wet Tropics officer to be stationed in the North (Stannard 1985). The Wet Tropics slipped from its position on top of the organization's agenda. 1985 became the ACF's "Year of Antarctica."

In the relative absence of input derived from national organizations during early 1985, those formal organizations based in Queensland became dominant partly by default. These state-level organizations could not so readily dump the issue; it was geographically in their domain. In Brisbane, the Queensland Conservation Council (QCC), the Wildlife Preservation Society of Queensland (WPSQ), and the Rainforest Conservation Society of Queensland (RCSQ) took a leading role. Also, the Cairns and Far North Queensland Environment Center (CAFNEC), based in Cairns, was included as a key part of the new Queensland-based Wet Tropics network. The Queensland organizations were still attempting to convince the Queensland government to nominate the Wet Tropics as World Heritage; the national organizations did not even attempt to pursue this course of action. As so often occurs, both state-level and national-level organizations perceived and pursued strategies in their own political sphere.

Of significant interest, also, was the emerging circulation of different types of political arguments justifying the forest's conservation. *Economic* arguments began to saturate the media; most of these directly emanated from Queensland-based organizations. One excellent example of economic rationality creeping into environmental arguments during this *Queensland phase* related to the building of a "canopy walkway" at Downey Creek. Downey Creek was "within 40,000 hectares of the rainforest catchment for the Johnstone River, 30 kilometers west of Innisfail" (Johnstone 1985). The area of the proposed walkway was at the center of a 200,000-hectare state forest which was being logged. The idea of a walkway through the forest was an attempt by local conservationists to save Downey Creek.

The editorial in the *Townsville Bulletin* applauded this proposal. The *Bulletin* regarded the canopy walkway proposal as a concept that could have a major impact on all future conservation-versus-development arguments; or, as in its own words, it "would allow us to have our cake and eat it too — to have virtually untouched rainforest, yet in conjunction with a multi-million dollar tourist development" (*Townsville Bulletin*, 3 November 1985). These arguments seem somewhat familiar and hardly surprising in the context of the late 1990s, where business is supposedly good for the environment and vice versa (without any inevitable trade-offs or irreversible ecological processes). In 1985, however, the concept of ecologically sustainable development was still in its infancy, as was the cooption and incorporation of environmental concerns by business interests. The walkway symbolized the entire tourist industry. Here was the answer to the perceived dilemma: development and conservation could co-exist; money could be made with the support of the greenies. Of particular interest, given this milieu, was the extent to which the conservationists were willing to compromise during this period. The walkway never went ahead, and Downey Creek lost its largest and oldest trees.

In the second half of 1985, the national organizations wished to reinstate the Wet Tropical Forests to the number one spot on the environmental agenda for 1986. They realized that Brisbane had become the seat of Wet Tropics power and, consequently, positioned branch offices in that city. TWS was greeted with some distrust by local environmentalists and, on arrival, was asked not to set up its fund-raising shops as these would cut into the local market (Lisle 1985). The ACF also established a permanent organizational base in Brisbane. The national organizations picked up where they left off, urging Canberra to nominate the area as World Heritage. The federal government responded to the lack-luster efforts of environmentalists during 1985 with "a master plan" for the long-term protection of North Queensland's rainforests, costing up to $200 million over the next twenty years.

The Brisbane epicenter of the campaign began to crumble in March 1986. Queenslanders had fought the Wet Tropics issue for many years without a break. With the "jettisoning" of the issue by the Queensland groups, the national organizations moved quickly to wrest the central role from them. The ACF's Antarctica campaign had "failed" in the short term, and TWS was now determined to revitalize its role in the Wet Tropics debate. Both national organizations moved to dominate proceedings. And so, the arena was set for the fifth and final stage of the campaign: the era of national elites.

Stage 5 and Conclusion: The Professional Elites

During the final eighteen months of the campaign before the 1987 federal election, an informal elite network of up to a dozen professional environmental activists now dominated all Wet Tropics environmental initiatives.[5] As a direct consequence of this dramatic shift in the movement's power base, the environmental movement became totally immersed in the federal election. This was quite remarkable, due to the fact that, in the past, party endorsements by environmental organizations (such as the QCC) had seldom occurred.

In addition to $70,000 of Labor campaign funds being directed via TWS into key marginal electorates, large sums of money were also accepted by this network from corporate Australia. Whether this was right or wrong in an ethical sense is another issue. What is important to glean from this situation is that these funds—massive when understood within the history of the movement in Australia—were accepted by certain movement participants without being recorded in organizational accounting records. One such person at the center of this exclusive network who personified this final stage was Jonathon West. West was the personal secretary of Barry Cohen, the environment minister, when he was appointed director of TWS just months before the federal election. Shortly after Labor leaders were re-elected, West left TWS.

Gone were the arguments about aesthetics and spirituality; gone, even, were those of science and economics; the era of political and bureaucratic expediency had arrived. The movement's electoral affiliation with the Australian Labor Party (ALP)—the political party then in government—was unrepresentative of the movement as a whole, but rather reflected the will of this elite network of powerful, professional activists.

With the declaration of 900,000 hectares of the Wet Tropics as World Heritage in 1988, some environmental activists have argued that the tactics pursued during this final stage have been vindicated. Indeed, this was an enormous win and ensured the creation of a independent statutory authority, the Wet Tropics Management Authority, which would attempt to juggle conflicting land-use needs and values for the area right throughout the 1990s. Wins tied to party politics, however, are often short-term gains for broad-based social movements. Creating such intimate ties with the Labor party also meant creating profound enemies for the movement within the conservative coalition. With the defeat of Labor in the mid-1990s the environment movement has suffered greatly in its capacity to deliver similar or even partial wins across a range of fronts. To some extent, it has become a victim of its own past partisanship, displayed in the last days of the Wet Tropics campaign. This situation is remarkably similar to that which has also emerged in the United States: close relationships forged under Clinton have now been punished under Bush.

The umbilical cord tied between them meant both the movement and the Australian Labor Party would share a similar plight. Luckily for the movement—and the last vestiges of the Wet Tropical Forests, which they bargained with—the "right" election result occurred in 1987. But what a risk, a risk which was taken without consultation from ACF and TWS members, let alone the thousands of other individuals, groups, organizations, and networks—not affiliated to either organization—which had fought, in their own way, to save the Wet Tropical Forests over the past decade (Doyle 1989, 44).

CONCLUSIONS

The Wet Tropics campaign went through a number of distinct phases when different networks of environmentalists took control of the campaign, with dramatic changes to the types of politics which were played out in each phase. This campaign illustrates beautifully the folly of attempting to take snapshots of even one campaign. As even at the campaign level, major changes in strategy, goals, and tactics evolve, or more vehemently assert themselves, over time.

As with the United States movement, the Australian green experience has been constrained by domestic concerns, particularly at the formal organizational level of the movements. This is hardly surprising in the context of mainstream conservation and wilderness organizations which have been so enraptured by playing major political party games that their goals often echo those of powerful political parties. Even today, this focus on a domestic polity persists, and this narrow gaze is not just confined to the wilderness networks. Even the more radical, non-institutionalized, anti-nuclear movement in Australia has very few operational linkages with anti-nuclear movements elsewhere. The most obvious case where some intersections would provide enormous strategic benefits is with the German movement (see chapter 7), where issues of nuclear transport and storage are even higher on the societal agenda. This lack of transnational networking is apparent on both sides, with just a smattering of more imaginative activists breaking the domestic mold by pursuing one-off, individualized "crossings."

Despite this narrowness, the Australian environmental movement remains one of the few dissenting voices in an increasingly sanitized and silent society. In recent years it has sought to address its shortcomings, and there are signs that, while maintaining an interest in *other nature,* there is a move toward a more human ecological approach, one which includes the resource distribution and access concerns which relate to people in the environments where they live: in towns and cities, in their homes and workplaces, not just *out there somewhere.* Specifically, this new consciousness—an environmental justice position—which was always part of the movements of the majority world, seeks to redress the rights of Australia's indigenous peoples who have been recolonized and disavowed of their land once again by the worst proponents of the wilderness position.

ANTI-ROADS MOVEMENTS

Environmental Movements in Britain

Despite the "pea soup" fog, at dawn the jumbo jet touched down at Heathrow Airport outside of London. After gathering luggage and moving gingerly through customs, I made my way to the car rental desk and within a half an hour I plunged onto the first motorway which would take me from the south of England to Newcastle in its northeast, where I would begin work at the University of Northumbria the next day. The weariness of the twenty-four-hour flight had no opportunity to grab me as I desperately peered through the fog, hoping to catch a glimpse of the M1 motorway sign which would show me the way. For three hours I traveled in a time capsule (not unlike the jumbo, but this time I had the controls), with no real indication that I was in England, or anywhere else. The language and music on the radio assured me that I was, but I had no other view than the road immediately ahead of me, and the cars swishing past me, seemingly moving at exorbitant speeds considering the lack of visibility.

At about 9: 30 A.M. the fog began to lift, and I began to catch fleeting glimpses of green in my peripheral vision, which, I told myself excitedly, was the English countryside. But despite the disappearance of the fog, I could see little due to the massive dimensions of the motorway and the enormous speeds the cars were traveling. At midday I was running out of petrol and decided to stop at the next town, fill the car up, and perhaps grab a pint and a bite to eat at a "quaint English pub" or something. But the motorway seemed to bypass English pubs and, in fact, bypass England altogether. After running the car dangerously low on fuel, I gave up. Instead, I stopped for petrol at a huge roadside complex which included self-serve petrol pumps, fast-food outlets, "refreshment centers," and even places where I could buy postcards to send back home. Apart from the postcards, there was little that I could define as English about this roadside "village." In fact, I'd seen exactly the same roadside conglomerations traveling across the United States, parts of Europe, and in my own country.

After driving the rest of the day into the early evening (I'd elongated the journey further by taking a wrong turn and ending up half-way to Manchester!) I finally arrived in the historic city of Newcastle-upon-Tyne. As I stared across the dark waters of the Tyne, once the home of thriving coal and shipping industries, I finally had some feeling that I was "somewhere else," that I was in England. The previous two days I'd been traveling in "transnational land," through airports, roadside stops, and motorways which could have been anywhere in the advanced industrialized world. Transnational land is a "place" built purely on equations based on the axis of time and money. In this manner, geological barriers and borders which define communities get in the way of hyper-trade. Mega- and hyper-highways simply bypass or plow through existing sites of meaning in a bid to reduce travel time for atomized traders, so enabling transactions to be further speeded up and providing increased access for these global traders. As will be discussed later in this chapter, this is exactly the kind of reasoning which has shaped British road transport policy for decades.

The increasing domination of massive trunk roads and motorways bypassing traditional English towns and cities and scarring the countryside was well advanced by the time of my arrival in England in early 1992. But it received an extra boost that year, when the Conservatives won the general election and, in part, regained power with the promise of further extending the already massive roads program. Despite opposition already existing in the British environmental movement to the increasing dominance of the automobile, 1992 was a stellar year for the anti-roads movement. After exhausting legal avenues, the anti-roads movement began to concentrate on nonviolent direct action as its major strategy against excessive road building. The battle for Twyford Down (believed by some to be the historic, mythical site of King Arthur's Camelot) reached center stage as local protesters, such as those who belonged to the Twyford Down Association (TDA), coupled with direct-action environmentalists from Friends of the Earth, Earth First! and the Dongas tribe (who were camped at the Down), involved themselves in nonviolent attempts at ecotage—bulldozer diving, tunneling, crane-sitting—designed to disrupt M3 road-building activities.

Despite the ultimate defeat of the Twyford Down environmentalists, this action led to many others with more successful outcomes throughout the 1990s and, in many ways, revitalized the British environmental movement, so much so, in fact, that many commentators make the argument that it became "an exceptional case": the most vibrant anti-institutionalized green movement in Europe.

■ ■ ■

INTRODUCTION

Due to the limitations of this text, coupled with a real attempt to provide some representative examples of the diversity of environmental movements across the globe, only two European movements have been singled out for this chapter-length treatment: England and Germany (see chapter 7).[1] The selection of these two national movements, however, does make some sense, as the German case is an excellent example of an anti-nuclear movement, whilst the one in Britain is seen as a particularly robust movement, in European terms, at the turn of the millennium.

There are, unarguably, massive differences in the green movement experiences of countries within Europe. For example, it would be ridiculous to assume that those nations which were once separated by the *iron curtain* and denoted by the terms *eastern* and *western* Europe would have the same sorts of environmental movements, or the same sorts of pressing environmental issues which forged them. It was not until the mid-1980s, for example, that environmental movements began to emerge in eastern Europe, nearly two decades after their birth in the West (see box 5.1 for eastern European movements).

Equally impossible to ignore are the acute disparities between those nations central to the formation of the European Union and those which inhabit the less affluent *periphery*.[2] Even amongst the nations of northern and western Europe there are major variations depending on cultural and historical differences, political opportunity structures, electoral systems, environmental perceptions; and many more bases for difference. It is true to say, however, that some western European movements do share, on the whole, certain key experiences which separate them from movements elsewhere on the planet.

Box 5.2 explains three subcategories of green movements in western Europe. Most western European movements share with their New World counterparts, such as Australia and the United States, an early movement, often evolving in the latter years of the nineteenth century, devoted to *nature conservation*. As in the case in England and Germany, nature conservation movements have remained as an integral part of green movements in the modern era.

In most parts of western Europe, humans have also been included within

Box 5.1

Eastern European Movements: The Case of Hungary

Prior to the mid-1980s, there was no environmental movement in eastern Europe to compare with those in the West. Those that did exist would have remained "underground" due to the authoritarian regime of the time.

The Hungarian ecology movement was born in the mid-1980s, but, given the constraints of mobilizing under the one-party state, it never attained an integrated organization. Rather, it existed in the forms of unconnected local citizens' initiatives, single-issue groups, and alternative lifestyle communities. Unlike ecology movements in France and West Germany in the 1970s, there was no unifying anti-nuclear group in Hungary, despite Chernobyl and the scandals surrounding the only Hungarian atomic power plant in Paks (Szabo 1994, 292).

Eastern Europe's major environmental problems include soil contamination, air and water pollution, and waste management. The heavy industrialization that occurred after the Second World War has been a major contributor to these problems as the governments of eastern Europe largely ignored environmental costs. Problems of environmental exploitation and degradation were addressed by an environmental movement that emerged following the collapse of Soviet Union control.

Initially, environmentalists were heralded as champions of democracy and dissent by the general populus. In Hungary, the protest against the building of an Austrian-funded dam on a Hungarian section of the Danube River provided a symbolic epicenter not only for the "ecologists," but also for many other forces of "democracy." Environmentalism, in this case, was used to undermine an authoritarian communist regime.

Following the apparent demise of socialism, the East became focused on moving to the "free market" systems of the West, and green interests became absorbed into mainstream politics. Once the green parties acquired a share of national power, the green movement declined. Despite enormous ecological problems facing the East, in the 1990s the green movement has substantially lost momentum (Chatterjee and Finger 1994, 66–67).

However, some networks within the green movement remain as a vibrant though informal voice in eastern Europe and continue to work to change the way in which new regimes respond to environmental degradation.

Source: *Adapted from Doyle and McEachern 1998, 71–74*

the green equations of mainstream environmentalism since the late 1960s. This more inclusive view of minority world environmentalism is often referred to as *political ecology*. Political ecology movements are dramatically different from those minority world movements, dominated by wilderness concerns, which have surfaced in the United States and Australia. Political ecology movements emerged predominantly in western Europe, largely in response to problems of advanced, industrial societies. So although there was still some emphasis on protection of the "natural" (nonhuman) environments, this was often subsumed by matters of an urban nature, where most *people* lived. As such, there was a strong *anthropocentric* or human-centered flavor to many of these movements. It was from these political ecology movements that the four pillars of Die Grunen sprung to life (mentioned in the chapter 7 introduction): ecology, participatory democracy, peace, and social justice. These ideological components did not just miraculously appear overnight in the West German Green party platform: their origins lay embedded in the compost heaps of western European mass social movements.

These movements were *post-industrial* in that they critiqued modern industrial society from a variety of angles, questioning the abilities of modern science and technology, bureaucratic political structures, and economic systems based on "growth at all costs" to deliver people to "the promised land" through *progress*. In fact, the *enlightenment* goals of industrial societies, it was

Box 5.2

Western European Environmental Movements

NATURE CONSERVATION MOVEMENT

The oldest branch of the environmental movement is the nature conservation movement, whose origins significantly preceded the evolution of the western European ecology and anti-nuclear energy movements. One of the main motives of the nature conservation movement during the nineteenth century was to preserve visible signs of human history in a rapidly modernizing world. Other traditional thrusts included bird preservation. More recently, the contemporary nature conservation movement is motivated by pollution problems.

POLITICAL ECOLOGY MOVEMENT

This movement emerged at the end of the 1960s in reaction to problems of industrialized societies. There was a strong urban focus, as well as attempts to protect relatively untouched "natural" areas. By the mid-1970s, environmental organizations usually controlled their operations. As western European traditional parties were unwilling to incorporate these needs into the governmental process, these organizations formed their own political parties (see chapter 5). Also in the 1970s, with close ties to other new social movements, it developed the "new environmental paradigm" view, which included, apart from ecological concerns over economic growth, a critique of science and technology and a preference for participatory politics. Although there was an interest in the welfare of other species, there was a strong anthropocentric "human ecological approach," with a nation-state political focus.

ANTI-NUCLEAR MOVEMENT

Although characterized as a New Left movement, in association with the previous category, this movement was primarily born of the desire to shut down power plants in western Europe (Whyl and Brokdorf in West Germany and Creys-Malville in France). Also, it attempted to promote the importance of the nuclear energy debate in European politics. It was one of the most radical, unconventional political players in the New Left environmental movement, with an emphasis on uncoordinated, decentralized actions. On the whole, it did not attempt to play neo-corporatist, formal organizational, and partisan politics.

SOURCE: *Adapted from Rohrschneider 1991; Doyle and McEachern 2001.*

Fig. 5.1. Green Park, London, 2001. The early British nature conservation movement interested itself, amongst other things, with the establishment of botanical parklands. *Author's private collection.*

argued, were actually issuing the earth a death warrant. The *post-materialism* of wilderness movements in North America and Australia (see chapters 2 and 4) is one such political manifestation of new social movements (NSMs) materializing from advanced industrial societies. Another set of outcomes was the political ecology movements, which were far less inclined to pursue higher-level goals such as the rights of "other nature." Instead, political ecologists argued for lower-level and more widespread systemic changes. They argued that incremental changes to the *status quo* or *business-as-usual* were not going to be enough to deliver salvation from what was widely perceived as an *environmental crisis.* Rather, fundamental, radical changes to the way people interacted amongst themselves, and with the rest of nature, had to take place.

These attacks on the modern industrial system—which the movement contended was poisoning the earth and depleting its finite resources—share some similarities with the movement case studies taken from the majority world in chapters 3 and 6. Both the western European political ecology and some majority world movements also critique Northern science and technology. There are, however, equally fundamental distinctions between these two groups. Minority worlds are advanced and/or post-industrial. Majority worlds are largely nonindustrial, preindustrial, or currently undergoing rapid industrialization. Usually in the majority world, industrialization, per se, is not seen as the culprit. Rather, most majority world environmentalists believe that the processes of industrialization are unduly controlled by large transnational corporations, minority world governments, and national elites. In effect, this situation is seen as minority world imperialism, understood in terms of its negative impacts upon people's livelihoods. As was argued previously, there is far more emphasis in the South on the necessity of its peoples actually reclaiming the means of industrial production, rather than challenging the appropriateness of different forms of technology and ecological management systems. In recent times, the political ecology movements of Europe, the environmental justice movements of the more affluent New World, and green movements of the majority world are increasingly sharing these agendas centering on a fair and equitable distribution of the earth's resources.

THE BRITISH ENVIRONMENTAL MOVEMENT

Like all national environmental movement experiences, they change over time. For every country which is the subject of a major case study in this book, entire histories could be written about alternate periods of green activism providing distinct phases in each movement's development. Britain is no different.[3] Peter Rawcliffe (1998), in the first broad-sweeping book on the British environmental movement since that written by Lowe and Goyder in 1983, divides the British experiment with green politics up into four such phases. The first phase is similar to that already discussed in the context of the United States and Australia. It occurred at the end of the nineteenth century and included the emergence of such organizations as the Royal Society for the Protection of Birds (1889), the National Trust (1895), and the Society for the Promotion of Nature Reserves (1912). In box 5.2 this is best understood as the birth of the *nature conservation movement*.

Rawcliffe places his second phase of movement development in the interwar years. At this point in history, organizations such as the Council for the Preservation of Rural England (1926) and the Ramblers' Association (1935) surfaced. The latter was notable for its deliberate adoption of decentralized structures. Phase three is the beginning of what is now known as "the modern environmental movement." Again, the timing is very similar to like periods already investigated in the United States and Australia. In chapter 7, also, it will become apparent that West German experience occurs at the same moment in history. This period saw an explosion in the numbers of diverse environmental movement organizations (EMOs). Prominent at this time were the World Wildlife Fund (1961), Friends of the Earth (1971), and Greenpeace (1967). This movement was underpinned by much broader green concerns than the earlier two phases and could now be characterized for the first time as a mass movement based on popular activism (Rawcliffe 1998, 16). In 1970, social commentator Nicholson reflected as follows: "Quite suddenly, the long struggle of a small minority to secure conservation of nature has been overtaken by a broad wave of awakening mass opinion reacting against the conventional maltreatment and degradation of the environment which man finds he needs as much as any other living creature" (Nicholson quoted in Rawcliffe 1998, 16).

Indeed the breadth of this green agenda in England and many other parts of western Europe was breath-taking. Although some organizations in Australia and the United States did adopt these wider societal goals, it was not the dominant experience of the movements as a whole. So, although the timing of the modern movements is shared between the New World movements and the Old World ones, the scope of their dominant agendas was very different: the New World really continuing with the "other nature" focus of the earlier period (albeit in far more radical ways); whereas the western European movements included a revolutionary envisioning of human societies.

The final phase which Rawcliffe discusses is from the mid-1980s to the present day. He records the fact that not too many national organizations formed during this stage, but there were substantial increases in the actual membership of preexisting ones. Internal organizational growth in preexisting organizations is just one factor indicating increased *institutionalization* within social movements (this theme will be discussed at some length later in the chapter). Interestingly, the growth and increasing legitimation of the established EMOs was coupled with a large increase of direct-action networks and informal groups working outside more mainstream organizations.

In some ways, despite the overall quality of Rawcliffe's broad sweep of environmental movement history in England, one suspects that the fourth and final phase could easily have been split again, reflecting two very distinct phenomena: the period up until the Earth Summit in 1992, when English environmentalists enjoyed unprecedented access to mainstream politics, and after this time, when many British greens became dissatisfied with the lack of real gains despite this level of institutionalization and began embarking on extra-institutional, direct actions for the remainder of the 1990s. Whatever the form of categorization or the reasons behind their appearance, these networks of more localized direct-action protest are most commonly understood as the anti-roads movement and will be the major focus of this chapter.

British Exceptionalism?

There are perhaps three key defining features of British environmentalism which separate its EMOs from those in most other parts of Europe. First, it is very unusual in that its anti-nuclear movement never really reached the levels of critical mass as experienced elsewhere in industrialized Europe. Indeed

FIG. 5.2. Nuclear power station, Kent, 2001. The anti-nuclear movement in England has not been as prominent as similar movements elsewhere in Europe. *Author's private collection.*

some political commentators in Britain do not even regard the anti-nuclear movement as part of the green movement at all. Brian Doherty argues that this has occurred in large part due to Britain's lack of reliance on nuclear energy due to its access to coal, gas, and oil reserves (Doherty, Paterson, and Seel 2000, 16). Even so, Britain still has nuclear power plants scattered throughout its countryside and its reprocessing plant at Sellarfield is one of the major such plants for the nuclear industry in the world.

The other key difference in the British experience within the European context is its lack of success at playing party politics. Despite the birth of the first green party in Europe occurring within Britain in 1973—the Ecology Party—green electoral representation has not proliferated as it has in other European countries. Elsewhere I have addressed this British green party political experience in some detail (see Doyle and McEachern 2001, ch. 5). What briefly needs to be said here is that the British electoral system—known as first-past-the-post—only rewards the most powerful parties which gain a majority of votes to the exclusion of those in the minority. In most parts of Europe, national governments, on the other hand, are elected within a *proportional system* of voting. Quite simply, this means that minority parties— like green parties—which win a minor, but substantial, portion of the votes gain a small number of seats in the parliament. This is exactly why the current federal government in Germany constitutes a red/green alliance. Even at European Union elections, these national electoral systems take precedence. In 1989 the British green party polled 14.9 percent in the European Union elections. This was approximately double the German vote. Although the German greens were awarded seven seats in the European Union Parliament, the British greens were not represented at all. In spite of these institutional barriers to national and European electoral politics in the United Kingdom, the greens have been more successful at the local level. In the mid-1990s there was anywhere between one hundred to three hundred green councilors scattered across England; 80 percent of these sat on local councils (parish, town, or community) (Hutchings 1994, 20–21).

Indeed, these two exceptionalisms which highlight British difference are two of the key drivers in the choice of the German case study in chapter 7. No other movement in the world, let alone Europe, has had such a successful green electoral movement or such a powerful anti-nuclear component. What is interesting within the context of this book, however, is that whilst the British practice concerning electoral politics may be unusual in Europe, it is the height of normality in the broader context of global environmentalism. In minority world countries such as the United States and Australia, along with most countries in the majority world, environmental movements have made few substantial gains in the electoral sphere. Rather, it is the German experience, coupled, to a lesser extent, with other European nations, which is the exception.

The third case for British exceptionalism relates to the spectacular increase in localized direct actions which occurred within the movement during the 1990s. A major European Community–funded project was launched in 1998 to examine environmental activism in Europe.[4] One of the early outcomes of this project was the understanding that more protest events (as measured by their appearance in the mass media) were occurring in England than in any other European nation throughout the 1990s. Indeed, at the very time when environmental protest appeared to be on the decline in many parts of Europe, in England green protest seemed to be increasing dramatically. Due to the results of this study, a strong case has been made for *British exceptionalism;* that is, as environmental protest wains in other parts of Europe (except in the case of the anti-nuclear movement in Germany, see chapter 7), it has actually increased dramatically in Britain during the most recent decade.

There are numerous reasons which could explain this apparent *exceptional* case. First, during the 1980s, Britain lagged behind much of western Europe in its environmental standards; so much so, in fact, that it was then known as "the dirty man of Europe" (Lowe and Ward 1998). As a consequence, it could be that, in some ways, Britain was merely catching up to the rest of the field as far as environmental awareness and policy-making was concerned. This is, of course, not a sufficient explanation. Doherty writes: "A more convincing explanation suggests that direct action began because there had been a growth of environmental consciousness in the 1980s which raised expectations that could not be met by existing EMOs; resources and repertoires for radical action were available through existing counter-cultural networks; and the provocative character of the government's road-building program provided a basis for the coalition of direct action groups and local anti-roads groups. While the causes of this rise in protest action may be based on contingent British circumstances, Britain is no longer exceptional, except in the current vitality of its environmental protest" (Doherty 2000, 17). Whatever the complex cocktail of arguments which account for this phenomena, the outcome was that radical and direct action campaigns increased in the 1990s in England. Most of these campaigns, protests, and actions were affiliated with the anti-roads movement.

ANTI-ROADS MOVEMENTS

Anti-roads movements in the minority and majority worlds are, again, vastly different.[5] Obviously road-building is a key indicator of industrialization and, as mentioned, the North and South are placed at different times in their development. In Asia, for example, roads are often projected by governments and international aid agencies as a means of promoting the transport of goods which will ultimately create growth whilst reducing poverty. Traditionally, protest in the South has concentrated on improving the quality of roads, rather than preventing them from being built, though this is changing. A more radical line is now being heard in the majority world. SUSTRAN is one such network which has recently surfaced. Its network includes members from several Asian countries including India, Korea, Malaysia, the Philippines, and Thailand (Sustran Network 2000). This umbrella group now portrays roads such as the trans-Asia highway not as something which will alleviate poverty, but as a further access point for minority-world companies and national elites to gain access to majority-world primary resources. During the late 1990s, in Manila, five thousand people were displaced by the building of a new city ring-road which had been funded by overseas aid money. In Vietnam protest currently mounts in relation to the government's plans to build a one-thousand-kilometer highway from Hanoi in the north to Ho Chi Minh

City in the south. Concerns of environmental activists are multiple. Rohde writes: "Concerns include the displacement of ethnic minorities, destruction of environmentally protected areas and the spread of HIV as people from the coastal areas move to less crowded regions inland. There is also concern at the danger of unexploded bombs along the route" (Rohde 1999, 13).

The Naxalite Movement in India is briefly mentioned in the next chapter. Though a forest movement, it is also an anti-roads movement. Whereas organizations like SUSTRAN make official their legal protest to aid agencies, the Naxalites violently defend their forests from the incursions of foreign capital. Roads are seen, in the light, as the first cuts into livelihoods of communities. In the South this is a common story: after the roads come the logging companies, then the mining companies, then the dam builders, and so the story rolls on (Kalland and Persoon 1997).

As discussed in the previous chapter, the first major campaign against road-building in the minority world occurred in Northern Queensland in Australia in 1983. Nonviolent direct action, including tree sitting, tripod-building, and locking on bulldozers, were some of the tactics used by a camp of green activists in a bid to stop the building of the Cape Tribulation road through the Daintree Wet Tropical Rainforest (Doyle 1994). Interestingly the activists did not refer themselves as "an anti-roads" movement; rather, they understood themselves as an environmental movement "protecting wilderness," as a "wilderness movement." As such, they cannot be regarded as an "anti-roads movement" in this work, as much importance has been placed since the beginning of this book on the preference for *emic* identity-building; that is, movements are defined by the participants themselves. Having said this, and this will be most apparent by this chapter's end, there were many close associations, both at the ideological and strategic levels, between this early Australian campaign and the anti-roads movements which formed a decade later in Britain.

Regardless of the argument as to which minority-world anti-roads movement formed first, without doubt, the most famous anti-roads movements occurred in Britain, and these movements will be the focus for the rest of the chapter. The modern, British anti-roads movement began in the 1980s but got up its full head of steam in the early 1990s. This movement became the most prominent part of the environmental movement in all of Europe for the rest of the decade. There are many parts which make up the ideology of the movement, but one thing is for sure; it was very much an anti-car movement. During the 1980s and into the 1990s there had been an aggressive road-building program put in place by the Tory government. Apart from changing the basic structure of the once renowned English countryside with huge, high-speed motorways, the creation of these new mega-roads also saw an immediate increase in Britons using cars. In 1952 there were 2 million cars in Britain, and by 1992, there were ten times that number: 20 million. Most significantly, a third of this massive increase in numbers occurred during the 1980s.

There is no doubt that the automobile has provided predominantly minority-world people with a mobility and convenience of which their ancestors never dreamed. Unfortunately, the dominance of the car and other petrol/gasoline-powered road vehicles has also led to profound changes to the very fabric of towns, cities, and lives. By accepting that car travel is normal, cities have expanded rapidly into the countryside, and the form of the car-dependent city is a sprawling one. Due to this car dependency, the inhabitants of the earth face enormous environmental problems. Apart from urban sprawl, there is a litany of other negatives associated with this "car culture" which many environmentalists, particularly in Britain, believe may ultimately lead the earth to "carmageddon." In an excellent book entitled *Winning Back the Cities* (1992), Newman and Kenworthy discuss the major impacts of automobiles on global warming due to carbon dioxide emissions. Smog also directly threatens health through contributing significantly to upper-respiratory diseases like asthma. Also, by continuing to build these high-energy, oil-dependent cities, many countries are overly reliant on the politics of Middle East oil (70 percent of oil reserves are here). Much money and many lives have been spent and lost in recent wars which have, in part, been waged to control the flow of these oil fields.

Another very obvious but lethal impact which cars have on societies is death directly inflicted through collisions. In the United States, for example, there are forty thousand deaths each year. This is over ten times more than were killed during the Twin Towers attack on September 11, 2001, but still there is no war on cars. Quite the contrary, in the United States, where there is much made of free trade, governments provide massive subsidies for fuel to allow the cheap running of large cars, whilst propping up local oil-based industries. Indeed, to be anti-car in the United States is to be "un-American." This explains the relative nonexistence of anti-roads movements in the United States and Australia.

Other less direct negative impacts are not so obvious, and more difficult to measure; but just as important. As streets and motorways become busier, they become less safe for pedestrians. Ultimately, there is a breakdown in communities, as street life itself becomes dangerous. This often leads to isolation and loneliness (Newman and Kenworthy 1992, 7).

By accepting car culture as "normal," the next "logical" step has been to extend the road networks. In Britain, the networks not only have been extended within cities, destroying communities which impede their linear progress, but have grown in number and in sheer size throughout the countryside. Much of the state-projected rationale behind these colossal programs of expansion is based on economic equations relating to *time savings*. Ultimately, the building of motorways is encouraged to provide the fastest travel times for commuters from point A to point B. Connolly and Smith explain this dominant argument in the British context: "Calculations of time savings are the dominant benefits of any trunk road proposal and represent the foremost quantification of the DoT's (Department of Transport) policy objective to assist economic growth by reducing transport costs. . . . Using economic valuation techniques, the DoT assigns a figure of 153.2 pence per hour per person for non-working time journeys (at 1985 prices)" (1999, 95).

There are many flaws in this purely economic rationalist approach. Obviously, many people, for environmental reasons, would be willing to sacrifice some time spent traveling. This economic rationale, however, understands anti-roads environmentalists not only as opposing the powerful cultural icons of the car and oil, but also as directly refuting the measurement of all natural goods through the lens of economic rationalism. In this manner, and others, the British anti-roads movement has rocked the very foundations of British society.

For a long time, there have been groups of concerned citizens lobbying for the cessation of road building through their villages, their suburbs, or their countryside. Many of these groups formed a coalition called Alarm UK, and, in the years between 1989 to 1993, it had limited successes through public inquiries in some anti-roads campaigns such as Preston, Crosby, Hereford, Norwich, and Calder Valley. More of a significant outcome for these local NIMBY groups during this period was a growing dissatisfaction with established democratic processes. (During this time, the NIMBY tag became less useful in describing their stance as, for example, to join Alarm UK activists had to agree against the "whole roads policy.") What was unusual about the anti-roads movement in Britain was that these originally more Not-in-My-Backyard (NIMBY) protesters were joined by other activists, often sourced from outside their communities, some of whom had a much bigger political picture concerning road-building. The NIMBY's increasing dissatisfaction with mainstream processes, coupled with their further politicization through association with more radical "outsider" activists, led to a powerful combination of previously disparate voices being joined together, and numbers swelled remarkably. As Robert Lamb, former director of Friends of the Earth in England, reflects, "All of a sudden we went from sitting in meetings of four or five people talking about bus routes . . . to a situation where we had thousands getting very angry about road building . . . [and] roads were where the real power lay" (Lamb 1996, 8).

In 1992 the first and definitive campaign of the direct-action networks of the anti-roads movement was at Twyford Down—mentioned at this chapter's outset—formed in opposition to the proposed M3 in Hampshire. This became the signature campaign of many similar campaigns to come over the next five or so years. Due to its singular importance, it is the subject of the major case study for this chapter. After Twyford, the anti-roads movement blossomed. From this point on protests started in Glasgow, Jesmond Dene in Newcastle, the M11 in east London and Solsbury Hill, near Bath in the West of England, and the M65 in Lancashire. From 1995 and 1996 another huge protest was mounted in Newbury in Berkshire. In 1997 action moved to Devon with protests against the A30 (Wall 1999, 65). Later that year, the anti-roads networks turned their attentions to preventing the building of Manchester's second runway (Griggs and Howarth 1999). Although declining somewhat in intensity (and moving onto other things) the anti-roads movement has continued to be active into the new millennium.

Doherty refers to these more radical outsider voices as "the second wing of the movement"; he writes,

> The second wing of the movement was represented by counter-cultural groups of protesters who took direct action against construction sites. British Earth First! Groups had been formed in 1991 and they provided the core upon which the new *non-violent direct action* (NVDA) movement was based.... There was particular interest in the alliances between dreadlocked and body-pierced radicals and "ordinary" local people. The tactics used to occupy sites threatened with destruction also attracted attention and served to delay construction and increased the costs of road-building.... These tactics were all used to make protestors vulnerable and to exploit the fact that evictors could not use excessive force in removing protesters. (2002a, 25)

Two key points come out of Doherty's comments here. First, these more radical networks of the movement adapted NVDA tactics already used in Australia and the United States (Doherty, Plows, and Wall 2001, 5). A particularly British adaptation was the building of underground tunnels. As further evidence of cross-national connections, tunneling techniques were used later in Germany as part of anti-nuclear campaigns.

The second point of interest relates to Doherty's hypothesis that these tactics symbolically made the activists more vulnerable, exploiting the fact that the road-builders were unable to use excessive force. In another work Doherty further expands upon the concept of *manufactured vulnerability* in the context of one specific NVDA tactic: tunneling (Doherty 2000). Tunneling had not been used previously in other first world direct actions. The reason for this is fairly obvious. Tree sitting and tripods make sense when the ecoactivists' objectives include preventing trees from being felled (see the United States in chapter 2 and Australia in chapter 4). Although, as aforesaid, tree sitting was used by anti-roads networks (where trees obstructed the road), tunneling was nicely suited to literally undermine the road-building process.

Doherty argues that the first extensive network of tunnels was created at Allercombe, Trollheim, and Fairmile in Devon in the route of the A30 (2000, 69). The tunneling at Fairmile was very impressive, with protesters remaining underground and avoiding eviction for nearly seven days. Similar tactics were used in the campaign against Manchester airport later in 1997,[6] and again in 1999 and at Crystal Palace. On these latter occasions eviction of the activists took over two weeks. Obviously, there are enormous risks to personal safety involved in living underground within a "homemade tunnel." Their success "depends upon the risks taken by the protester and the care taken by evictors to avoid causing injury" (Doherty 2000, 70). Doherty writes of this manufactured vulnerability as follows: "One way of defining the novelty of the tactics used by ecoactivists is to point to the manufactured character of their vulnerability. The deliberate use of vulnerability is the moral force of all NVDA, but the ecoactivists were not in themselves vulnerable to any major violence from opponents or the authorities, nor could they hope to provoke or expose it. Blockaders in liberal democracies in the past have usually been removed quickly by police and such tactics have become too routine to be effective. . . . Ecoactivists in Britain and elsewhere have used technical devices to manufacture their own dangers in order to make their bodies vulnerable" (2000, 70).

There can be little doubt that the success of these tactics in Britain relies

Fɪɢ. 5.3. Southeastern England, 2001. The anti-roads movement opposed the building of vast networks of major highways which plow through the English countryside. *Author's private collection.*

heavily on the more peaceable traditions of the police force in that nation.[7] Within Europe, chapter 7 provides a stark comparison when reviewing the activities of the German police in relation to protests against the transportation of nuclear waste. An even more dramatic contrast is the comparison with anti-roads activism and other forms of environmental activism in the majority world. In both chapters 3 and 6, concerning the Philippines and India, there is no attempt by activists to *manufacture* vulnerability as vulnerability does not need to be built, it *exists* a priori. Indeed, a majority-world activist rarely needs to act symbolically. Often the lines in the sands are drawn between the powerful and the powerless. Danger and death are imminent. This is another huge dividing axis which separates environmental activism between the minority and majority worlds, and this theme is revisited in chapter 6, as well as in the final conclusions to the book.

What remains for us to do in this chapter is to investigate the details of one particular anti-roads campaign in Britain. For, as it has been proven in each chapter of this book, it is in the detail of specific campaigns that the richest vein of stories describing noninstitutional ecopolitics are told. Let us turn, therefore, to the most famous anti-roads campaign in Britain: Twyford Down—the late twentieth-century fight for Camelot.

THE BATTLES FOR TWYFORD DOWN

Twyford Down, the site of two scheduled monuments and two more sites of special scientific interest (SSSI), is one of the most protected and revered sites in England. For twenty years there had been extensive public opposition to the building of a three-mile section of the M3 which would desecrate these sacred British sites. Most of these actions had pursued legitimate channels, including legal pathways under both British and European law. After the first SSSI was destroyed the protest was basically abandoned by two of the major players: the Twyford Down Association (representing local people) and the Friends of the Earth, by now a huge, semi-institutionalized organization. Under threat of a court injunction, FoE strategically retreated. In an article on British transport policy and the anti-roads movement, Rawcliffe writes, "However by this point a grassroots group of protesters had established a camp on the second SSSI. Calling themselves the Dongas Tribe after the ancient routes that crossed the Down, their number quickly swelled to nearly 100 people. . . . The group successfully disrupted construction using various forms of non-violent action. . . . By August, more than 30 demonstrations were held involving between 4 and 500 people—an unlikely alliance of Tories, travelers and eco-radicals" (1995, 32).

The media found this uniting of "strange bedfellows" fascinating and, in turn, so did Britain. Who were these three groupings to which Rawcliffe refers? First, the Tories symbolized those people from the more conservative side of politics, interested in the preservation of the "English countryside" and the preservation of sacred sites. Obviously, many individuals involved in the Twyford Down Association, although officially withdrawing from the protest, did not just disappear. Indeed, frustrated as they were by years of fruitlessly pursuing legal channels, they were invigorated by the direct-action tactics of the Dongas and the ecoradicals.

The Dongas tribe is an interesting phenomenon. In some ways they were invoking certain elements of indigenous politics and, in turn, identifying somewhat with issues of ancestral domain that many commentators almost exclusively use in the context of the third world. In actual terms they identified themselves with Aboriginal societies in Australia and Native Americans in South and North America (Lamb 1996, 7). These were early visible signs that this new wave of environmentalism was breaking down the walls imposed by domestic-centric politics and beginning to perceive a world outside of Britain, outside of Europe. Moreover, as discussed in the final chapter, a new globalization of noninstitutionalized activism was beginning to emerge from this fresh outlook.

Many of the Dongas were *neo-tribalists* challenging the globalization of advanced industrial society. Along with this neo-tribalism was "mythological commitment to the land, believing that Twyford Down was the site of King Arthur's Camelot" (Wall 1999, 71). In a simply brilliant book, jam-packed with fascinating direct quotations from Twyford Down activists, Derek Wall argues that the identity of the Dongas was far more complex than the preceeding quotation of Rawcliffe's reveals. Indeed, the identity of the Dongas only emerged *after* the protest camps had been set up. Wall includes in his book the comments of a camper called "Jazz," who claims that the Donga identity fails to show the scattered affiliations of the original campers: "Initially people at Twyford were quite a muddled bunch. There were pagans and there were anarchists, and there were people coming from all walks of life and from the established green movement, from FoE and the Green Party. So I originally came across something called EF! [Earth First!] at Twyford, but it was so muddled in that I didn't pay an awful lot of attention to it. The identity was the Dongas . . . ancient medieval trackway. . . . We had a meeting and passed a little totem pole around. We declared it an autonomous territory and called ourselves—loosely, all this collection of different people—'the Dongas Tribe'" ("Jazz" quoted in Wall 1999, 69).

The third group Rawcliffe names—ecoradicals—also have blurred boundaries of identity. Some saw themselves as part of the Dongas, other perceived themselves as separate, and the latter scenario led, in time, to internal conflicts at the protest camps. Many of these so-called ecoradicals were from a green direct-action *nonorganization* or loose network known as Earth First! This nonorganization had been very active in both Australia and the United States, predominantly in forest and wilderness conflicts. After some early attempts to start up in England had been met with a luke warm response, the focus from forests to roads led to a mass adoption of some of the Earth First! nonviolent direct-action tactics. Obviously, the issue of rainforests and hardwood timbers did not appeal to the sensibilities of most Britons. Likewise, the *political ecology* component of the roads issues, that is, the ecological impact upon humans, was far more suited to the European green theaters of protest than the wilderness/*deep ecology* focus on "other nature."

The identity of many Earth First!ers was almost as loose as the Dongas, with many individual groups with different names—like Earth First! UK, Earth First! Bath, or Earth First! Brighton—forming around "affinity" groups based on place and preexisting friendship, mixed with new networks. The overriding characteristic of Earth First! was its members' relative youth when compared to members of established green NGOs like Friends of the Earth, who were once considered at the radical, cutting edge of the green movement in Britain and in many other parts of the world. Roger Higman, FoE's transport campaigner, remembers the protest as follows: "They seemed incredibly young. Clearly they cared but we thought that they were very confused, very inexperienced. We'd been used to dealing with local residents, all basically ordinary people in the area. And our own activists were mostly thirty-something's, people with jobs that also let them to pursue campaigns on subjects they cared about. All of a sudden you had kids, scruffy kids. They had hardly any knowledge about anything else in the roads program, this was just the one road they'd heard of. They wanted to fight for every tree" (quoted in Lamb 1996, 7).

The age issue is an important one. As discussed in this chapter's conclusion, whilst many more mainstream green NGOs were becoming somewhat professionalized and institutionalized, here was a group of younger people who had not necessarily been involved in ecoprotest before. Some were fresh and free from past campaigns, baring few scars from previous ecobattles. Again, it would be an over-simplification to simply draw a line between older and younger activists. Alongside the more youthful were older green activists, more politicized but profoundly unimpressed by the more mainstream line which many EMOs were now taking. They were very uninspired by FoE stepping back at Twyford for fear of breaking a court injunction. Importantly, whilst younger activists inspired others by their risk-taking activities, older activists "educated" them in the broader green picture.

The Dongas were evicted on 9 December 1992 by a private security firm and retreated to a woodland near Winchester. Friends of Twyford Down was set up to continue the fight (Wall 1999, 72). Wall recounts that anti-roads direct actions continued on almost a daily basis throughout all of 1993. There were many different forms of direct action, from locking on to dumper trucks, "digger-diving," the burning of heavy earth-moving equipment, to peaceful gatherings of activists for weekends of fun, friendship, and community-building. At the final hour, Camelot Earth First! appeared and, "entering a cutting at 7.30 A.M., immobilized machinery" (quoted in Wall 1999, 73). Despite the sheer effort of protest continuing, but becoming more piecemeal into 1994, the road extension was built.

Regardless of the direct defeat at Twyford Down, the green movement had far more victories which would lead to medium and long-term gains. Apart from many activists inspiring numerous other anti-road campaigns across Britain in the mid to late 1990s, NVDA activists expanded their repertoires to include more offensive actions, rather than purely defending themselves from the onslaught of "progress" personified in the forms of the police and private security firms enforcing the road-building program of the state. As a consequence, in 1995, Reclaim the Streets (RTS) began to take hold. Activists seized streets and held parties. After London, these street parties spread elsewhere in England then to other parts of the world, including as far afield as Australia. In April 2001 in Adelaide three hundred protesters set up seats in the middle of the city in a bid to "reclaim the streets" for a day. Seventy police moved in and arrested six people for having "too much fun" (Plane 2001, 4).

What is fascinating here is that NVDA techniques first used to stop the Cape Tribulation Road from being built through the wilderness zones of North Queensland had migrated, alongside those from North America, to Britain.[8] These techniques had taken hold in the anti-roads movement. Following on from Twyford, with later adaptations of tunneling at Newbury, and then the more proactive Reclaim the Streets phenomenon, these honed traditions were now reinjected back into places like Australia, North America, and Germany. The campaigning strategies and their tactical handbooks had been expanded in the process. It is almost impossible to assess the success of Twyford Down ecoactivists simply on the short-term basis of failing to stop the road.

But in the medium term, and as far as more quantifiable results are concerned, the Twyford legacy has also produced other major wins. During the late 1990s, road-building in Britain was slashed by two-thirds. Unfortunately, despite policy promises to the contrary, trunk road building still continues under the "New Labor" government of Prime Minister Tony Blair. Consequently, the anti-roads movement still has work to do. In March 2001, a Hastings Alliance was launched in relation to plans to build twenty-one kilometers of new roads to bypass Hastings. This alliance includes a combined membership of 2 million, involving such massive institutionalized organizations as the Council for National Parks, the Royal Society for the Protection of Birds, the

Worldwide Fund for Nature, as well as Friends of the Earth. What the Twyford radical direct-action activists did was to place the issue of road-building back into the spotlight, just as the mainstream environmental NGOs had packed up their bags and gone home. Now these NGOs see anti-roads campaigns as central to their daily business. In many ways the job of the direct-action generation has been done, and they will probably reemerge in some other more hotly contested political site.

A fitting way to end this case study is to quote directly from a FoE U.K. press release entitled "Hastings Alliance Launched" (14 February 2001). FoE, once pilloried for showing fear at being litigated against at Twyford, was now leading the EMO charge in this "second Battle for Hastings." Despite years of continuous anti-roads campaigns, FoE still had one of its major weapons intact: its participants' sense of humor (Rohde 1999, 7). "Late Anglo Saxon monarch King Harold will visit the Department of Environment, Transport and the Regions today to warn John Prescott (deputy PM) against building two new bypasses around Hastings. The King, in full period armour and wounded by an arrow, will be accompanied by a retinue of retainers. Their shields will bear messages" (FoE 2001).[9]

CONCLUSIONS

In the first chapter of this book, I outlined major themes which would be investigated in the course of discussion and made mention of Rootes' position that institutionalization was "the strongest story line" within British environmental movements. There can be no doubt that English environmentalists were slower than many of their western European contemporaries in gaining significant access to governmental power. By the early 1980s, in Sweden, Denmark, Germany, and the Netherlands, for example, governments had taken environmentalists' concerns very seriously and had implemented wide-ranging programs of legislative reform. During the mid to late 1980s England finally caught up with other parts of Europe in that its movement began to make ground within government circles.

Some commentators on this trend (Diani and Donati 1999) argue that this institutionalization of the movement in many parts of Europe has led to a shift away from the politics of mass protest toward professionalized protest organizations and public interest lobbies. Even in the specific case of Britain, similar analyses were being made up until the very early 1990s (see Rootes 1995; Rudig 1992). It was thought that access to the state and business provided to mainstream green NGOs, which had dramatically increased in terms of size, power, and financial security, would also result in the more radical, illegitimate, and direct-action environmentalists disappearing into the distance. The argument was as follows: environmentalists had succeeded in gaining the ears of those in power (indeed, in many cases they had become indistinguishable from those in power); why, then, was there a need for more radical, outsider tactics?

Van der Heijden lists three indicators of social institutionalization: organizational growth, internal institutionalization, and external institutionalization (1997, 31). Rootes measures certain British EMOs against these criteria, and, in all three cases, the British movement provides more than enough information which leads to the conclusion that "the British environmental movement is in an advanced state of institutionalization" (Rootes 2000, 12). As mentioned earlier in Rawcliffe's description of his "fourth phase," rather than new formal green organizations being formed in the past decade, established organizations have gained substantial footing with increases of membership, rather than new organizations typically being spawned. Between 1971 and 1981 traditional environmental organizations like the National Trust and the Royal Society for the Protection of Birds grew fourfold and doubled again between 1981 and 1991. Political ecology organizations like FoE and Greenpeace also swelled dramatically in the 1980s. Donors and members of FoE increased by a factor of six and Greenpeace subscribers increased by tenfold (Rootes and Miller 2000, 13).

Apart from organizational growth, EMOs also became more internally institutionalized. This can be measured by an array of indicators, including internal decision-making structures, how resources are garnered, and relationships between professional activists and members/subscribers. Another indicator which Rootes uses relates to the form of action taken by national EMOs: "the snapshot [that] emerges of British EMOs in 1999 is one of organizations more engaged in lobbying government, informing the public, attempting to mobilize public opinion via the mass media, and publishing scientific reports rather than engaging in mass demonstrations or more radical forms of direct action" (Rootes and Miller 2000, 16). This leads onto the third criterion of Van der Heijden's: external institutionalization. Quite simply, most green EMOs are now part of the policy-making processes of governments and businesses rather than being in an aggressive opposition. This has occurred, though admittedly to a lesser extent, in political ecology organizations like FoE and Greenpeace just as it has occurred in the more conservative nature conservation organizations. As Doherty writes,

> During the late 1980s and early 1990s, groups like Greenpeace and FoE were becoming institutionalized. They were reorganized in the 1980s to become more professional organizations using direct-mailing techniques to maintain large membership levels. Rising public support for environmental issues meant that by 1989 even figures like Margaret

Thatcher—who had included groups like FoE in the early 1980s in her definition of "the enemy within"— . . . were learning to adopt "green-speak." . . . This reached a highpoint in 1992. . . . Both FoE and Greenpeace had achieved "insider" pressure group status and were fronted by "establishment" figures for part of this period. Practical advice to business and government was replacing critical and confrontational campaign strategies in both organizations."(Doherty 2000, 16)

There can be no doubt, then, that the major networks of the British movement have become institutionalized. But where some commentators get confused is that they imagine that this increased access by major parts of the movements entails the dissolution of more radical voices. Granted, it becomes far more difficult for these voices to be heard through EMO and state-oriented forums. And, no doubt, this increased access by some powerful players may create a quietude surrounding green issues for a period, in that the public accepts that environmental issues are being addressed adequately and are "under control." The point remains, however, that environmental problems still exist on a scale beyond imagination, and that networks of environmentalists do become increasingly frustrated by the appeals-to-elites tactics of mainstream EMOs. The road program continues under New Labor, and basic environmental legislation is often not enforced. With this frustration and loss of faith in established legal mechanisms, there continues to be an opening for some networks to reassert their outsider status (both outside the state as well as outside established green NGOs).

Earlier, the four phases of Rawcliffe's history of the British movement were presented and I suggested that the final phase could be quite usefully divided into two periods. I reassert that claim here. The first phase, during the 1980s, saw huge growth and increasing institutionalization in the movement. From 1992 to the present entails a more neoteric phase. After a period of relative silence, as it appeared that green issues were positively being incorporated into mainstream economic rationalist agendas, newer and highly amorphous networks of Generation X-ers established their own direct action agendas, whilst established green organizations still further institutionalized.

Since the 1980s all green movements in the minority world have attained increased access to established power bases. As a consequence to increased access to power and money, there have also been trade-offs. One of these is the removal of the mainstream EMOs from their grassroots constituents. With their increasing professionalism and conservatism there has also been a "graying of the greens," particularly from the mid-1980s until the early 1990s. Some commentators predicted the death of the movement in western Europe occurring due to the fact that green concerns were now "part of the furniture." Instead, a newer, particularly vibrant strand of direct-action environmentalism has emerged in the more-affluent countries. Many of these activists are disturbed about the inadequacy of the mainstream green NGOs to deliver on issues of substantial environmental reform. They are from a younger age bracket (although there are still important members of these networks who are from earlier, countercultural/environmental movements), and they are more connected with the green agenda of movements based in the majority world.

This last point is an interesting one. These newer green activists do relate much of their agenda with the issues of corporate-controlled globalization. They became politicized during the anti-roads campaigns and are now moving into anti-globalization protests. Welsh argues that many of these newer greens have networks spanning several continents: "The better known connections include those between the Zapatistas and environmental and social justice groups from a range of other countries. Other significant linkages include those with the Indian sub-continent where Vandana Shiva is particularly prominent" (Welsh 2001, 19). These new global linkages will be taken up in the final chapter.

As also argued in the conclusion to this book, social movements have a very different social form than formal organizations. The "iron law of oligarchy," which formalizes organizations over time, is an analytical tool designed to understand formal organizations, not new social movements. As has been already demonstrated in the chapter on the United States movement, and as will be later revealed in chapter 7 on Germany, this increased institutionalization does not always mean that *all parts* of a national movement experience can be incorporated into the system. There will always be parts of the movement which will reject increasing professionalism and institutionalization. Chris Rootes writes: "The institutionalization of environmental activism in Britain has indeed proceeded apace, particularly in response to new opportunities created by political elites at international, European and national levels. . . . [Yet] as recent British experience shows, there are significant strands of environmental concern and activism that resist institutionalization. Indeed, the new wave of radical groups such as Earth First! deliberately resist forms of organization that are susceptible to institutionalization. It remains to be seen whether the rise of a radical environmentalist counter-culture will prove durable, or to what extent it is, in Europe, a peculiarly British phenomenon" (Rootes 2000, 53).

If institutionalization does becomes complete, then environmentalism ceases to be a social movement. With the sheer enormity of global and local environmental issues which confront our lives, this seems highly unlikely for the foreseeable future.

The absolute diversity experienced at Twyford was nothing new, but it certainly reasserts the point that this diversity still exists and that not all sections of the movement are becoming institutionalized. Younger activists joining with the more radical of the older greens have led to the reinvigoration of the green movement in Britain. Despite the institutionalization, new and vibrant traditions are being born. The green movement is still alive in the United Kingdom, breaking out of its box just when its last rites were being read. The very definition of a new social movement is a human collective form which is changing, ever amorphous, ever recasting boundaries of identity.

RIVER MOVEMENTS

Environmental Movements in India

I arrived outside the "offices" of the Narmada Bachao Andolan (NBA) in Baroda, the sun still not fully risen at 6 A.M. The NBA is the key environmental organization involved in the campaign against the building of the huge Sardar Sarovar Dam Project (SSP) on the Narmada River in central-western India. The office was on the second floor of a small apartment building, and as I climbed the stairs I muttered to myself that, surely, I must be in the wrong place, that the world-renowned NBA would have grander offices than this. I was wrong. A small sign on the door told me I was in the right place. I knocked tentatively and eventually an elderly tribal man beckoned me to enter. He pointed to the floor which was full of ten to fifteen or so sleeping bodies. We picked our way over them. He showed me the toilet, and then he went back to sleep.

After washing my hands and face, I came out and there was nothing else for me to do but to lie down on the floor, using my bag as a pillow. I tried to rest but I was still wired from the all-night bus trip and, as a student of environmental movements, to be here was just too exciting. After half an hour of trying to lie still while brain buzzing, the human form next to me stirred. A few seconds later it became apparent that it was a woman, and a few more seconds after that it occurred to me that I was lying next to Medha Patkar, who many people within Indian environmental movements regard as the female, modern-day equivalent of Mahatma Gandhi. With over a billion people in India, it always amazed me who I came across!

Immediately on waking, Patkar began answering my questions relating to the campaign and the movement. The rest of the bodies in the room began to stir. Some were tribal leaders (*adivasis*), some were small landholders (*patidars*), and others were activists working out of this office: all were part of the Andolan (the movement). Patkar explained that the previous evening an NBA meeting had been held until 3 A.M. to discuss strategy for an upcoming court case in New Delhi (March–April 2000) which saw the Indian state attempting to remove restrictions on the height of the dam wall at Sardar Sarovar. She explained that for every meter built on top of the existing forty meters, additional villages would be flooded.

There was only time for basic ablutions and the preparation of tea. Although it was now only 7 A.M. in the morning, the campaign had recommenced. Small groupings of people gathered again in separate circles in the same room that they had slept in, and discussion began again. Actions were allocated to specific people; instructions were given. This pace and commitment has lasted for fifteen years! I was introduced to two men, one an adivasi from a submergence zone, who had already lost his home, and the other, a young activist—Sanjay—who had been living in a particular local community in one of the proposed submergence zones for the past eight months. These two people would be my guides as I sought to visit the actual site of the Sardar Sarovar Dam, which was surrounded by tight military security. We gathered our possessions and left the NBA office immediately.

More bus rides out from Baroda; a journey through drought; entire communities digging unmapped and illegal canals and ditches from limited water supplies which are going to be sent elsewhere. I talked to Sanjay about the campaign. After some time I asked him about how he got involved with the NBA. He explained that he was an accountant doing the books for a school in Maharastra which Medha Patkar visited one day. On that day he became convinced that he must dedicate his working life to the poor and displaced indigenous peoples of the Narmada Valley. He spoke to me of the teachings of Gandhi, about the importance of leading a truthful life.

We managed to get hold of a jeep for the last part of the journey. I was taken through numerous security checkpoints and was quizzed as to the purpose of my visit. There were so many enemies of the dam, so many enemies of India, it was explained to me by one particular bureaucrat. I could not explain that I wanted to meet and interview people who had been displaced by the rising waters. Instead, it was alright to pass the final checkpoint if my sole objective was to see the dam wall itself, to marvel at this engineering feat, as long as I didn't take photographs. The jeep climbed past the first villages that were now no more. I found out later in interviews that some people had been moved to higher ground, to dwell in galvanized iron huts which were scorching in summer and freezing in winter. In my own country we referred to such constructions as sheds; here, they were promoted by the public relations people for the dam as "purpose-built dwellings." Others from the low-lying villages had moved into dwellings provided by the project as part of employment packages. There was, in many instances, a degree of shame attached to inhabiting these dwellings. Still others had moved away from their homeland to the towns and cities of India, just part of a massive movement of people away from rural lifestyles to urban ones: a transmigration far larger than the agrarian and industrial revolutions combined.

These people left their sacred place with a small amount of compensation in the form of bits of paper with numbers on them: money, something which was rarely seen before, foreign objects, part of a world with markets and bazaars so big that an individual could not even see them. Trading on a global scale.

One thing I was certain of as we moved to the apex of the range of hills which surrounded the dam. These villages were not displaced and then moved somewhere else: they had been annihilated. I looked at the dam wall and the military looked at me. I did not see the great "modern temple of India," which Nehru had promised to his people some fifty years before. I saw a wall of concrete already crumbling with the last monsoon. I saw channels, which were meant to deliver water to the outlying regions—such as Kutch—with huge cracks and no lining. I saw no evidence of drainage works which would be necessary to guard against salinization after the flooding and irrigation that would ensue. I saw an environmental disaster.

We moved away from the dam face, down into the settlements of which I have already spoken. I was invited into Bahati's home and offered water: the land beyond mineral water, a land where women must walk twelve miles a day to gather a container of water relatively fit to drink, despite the close proximity of the dam. We talked at length of the many hidden human issues involved with displacement—just one person's story in a million such stories.

I said good-bye to Sanjay at a small jetty. He was returning upstream to a village across the border, in Maharastra. He looked ill with malaria and exhausted. He asked me when I would be back. He told me that I would be welcome, that I needed more time to spend with the villagers. But, unlike the people I had met near the river, and the millions more which lived upstream, I had a pass out: back on the bus to Baroda and the offices of the NBA and, eventually, back on the bus to Udapur, back on the train to Delhi, back on the plane to Australia, back to a world which was relatively safe and secure, a place where the roll of the dice had fewer numbers, a place where environmental movements fought to protect trees, koalas, and whales.

■ ■ ■

INTRODUCTION

This chapter moves again from the minority world to the majority world. In chapter 3 we discovered that much environmental activism in the majority world does not include the same active engagement with mainstream party politics and business-as-usual as is often evidenced in the North. Rather, there are usually very clear lines drawn between those who suffer due to environmental degradation and those who benefit. Consequently, as the aforementioned case of environmental activism in the Philippines revealed, majority world environmentalism is usually characterized by more *structuralist* understandings of power, and this is reflected in campaign strategies and rhetoric.

It would very simplistic, however, to imagine that all green movements in the South were the same. Although sharing some important traits, there are a multitude of deep-seated variables. For example, the movement in India, although sharing the Filipino penchant for extra-institutional activity, is ardently *nonviolent.* The structural division between the *haves* and the *have nots* is just as well etched as in the Filipino experience, but most green strategists in India pursue their environmental goals without recourse to militant defense. Obviously, this difference, in part, occurs due to cultural distinctiveness. The fact is that despite the impact of Northern dominated, corporate-controlled globalization, cultural diversity, such as witnessed through various religious and philosophical practices, is still the norm, rather than the exception. Consequently, Indian environmentalists, surrounded by Hindu, Jain, Sikh, and Buddhist philosophies (to name a few), will invent ways of eco-activism which loosely fit into these preexisting frameworks. The predominantly Christian and Islamic beliefs encountered in the Philippines may be less rigorously entrenched in principles of nonviolence.

One such nonviolent campaign, based on the teachings of Gandhi, centered on the fight for the Narmada River in India. This campaign has dominated the ecopolitical landscape of India for over a decade and a half, emerging for the first time in the mid-1980s and continuing until the present day. Anti-dam or pro-river movements are the focus of this chapter, with particular mention of the campaign fought against the construction of the Sardar Sarovar Dam on the Narmada River in western-central India.

ENVIRONMENTAL MOVEMENTS IN INDIA

India is usually seen as a third world nation, with vast numbers of citizens experiencing a poverty which is hard to comprehend from a first world perspective.[1] The power of the state in India demands attention here as it informs the shape and style of the politics of resistance. India boasts the world's biggest democracy, but it is a democracy controlled by an extremely powerful, centralized bureaucracy based in New Delhi. So powerful is *the Center* that it has managed, amongst other achievements, to partly check the advances of minority world corporations as they have sought to cross nation-state boundaries. As a result, such symbols of corporate globalization as Coca-Cola and McDonalds have suffered partial knock-backs in the establishment of their franchises there. Accordingly, the Indian state still controls such basic infrastructure as education, health services, public transport, and many other services. Moreover, due to the primacy of the state in defining Indian citizens' lives, it is seen as the sole provider of either a good and just livelihood, or one full of poverty and destitution. For a combination of reasons, for the majority of South Asia, it is the latter scenario which rings more truly. Due to the desperate levels of poverty, malnutrition, and disease, it is the state, through its inability to provide for the majority, which is seen by its environmentalist critics as the main culprit in its development schemes which, in their environmental devastation, seem to provide little comfort for most Indians. In the case of the Philippines, as in most other countries in the majority world, transnational corporations have been largely demonized in their role as chief exploiters; but in India, the state itself is often perceived by environmental activists as the key villain. Ashok Swain writes on Indian environmental movements as follows:

> India has been successful in maintaining its democratic structure since independence in spite of its multiethnic, multireligious, and multilinguistic society. This "Indian wonder" is now passing through a period of transition. Crisis has become the refrain of political scientists and political economists describing the present state of Indian democracy. . . . As part of these new, organized protests in India, environmental movements have grown in frequency and intensity and involve people from all social strata. This popular opposition, directed against some of the developmental policies adopted by the state . . . revolve[s] around competing claims over renewable natural resources; they also manifest the struggle for the rights of victims of environmental degradation. (Swain 1997, 818)

This situation, of course, is rapidly changing. Increasingly, transnationals are crossing South Asian borders, and basic services, however inadequate, are becoming privatized. As this trend continues, it is feared by environmentalists that the Indian people may suffer even more. For the purposes of this chapter, however, it is the position of the Indian state, as the major development player, which has shaped environmental opposition. As a result, most environmentalists operate outside of the state, with some vibrant exceptions. There is no large and powerful band of New Delhi *beltway* environmentalists who have breakfast with the president or prime minister, as is the case ex-

FIG. 6.1. Slum Dwellings along the railway tracks, New Delhi, India, 2000. With massive movements of people from rural areas to cities, huge numbers of Indians are now coalescing in new cities on the periphery of established cities, without any of the basic infrastructure for living; environmental movements struggle to provide basic shelter, clean water, and adequate nutrition. *Author's private collection.*

plained in the U.S. movement (see chapter 2). Most environmental conflict is just that: conflict, albeit usually nonviolent, in places on the destitute periphery, where humans and nonhumans alike are literally pushed to the wall of extinction. Sometimes these walls are built of bricks and cement, and sometimes these monuments of state development are referred to as *mega-dams.*

Before we move onto movements against mega-dams, some mention must be made of the first emergence of the broader environmental movement in India. One of the earliest, most famous, and trend-setting environmental campaigns occurred in the early 1970s in the mountainous area of Uttar Pradesh, known as Uttarkhand, west of Nepal: the Chipko movement.

Uttarkhand is an ethnically and ecologically distinct region with a small population; once very rich in resources, it has now been ruthlessly and continuously extracted by outsiders. After the end of the India-China border conflict in 1962, much road-building was instigated throughout this area, opening up its resources of timber and limestone (Karan 1994, 33). Road construction to reach the resources led to deforestation, which further led to erosion, landslides, and loss of soil, forest, and water resources. Forests were logged for their economic value without concern for the needs of the Himalayan people. India lost 3.4 million hectares of forest between the years

1950 and 1972 and 9.2 million hectares in 1972–1975 and 1980–1982. (Banuri and Marglin 1993, 28). This inevitably caused serious economic and social dislocation in the Himalayan communities. The local people who lived in the area were greatly affected, namely Hindu and Muslim subsistence farmers and artisans as well as Tibetan-speaking Buddhist farmers, herdsmen, and traders. The beneficiaries of this development were entrepreneurs, usually absentee landlords from the plains, but the costs of the massive environmental devastation which followed, including huge floods, were incurred by the local inhabitants.

The Chipko movement began three decades ago during Gandhi's movement of nonviolence. Prior to this, social protests were quite violent but did instigate collective actions of the peasants for future demonstrations. Women in the hills of India were involved in many protests before the actual Chipko movement arose. All of these earlier protests prepared the women for the Chipko movement, which ended up being a success because of the women's strength and achievements. Women had an interest for sustenance activity based on forest protection while many of the local men had interests for commercial activity (Shiva 1989, 71).

The Chipko movement has gone through many different modes of action and protest and the participants have certainly practiced many different techniques in order to achieve change. By the 1970s the organizational base of the women was ready, and more frequent protests occurred concerning the rights of the people to utilize the forest produce. A major signal that the Himalayas were dying was in 1970 when a major flood inundated several villages and fields (Shiva 1989, 74). When this occurred, the women were the first ones who realized the connection between the flood and deforestation because they were the ones working amongst the forests every day. Soon after, vigilance parties were formed to keep an eye on axe men until the government was forced to set up a committee which recommended a ten-year ban on commercial green-felling in the Alakananda catchment (Shiva 1989, 75).

Chipko then started mobilizing for a ban on commercial exploitation throughout the hills of Uttar Pradesh. In 1972, several demonstrations were held by the women in the hills to demand an end to the contractor system of forest exploitation and to demand the state to stop permitting the cutting of ash trees. Meanwhile, a sporting-goods company arrived with a permit to fell fifty ash trees. The people (mostly women) decided that they would attach themselves to the trees. This type of resistance was chosen because if a wild animal came face to face with a mother and a child, the mother's natural reaction would be to hug the child and this was how the women felt toward the forests (Bahuguna 1990, 115).

Through this form of nonviolent resistance, the women were able to drive many tree fellers out of the forests on several occasions. Women continued to hug the trees to protect them from the axe men in further situations. In 1974, the government allowed the cutting of twenty-five hundred trees in the Reni Forest, but the women, again, hugged the trees to protect them. The women quickly mobilized, confronted the contractor's men, and forced them to back down (Calman 1992, 93).

Women may have been the backbone of the protests, but increasingly there was active participation by all social groups in India. It could be stated that were it not for the women noticing the effects of the commercial deforestation and acting upon them first, the protests would not have been nearly as strong. Women played a strong role in the movement and made it the success that it was. The women of the Chipko movement not only protected the forests and their society, but the movement added to the world's consciousness of environmental issues. Major afforestation programs have since been launched, and women's movements still continue to fight for a rational forest policy in India (Bahuguna 1990, 120). Karan describes this hallmark movement as follows: "From that action arose the Chipko environmental movement. More than a dozen major and minor incidents of confrontation occurred during the 1970s. . . . Going from village to village, the Chipko activists prepared for each confrontation by informing people of the movement's purpose and inviting their participation. . . . By the late 1980s the movement had splintered into two groups that have broad grassroots support and advocate participatory methods which respond to local issues in the context of local social and cultural traditions" (1994, 34).

These Gandhian methods of noncooperation and resistance would be the mainstay of all environmental movement activity in India, including anti-dam movements, until the present day. This experience of nonviolence also meandered beyond India, impacting on peace and environmental movements across the globe in alternate ways. The gender-specific nature of activism is a defining factor of environmental grassroots politics in India, and in the majority world in a general sense. The Green Belt Movement in Kenya is another excellent example of women revegetating massive tracts of land, as well as moving toward more direct, participatory models of democracy and resource allocation.

ANTI-DAM MOVEMENTS

Mega-dams are a bit like nuclear power. Just when the minority world comes to terms with their inherent dangers, the majority world embraces them. More to the point, however, is that fact that Northern-based transnationals are hawking these outdated and dangerous engineering technologies in the third world as they exhaust first world markets and welcomes. At this time of writing, there is a veritable explosion of mega-dam building in the South, from Turkey to Thailand to South Africa, from Indonesia to China (see box 6.1 for the anti-dam movement in China). This is occurring in spite of the findings of the final report of the World Commission on Dams (WCD) in November 2000. The 404-page report argues that the electricity generation, flood mitigation, and water provision of these large dams has not lived any-where near up to developers' claims. In addition, the report concludes, "Large dams have forced 40 to 80 million people from their homes and lands, caus-ing extreme economic hardship, community disintegration and an increase in mental and physical health problems. Indigenous, tribal and peasant com-munities have been particularly hard hit. People living downstream of dams have also suffered from increased disease and the loss of natural resources upon which their livelihoods depended" (WCD Report, November 2000).

In every country where such a dam is being built there is an environmen-tal movement which opposes it. Movements against mega-dams have grown in stature since the early 1980s. In their groundbreaking work in 1984, Ed-ward Goldsmith and Nicholas Hildyard wrote of the vast societal impetus be-hind the building of large dams and the enormous obstacles which environ-mental movements and others faced in their opposition to such enterprises. They state, "To add to their difficulties, they (environmentalists) must also confront the entrenched belief that large-scale water development schemes (with their resulting hydroelectricity) are an essential part of the process of economic development—a process which we have been taught to see as the only means of combating poverty and malnutrition, and assuring health, lon-gevity and prosperity for all. To challenge dams is thus to challenge a funda-mental credo of our civilization" (1984, 231).

There is no space here for an in-depth critical analysis of the phenomenon of mega-dams.[2] It is important to understand, however, that anti-dam move-ments do challenge basic assumptions intertwined with the pillars of Western progress. On the other hand, anti-dam movements can easily be viewed in a more positive light: as *pro-river movements* led by political advocates for more sustainable and equitable management practices of river systems and the valleys of humans and nonhumans which coalesce around these sources of life.

The early to mid-1980s saw the first anti-dam movements born into the minority world (McCully 1998, 316). Probably one of the most famous of these early protests was the campaign to save the Franklin River and its sur-rounding forests in Australia. These anti-dam environmentalists fought the powerful Tasmanian Hydro-Electric Commission (HEC) in the late 1970s, with the campaign crescendoing to a peak in 1983, at the very time the Save the Narmada Movement was beginning to catch the attention of the Indian population.

Box 6.1

Three Gorges Dam, Yangtze River, China

The Three Gorges Dam on the Yangtze will be the largest hydroelectric dam in the world. It stretches nearly a mile across and towers 575 feet above the world's third longest river. Its reservoir stretches over 350 miles upstream and has forced the displacement of close to 1.9 million people. Construction began in 1994 and is scheduled to take twenty years and over $24 billion.

In its campaigns against the dam, International Rivers Network has been calling attention to the environmental and social impacts of the project along with the international companies and banks necessary for construction. In September of 1994, IRN, and a coalition of U.S. environmental, developmental, and human rights groups, encouraged the U.S. administration to withhold financial support for the U.S. companies eager to bid for the project. After more than a year, the National Security Council concluded that the U.S. government should stay clear of the controversial Three Gorges Dam. In May of 1996, the U.S. Export-Import Bank announced that it would not guarantee loans to U.S. companies seeking contracts for the dam. In addition, the World Bank, traditionally the largest funder of dams in developing countries, has also refrained from financing Three Gorges Dam.

Despite the warnings and protests by Chinese citizens and the media attention surrounding the project, major banks and government export credit agencies have been quick to fund-raise for the dam. IRN is currently holding U.S. investment banks, namely Morgan Stanley Dean Witter, responsible for financing the dam through the underwriting of China Development Bank (CDB) bonds, a government-run development bank that funds infrastructure construction. Morgan Stanley Dean Witter, through its joint venture, China International Capital Corporation, has been an advisor to the Three Gorges Project Development Corporation on international fund-raising possibilities since 1995. Approximately 65 percent of the Three Gorges Dam construction costs are financed by the CDB. Also being targeted are Goldman Sachs and Co. and CS First Boston, whose $1 billion PRC general obligation bond offering at the end of 1998 reportedly funnelled $200 million to the dam. In response to letters sent by IRN questioning the wisdom of the banks' involvement, representatives claim they had received assurances from CDB officials that none of the funds raised from the bond underwriting are going toward the dam. However, U.S. bank representatives have not been able to provide copies of such assurances nor have they been able to explain how those assurances are being monitored.

SOURCE: *Adapted from http://www.irn.org/programs/threeg/.*

The battle for the Franklin was a wilderness and forests campaign (see chapter 4) as well as an anti-dam campaign. Patrick McCully, in his excellent study on the politics of big dams, explains that the Gordon-Below-Franklin Dam "would have flooded part of one of the last great temperate wildernesses of the Southern Hemisphere. It would have inundated rare temperate rainforest, one of Australia's most spectacular gorges and archaeologically important caves with evidence of occupation 20,000 years before" (1998, 322).

In December 1982, environmentalists staged several blockades at the construction site of the Franklin dam. At its peak, twelve hundred demonstrators were arrested during this "nonviolent action," and in the interim the Franklin area was classified as a World Heritage site (Doyle 2000). Eventually, the "anti-dam," newly elected Labor Party had to take the issue to the High Court, which ruled that the Commonwealth government's external affairs powers "allowed Federal legislation giving domestic effect to international treaties, such as the World Heritage Convention, to prevail" (Tighe 1992, 126). The Franklin River and its surrounding wilderness had been saved.[3]

The Franklin dam campaign epitomizes anti-dam movements in the more affluent minority world. It provides stark contrast with those movements now so prominent in the South. There are vital demographic differences which influence these contexts. Millions of people work and live in the valleys to be dammed in the South (including the indigenous peoples), whilst most indigenous peoples in the North have been removed from dam project sites a very long time ago. The campaign for the Narmada River is the most famous of these current struggles in the majority world.

THE NARMADA CAMPAIGN

The environmental protest with the biggest profile in India over the past decade and a half is, without doubt, the campaign fought over the damming of the Narmada River in Western India (Swain 1997, 7).

> It is said that Shiva, Creator and Destroyer of Worlds, was in an ascetic trance so strenuous that rivulets of perspiration began flowing from his body down the hills. The stream took on the form of a woman—a beautiful virgin innocently tempting even ascetics to pursue her, inflaming their lust by appearing at one moment as a lightly dancing girl, at another as a romantic dreamer, at yet another as a seductress loose-limbed with the lassitude of desire. Her inventive variations so amused Shiva that he named her Narmada, the Delightful One, blessing her with the words, "You shall be forever holy, forever inexhaustible." Then he gave her in marriage to the most lustrous of all her suitors, the ocean, Lord of Rivers. (Mehta 1993, 8)

The Narmada Bachao Andolan (NBA) has been fighting an environmental campaign against the damming of the Narmada River since the mid-1980s. The damming of this mighty river means the displacement of hundreds and thousands of people (if not millions) from the valley floor. Critics of the dam-building see it as a symbolic and hollow nation-building exercise which ultimately delivers more water, electricity, and money to those in India who already possess an inequitably large share of wealth, resources, and power.

The Save the Narmada Movement commenced in the 1980s as a battle for

FIG. 6.2. The banks of the Narmada River, India, 2000. This plaque was unveiled by ex-Indian prime minister Nehru, who claimed that dams such as the Sardar Sarovar would become the "modern temples of India." *Author's private collection.*

the resettlement and rehabilitation of people being displaced by the proposed giant mega-dam—the Sardar Sarovar Project (SSP)—in the Indian state of Gujarat. The SSP is just one of a number of major dams being built on the Narmada River, the fifth largest river in India. Sheth writes, "The reservoir will submerge about 37,000 hectares of lands, of which about 11,000 hectares are classified as forests. It will displace about one lakh (100,000) persons of 248 villages (19 of Gujarat, 36 of Maharashtra and 193 of Madha Pradesh). The anti-project activists give more than double this figure as the project-affected persons (PAPs)" (Sheth 1997, 253).

The exact numbers of displaced persons are obviously debated vociferously by different parties, but they must be understood within the larger context of displacement which mega-dams have brought to India. In a popular book which shook India on publication in 1999 (*The Greater Common Good*), Arundhati Roy estimates that at least 33 million people have been displaced by mega-dams in India over the past fifty years. Roy writes of the ecological carnage of big dams: "Big dams started well, but have ended badly. . . . They're undemocratic. They're the Government's way of accumulating authority (deciding who will get how much water and who will grow what where). They're a guaranteed way of taking a farmer's wisdom away from him. They're a brazen means of taking water, land and irrigation away from the poor and gifting it to the rich. Their reservoirs displace huge populations of people leaving them homeless and destitute. Ecologically too, they're in the doghouse. They lay the earth to waste. They cause floods, water-logging, salinity, they spread disease" (1999, 7–8).

In the months directly preceding my visit to the NBA, I had been working in the north of India. During this time I had discovered that many Indian elites—largely academics and bureaucrats—had deep-set, although largely unsubstantiated, opinions on the politics of the NBA. It seemed as if the NBA not only characterized the modern environmental movement in India, but also was now a symbol of all nonviolent dissent against the normal practices of the Indian state, as well as against the globalization of free market economics. Outside of India, also, the NBA has become a cause celebre, a champion of the South against the excesses of the North.

Given this almost epic standing, the NBA has created some serious enemies. The NBA is demonized from many angles. Sometimes it is portrayed as a middle-class movement of urban greenies and do-gooders stirring up trouble amongst the tribal and other small landholder communities of the Narmada Valley. At other times, the movement is depicted as being either controlled or funded by, or in too close liaison with, international environmental organizations, which ultimately may be serving interests other than those which are strictly Indian.

Both these arguments against the NBA have little standing. First, it is obvious that there are some more middle-class activists, such as Medha Patkar, in the movement. Few social movements have ever flourished without input from this sector of society. Regardless of this fact, however, most of the NBA personnel are made up of *adivasis* (indigenous peoples) as well as small lowland farmers living in submergence zones. In interviews during my own visit to the Narmada Valley in 2000, I found that those activists who were not originally from the valley received eight hundred rupees a month (twenty dollars) to live on; and all had been instructed to never accept money from well-meaning "internationals" (such as myself) to supplement wages and expenses, as this was contrary to NBA policy. Grassroots activism in the third world means living with a community under threat, becoming a positive conduit for the community to the outside world.

Due to the length and intensity of the campaign, there is no opportunity here to provide a full chronological account of the campaign, as it has been championed by its key NGO proponent, the Narmada Bachao Andolan (NBA) (Save the Narmada Movement).[4] It is largely sufficient to assert here that the strategies of the NBA have been diverse and multitudinous. There have been court actions and intensive lobbying efforts at every level of Indian and international societies. Just a few events within this vast campaign can be touched upon here. First, as aforementioned, the Narmada issue, more than any other environmental campaign in India, managed to unite a wide variety of social movement actors who were previously fighting disparate and more localized campaigns. At its Harsud Convention in 1989, for example, forty-five thousand people attended, including project-affected persons (PAPs) and activists belonging to approximately two hundred NGOs (Sheth 1997, 255–256).

Next, in 1992, the Save the Narmada Movement, linking with United States NGOs, the Environmental Defense Fund, and the Friends of the Earth (Sheth 1997, 72), briefly moved the campaign to Washington in its efforts to place international pressure on the World Bank to withdraw its funding for the project. The NBA managed to ensure the withdrawal of the World Bank's funding of the project. This was a huge win with the World Bank's reputation almost permanently tarnished in future "development" projects across the globe. No doubt, the Narmada campaign contributed heavily to the World Bank's future decision not to become an active partner in the aforementioned Three Gorges Dam Project in China.

In 1995, the NBA took its fight to the Indian Supreme Court and won a four-year stay on the continued construction of the huge Sardar Sarovar Dam. In October 2000, the Supreme Court, however, decided to allow the construction of the dam to a height of 138 meters, as originally planned. The Gujarat State Government and the National BJP Government hailed this decision as a victory for the people and a defeat for the NBA. The NBA begs to differ, for the battle for the Narmada has always been more than just whether a dam was going to be built or not. In an interview with "Shripad" (a senior activist within the organization), it was made quite clear that the goal of the struggle was always much broader: "The goal has always been to empower people to fight for their own rights; to create a just society; to create a space in that society for justice and environmental responsibility" ("Shripad," personal communication, 2000).

Most of the NBA's work has been built on educating and mass mobilizing the people of the villages which are directly threatened by the project. From this support and education, the people themselves, through solidarity forged across tribal/class/caste boundaries, have found voice and some semblance of political power to contest the previously uncontestable, to confront, face on, the might of transnational capital—in the form of the World Bank and other companies—and the authority of the centralized Indian state.

One trend in this vast environmental campaign is without question. From its early beginnings, with its focus purely on human displacement, gradually the focus of the Save the Narmada Movement shifted to the protection of the ecological integrity of the valley and the pursuit of environmental justice for the entire valley (Karan 1994, 6). The NBA and the broader movement, and its charismatic leaders, Babe Amte and Medha Patkar, have pursued numerous successful, nonviolent actions of *satyagraha* (literally, "firmness in truth"). In 1994, for example, at a "dharma" every protester's hands were tied to symbolize their commitment to nonviolence. This did not stop the protesters from being badly beaten by police, but won the movement a deep respect from many parts of the Indian populace.

It is almost unfair to single out any one person in the long Narmada campaign. So many people have devoted their lives to this cause—literally. The story of Medha Patkar, however, encapsulates a style of political activity synonymous with the campaign. Patkar was a social scientist attached to the Tata Institute for Social Studies in Mumbai when, in 1985, she became enmeshed in community mobilization in the submergence zone villages of the SSP. Since that time Patkar has put her life on the line so many times for this cause that it is impossible to list. For example, in late 1990, after pursuing a range of more mainstream political actions, Patkar and six others started an indefinite hunger strike. Ultimately, after twenty-two days of fasting the police moved in to make arrests. On another occasion, in 1993, Patkar and a *samarpit dal* ("band of the dedicated") refused to move from a submergence zone. Instead, they decided to "meet the waters," as the Narmada, their sacred mother, now dammed, rose to claim their villages, their past, their future, their lives. In the Indian environmental movement context, regardless of the level of desperation, almost always this direct resistance is nonviolent, based on satyagraha.

In many parts of the world strict nonviolence is no longer a defining characteristic of environmental action. In the United States, for example, the eco-saboteurs of deep ecological "non-organizations" such as Earth First! believe they have a right "to defend mother earth" with militant actions. In Britain, animal rights organizations and the anti-roads movement have consistently used violence against property to pursue their goals (Wall 1999). As will be discussed in the next chapter, recent struggles against the transport of nuclear waste in Germany have also become quite militant. In the Philippines, this level of violence includes the right to pursue guerilla warfare in order to protect people's access to a livelihood when threatened by the activities of giant multinational mining corporations. In anti-dam and broader environmental movements in India, however, the most important shared ideological component of the movements is nonviolence.

Mahatma Gandhi's teachings have also emerged as a powerful influence in the Australian anti-dam context, due largely to the merger of the peace movement with the environment movement in the late 1960s and early 1970s (Summy and Saunders 1986). One of the key campaigns of the peace movement had been against nuclear war, and this focus was extended in the 1970s to include opposition to uranium mining, which was seen as part of the "nuclear cycle" contributing to nuclear militarization. In addition, nonviolent techniques also infiltrated the early Australian movement from the United States Movement for a Free Society, again, in the early 1970s. Finally, the Tasmanian Wilderness Society, which was the key NGO during the battle for the Franklin, possessed a very influential network of Quakers (or Friends) who helped shape this nonviolence focus.

In the case of the Narmada, the ever-dominant philosophy of nonviolence is at times overwhelming. Indeed, the existence of an ideology of nonviolence is one of the centrally defining characteristics of what can, and cannot, be classified as an "environmental" campaign in India. In a work on environmental politics in India, Sumi Krishna (1996) attempts to explain why the more violent/militant "tree wars" of the Gonds of Adilabad, the Naxalites, and the Jkarkland Movement in Southern Bihar are not regarded either by the environmental movement in India or by the Indian ruling elite as part of their shared terrain. Krishna argues that the dominance of the ideology of nonviolence and its concomitant distaste for militancy within the Indian green movement, among other factors, explain this border between two movements with many similar goals, such as the empowerment of poor people against the encroachment of the state and multinational interests (1996, 152).

It is critically important, however, to understand the deep differences between minority world and Indian understandings of nonviolence. The Franklin protest, in Australia, was nonviolent in that people passively gave themselves up to police for arrest and did not inflict violence on their opposition. This Western definition, however admirable, is an extremely narrow understanding of nonviolence when compared to NVA (nonviolent action) as practiced by the NBA and its supporters (Doyle 2004b).

The Narmada NVA experience is different in its level of risk as well as its depth of philosophy and broadness of purpose. In the NBA's case, the failure to act on behalf of the environment and its people would lead to a massive displacement of people. In turn, for these people this leads to a loss of a basic environmental security and denies access to adequate shelter, water, and food sources (Doyle 2004a). Even worse is the decimation of tribal meaning systems with the dispersal of families and other collective forms based on common kinship. This situation leads to sickness, both of the body and the spirit, and, on many occasions, death. In the wealthier nations of the North, although there are many dedicated activists, most environmental campaigns do not lead to the activists' loss of home or life. For example, how many Franklin protesters were willing to die for their cause? In the Indian magazine *Frontline,* which has covered all aspects of the Narmada dispute since its emergence, the level of risk was made quite clear: "By the monsoon of 1993, villages nearest to the dam site, at Kervadia in Gujarat, faced submergence, and Patkar was forced to use the card of 'jal samarpan': threatening to drown herself in the floodwaters if the Government did not halt construction and constitute an independent review of all aspects of the SSP" (Swami 1994, 116).

As touched upon previously, on numerous occasions Medha Patkar and

Fig. 6.3. Medha Patkar and other Narmada Bachao Andolan organizers meet to discuss strategy at NBA headquarters in Baroda, Gujarat, India, March 2000. *Author's private collection.*

supporters faced death, either through extended hunger strikes, through beatings ministered by officials, or through refusal to leave villages threatened with submergence: a willingness to meet the waters. Satyagraha, however, is more than just a case of heightened risk; it is a term which embraces an entire way of living rather than just being a "passive resistance" tactic at a time of conflict. At the personal level it may relate to vegetarianism and acts of self-discipline. At the societal level, nonviolence is *noncooperation.* It is a dramatically radical political philosophy which strikes at the very heart of the modern nation-state, promoting decentralization and direct participation in decision-making. Baviskar contends, "The slogan of 'Our rule in our villages' calls for non-cooperation with the state, the Gandhian method of passive resistance against exploitative authority. *Jan andolan* (people's movement), or decentralized and non-violent collective action, is posited as a political alternative to the dominant political system . . . [and] village self-government is theoretically consistent as a form of decentralized political action that tries to create a political alternative to mainstream politics" (1995, 224–225).

Although there were many occasions when traditional political and legal avenues were pursued by the NBA and its supporters, it was always, first and foremost, a mass mobilization campaign designed to empower the *adivasis* (indigenous peoples) and small Patidar farmers (landholders with five to ten acres) directly threatened by the dam. The philosophy and practice of nonviolence in organizations like the NBA has led to the education, empowerment, and mobilization of Indian villagers in the valley. Prior to this empowerment, for the fifty years since India has gained nationhood, most of these people had no formal education, no subsidized food, no health care; and, on the few occasions when there has been government contact—in the words of Himanshu Thakkar of Delhi's Center for Water Policy—"it has created points of access into forest society with a view of exploitation on behalf of the state" (Thakkar, personal communication 2000).

The struggle for the Narmada—"the Delightful One"—and all her peoples continues.

CONCLUSIONS

The differences and similarities between anti-dam campaigns in the North and the South are many. The first relates to what, at first glance, appears to be the shared philosophical and tactical position of nonviolence. A closer look, however, reveals deep rifts in the interpretation of the concept as practiced by movements in either the minority or majority world. The second brutally obvious difference between the two movements relates to the alternative positioning of the human being in relation to nature/environment: there can be no more profound difference than this.

I have made the point often in this book that the minority world concept of "environment" usually denotes an instrumental nature, out there somewhere, away from humans, a nature which can be molded, used, and perfected by humans. In this manner, environment, in the more affluent North, has been dominated by issues such as wilderness (mainly forests). The term "wilderness" relies on a concept of "true nature," as it was without the imprimatur of humans stamped upon it: the Christian garden before the great sin. In Judeo-Christian societies, the human–other nature split is a defining feature of its cosmology. Consequently, movements in the North bearing the green cloak may be dominated by questions such as which particular parts of nature must be hermetically sealed from human access; or, more profitably, how can this external environment be managed more efficiently.

According to Tagore, Indian society, on the other hand, has emerged from a "forest society" and has always seen humans as part of nature rather than separate. He writes, "The culture of the forest has fuelled the culture of Indian society. The culture that has arisen from the forest has been influenced by the diverse processes from species to species, from season to season, in sight and sound and smell. The unifying principle of life in diversity, of democratic pluralism, thus became the principle of Indian civilization" (quoted by Shiva 1992, 196).

Obviously, many other religions—such as Hinduism, Islam, Jainism, etc.—as well as non-religious ideologies have been layered, palimpsest-like, over this original cosmological script; so the origins of this human inclusiveness in nature in modern India are confused by the overlaying of other types of boundaries of identity. In actual practice, therefore, certain sectors of Indian society are just as dismissively dualistic as Western societies when it comes to their separation and treatment of "other" nature. For example, Indian political elites often describe the activities of environmentalists by referring to them as "boys and girls interested in saving tigers and trees" (Baviskar 1995, 235). Baviskar continues, "Such an understanding of what is 'environmental' echoes the thoughts of those who see development as an essentially benign process, marred only by a few regrettable externalities such as environmental pollution. 'Tigers and trees' are perceived as trivial concerns, luxuries that elites can afford to indulge in, since they have already gained the benefits of development. This interpretation of the conflict as 'environment versus development' has tended to prevail in government discourse."

Of course, this is another example of the power of the environment as a symbol. Different sectors in different societies define it differently for both substantive and strategic reasons. Some seek to expand its umbrella; others seek to reduce it. In Baviskar's quotation, it is evident that certain sections of the Indian elite seek to limit the boundaries of identity of the Indian environmental movement by publicizing their denigrating interpretation of the narrow focus of green activists. Often, this "tigers and trees" focus is then discursively connected to the fact that Indian NGOs are simply pawns of the North, promoting post-materialist agendas.

But even sidestepping these religious/cultural divisions/explanations, it must be said that in many cultures in the South, regardless of religion, the human/nonhuman nature split is not as evident within environmental discourses. Most environmental issues in the South, as perceived by the bulk of the environmentalists themselves, are human survival issues such as sustainable shelter, food, and water supplies, employment, and disease control (Doyle and McEachern 1998, 2). Consequently, the luxury of pursuing nonhuman welfare issues is not available to most people. In this manner, through obvious necessity, humans are not regarded as separate from the rest of nature: the ecological degradation/human devastation nexus simply presents itself. The well-known Indian environmentalist Vandana Shiva comments, "The ecology movements that have emerged as major social movements in many parts of India are making visible many invisible externalities and pressing for their internalization in the economic evaluation of the elite-oriented development process. In the context of a limited resource base and unlimited development aspirations, ecology movements have initiated a new political struggle for safeguarding the interests and survival of the poor, the marginalized, including women, tribals and poor peasants" (1991, 19).

Environmental issues in India, in this regard, are more central to questions which challenge status quo, "grown-up" politics. Although wilderness networks still exist within South Asian (Indian) environmental movements, they are in a minority. Environmental movements in India, as with most of the majority world, perceive issues of social justice and equity as central goals. In short, it is not just a question of which parts of nonhuman nature are protected, but rather issues of the maldistribution and overconsumption of resources dominate these green agendas. There is very little which is post-materialist about the political reality of India. The post-materialist thesis, sometimes (but far from always) provides a suitable description of green movements in the minority worlds of the North, but has very little applicability in the South.

This construction of green alternatives is a distant dream in most cultures. In other parts of the world, though few in number, the creation of green alternatives has shifted from movements of radical resistance to pragmatic governance. The green kaleidoscope now turns to the extraordinary case of the modern German environmental movement.

ANTI-NUCLEAR MOVEMENTS

Environmental Movements in Germany

I landed in Singapore in the middle of the night. Even by plane, Europe was at least two stops away from Australia. I had six hours between flights and drifted aimlessly around the world within a world which is Singapore airport—browsing through books, reading and sifting through some papers, sitting and staring. On one particular circuit of the complex I noticed a larger than usual crowd gathered around a vast television screen beaming in BBC world news. There was a palpable tension in the bodies and faces of those huddled together.

I moved toward the screen. An anonymous gaunt face greeted mine: he was pushing out through the crowd, past me, pushing in.

"There's a war," he said as if he knew me. "They're bombing Bosnia."

The television receiver told the story of the early stages of the United States–led NATO air strikes on Serbian-held territory in March 1999. Before my flight to Frankfurt, I spent the next few hours inhaling visual tidbits of tightly controlled information released by the NATO military command.

The flight was delayed while a new course was plotted to avoid the strike zones in south-central Europe. While flying north over Moscow, then back down into Germany, I tried to gaze through the darkness and pondered the many bombs which had been dropped on European soil since the first celebrated flights of human beings began, nearly a century ago.

The tension I first witnessed around the television set at Singapore airport remained amongst those on the flight and, upon landing in Germany, it seemed, if possible, to raise a few notches higher. Every television set, every radio, every countenance, every conversation addressed the same issues.

I'd traveled to Germany to gather information from movement intellectuals/activists on the enormous gains that German environmental movements had won over the past two decades. No other nation-state had been ruled by a green party (in Germany's case the Greens ruled in coalition with the Socialist Democrats).[1] Since the heady days of the early 1980s, when Die Grunen politicians first entered the West German parliament, eschewing ties and suits and replacing them with jeans and casual, open-necked shirts, the German green movement has achieved so much. Its four pillars of peace and disarmament; representative and more participatory forms of democracy; social equity, justice; and ecology have been the inspiration of most political ecology movements, specifically in the first world.

Real gains have been made by both the Green party and the broader environmental movements which gave birth to it. The party has put into place a program for the phasing out of nuclear power over thirty years; it has paved the way for dramatically reduced greenhouse emissions; it has put into place much tougher legislation to reduce German industrial pollution; it has supported those who quest for alternative forms of energy production; it has led the way in the European Parliament on challenging the technologies of genetically modified foodstuffs; and, most importantly, it has challenged existing electoral and parliamentary orthodoxies: for example, it has rotated office bearers on a two-year basis (although this practice has now been abandoned) and has set clear and enforceable targets ensuring that more women take part in the business of the party/government.

Over the next few days of traveling through this nation which has championed a red-green political experiment, the tense conversations I had overheard on my arrival at Frankfurt airport had become even more focused: "Would Germany's military become involved in the Bosnian crisis?" Within a week of the commencement of the bombing, Joschka Fischer, leader of the Green party and now minister for Foreign Affairs in the red-green government, answered this oft-asked question in the affirmative. Germany committed its air force to the NATO bombing of Bosnia; NATO later turned its explosive might onto the ancient Slavic capital of Belgrade. This was the first time the German Luftwaffe had involved itself in an offensive military action since World War II. The magnitude and gravity of these actions profoundly affected all German people with whom I talked. But the most deeply perplexed were the Greens themselves, both party and mass movement participants.

My brother, Greg, was living and working as a musician in Vienna and we arranged to meet for Easter in Munich, a halfway point. On the train trip down I sat next to a woman named Monika. After our initial meeting, our conversation quickly moved to the same dialogue taking place all over Germany. After some time she admitted that she was a local member of the Green party and that she was shocked and disenchanted by the militaristic gestures made by Fischer and his pragmatist supporters. She asked me, "What happens to the house when the pillars are removed? Does it topple over?"

She was referring, specifically, to the peace and nonviolence principle of the Greens, one of the four keystones of the party's foundations. I had no answer for her. The party had already survived severe ideological rifts in the mid to the late 1980s between the "realos" (realists) and the "fundis" (fundamentalists); and it had survived German reunification in 1990, despite some serious reluctance on behalf of some in both the West and East German parties. But this decision of Fischer's seemed to shake the very temple of green itself.

One week after the beginning of the bombing, large, spontaneous, and nonviolent street demonstrations took over the center of Munich. The anti-war stances of the demonstrators were heightened by the occasion of Easter, a time to reflect, in Christian countries, on the folly of human intolerance and the yearning for peace and goodwill. Serbs living in Germany, and their supporters, gathered in a protest meeting closely monitored by German police. The protestors wore "bulls-eyes" stuck onto their backs, with the words "NATO target" written alongside.

At the same time, in front of the Munich Rathaus, disenchanted environmentalists and other peace activists rallied in opposition to the Greens in government. One man, dressed in a World War II Nazi helmet, had inscribed it with the words "Die Grunen?" Many of the speakers in front of the Rathaus ended with this rhetorical sentiment: "Is this the cost of power? If it is, then we don't want it."

That day, one thing became certain to me as a spectator/participant within these emotionally charged protests. The broader ecological movement, from which the party in government had emerged, had not, contrary to the comments of some analysts, disappeared on the party's rise to ascendancy. It is true that Green concern in Germany had gained a level of administrative institutional access which has never been witnessed anywhere before; but this reality has been used in an ill-founded manner, on too many occasions, as a premise for imagining that the noninstitutional elements of the movement have waned or, even more inaccurately, ceased to exist. Instead, the green movement has remained a connected but separate entity, continually demanding that the party keep true to its four-pronged holy grail; and, at the same time, it has diverted much of its more multilayered, amorphous energies and strategic purposes to multifarious forms of extra-parliamentary politics.

On this occasion, however, the gulf between the Green party and the green movement had never been so vast.

■■■

FIG. 7.1. Anti-war rally, Munich, Germany, September 1999. *Author's private collection.*

INTRODUCTION

Moving from India to Germany is a dramatic real and metaphorical journey. In this chapter, again, we step through the portal: leaving the lives of the earth's majority and entering into the ecopolitics of the smaller, more affluent world. To say that these two experiences are worlds—if not universes—apart, is not overstating the case.

It is simply not possible to write a book on environmental movements without paying homage to the German experience. It is, without doubt, the most famous of environmental movements. Anti-nuclear movements are just emerging in the third world at the same time as nations like India and Pakistan are adding "nuclear capabilities" to their military arsenal. In the minority world, in the United States, U.K., Australia, and Germany, anti-nuclear sentiments have informed an environmental position to differing degrees since the late 1960s. In Germany's case, the anti-nuclear position has been the most prominent green issue since the emergence of its environmental movement, and this issue—and the networks that surround it—continue as powerful threads of ecoactivism to the present day.

In chapter 5, we reviewed the activities of the British movement. It was argued that the English experience has been shaped by the traditions and ideology of *political ecology*. The German movement, which began in what was West Germany, shares this ideological past, but even more so. Indeed, it is *the* quintessential political ecology movement.

THE ENVIRONMENTAL MOVEMENT IN GERMANY

In Germany, the environmental movement is usually referred to as the *green* or the *ecology* movement.[2] There are both subtle and substantive differences in meaning here but, for the purposes of this text, these terms will be used interchangeably with *environmental* movements.

Germany is a powerful and wealthy, advanced industrial nation. In 1990 the Berlin Wall came down. The wall had physically separated West Berlin from East Berlin and had represented a broader separation between East and West Germany (as well as between eastern and western Europe). Two Germanys had previously existed since 1945, from the end of World War II. The Germany of the West was a capitalist nation, whilst East Germany ran its society by socialist principles. Post-unification, all of Germany is now one nation, aspiring to capitalist economic and cultural ideology. Also, the green movement in Germany has had to make this transition to reunification, with varying degrees of success.

In the late 1960s, West German political ecologists comprised one of three strands which made up the modern environmental movement. Dieter Rucht writes of these early years:

> First, local and independent citizen action groups mushroomed and in part, also united in regional, state-wide and national organizations such as the Bundesverband Burgerinitativen Umweltschutz (Federal Alliance of Citizen Initiatives for Environmental Protection; founded in 1972). These groups' early risers were mainly focusing on specific issues such as air pollution, individual transport, and nuclear energy. Second, pre-exiting organizations for nature conservation became re-vitalized and, to some extent, politicized. An outstanding example is the Bavarian-based Bund Naturschutz (Alliance for Nature Conservation; founded in 1913) which renewed its program and leadership in the early 1970s and was instrumental in founding the Bund fur Umwelt und Naturschutz

Deutschland (BUND) in 1975. Third, loose networks of individuals and groups adhering to a more general concept of political ecology emerged. They saw an urgent need for a radical change of industrial societies, promoting ideas of decentralization, soft technology, an ascetic and ecologically friendly lifestyle, and sometimes even industrial devolution. (Rucht 1999, 2)

During these early years of the modern West German movement, both state and federal governments passed important environmental legislation and set up strong administrative systems to enforce it. For example, with changes in the Constitution, regulatory powers relating to waste disposal, clean air, and noise abatement were transferred from the lander (state) to the federal government in 1972 (Brand 1999, 38). Despite these early moves by the state to embrace environmental concern, most environmentalists remained unconvinced about the ability of existing institutions to cope with an *environmental crisis.* This situation was further exacerbated by the OPEC oil crisis which shook the world in 1973 and the global recession which immediately followed it. The federal government moved from being "a driving force of environmental protection to being a brake upon it" (Brand 1999, 39). As was evidenced in the cases of the United Kingdom, Australia, and the United States, despite early legislative gains, environmentalists during the 1970s were largely regarded as antagonistic to the state, as political outsiders. In this light, the environmental position was widely understood to be the polar opposite to economic growth, employment, and progress. In West Germany the movement began to involve itself in more militant conflicts relating to nuclear power.

The 1980s saw a change which, again, uncannily echoes with the history of Australian, British, United States, and many minority-world movements. During this new decade, environmentalists would make a remarkable transition from rank political outsiders, as hordes banging on the ramparts of the citadel, to political insiders, cementing environmentalism into the politics of the everyday. There are numerous reasons for this, but it is obvious that the state, at least in part, began to accept the legitimacy of some of the environmentalists' more moderate claims and, even more importantly, saw electoral gains in accommodating these concerns (Fuchs and Rucht 1994). In addition, some dominant networks within green movements became more pragmatic and accepted that there might be some gains made by engaging with existing institutions of the state and of capital production. It was during this period that the world saw a parliamentary wing of the movement emerge forcefully as a new party: the West German Green party—Die Grunen. It is to this phenomenon that we now must turn our attention.

In chapter 1, it was mentioned that this work would only concentrate on noninstitutional elements in environment movements. Why then are we looking at green electoral politics in Germany? The answer lies within two facts. First, to ignore the German Green party—the electoral manifestation of an environmental movement—leaves a huge hole in this story. Indeed, it is the party political element of the German experience which clearly sets it apart from the rest. Second, when it first appeared on the electoral scene, Die Grunen, as strangely as it seems, classified itself as "an anti-party party." In doing so, it challenged the very structure and operation of party politics. The late Petra Kelly, a famous leader of the party in its early days, discussed this very point as follows: "As Greens, it is not part of our understanding of politics to find a place in the sun alongside the established parties, nor to help maintain power and privilege in concert with them. Nor will we accept any alliances and coalitions. This is wishful thinking on the part of the traditional parties, who seek to exploit the Greens to keep themselves in power. . . . We are, and I hope we will remain, half party and half local action group—we shall go on being an anti-party party" (quoted in Dobson 1991, 193–194).

So apart from championing the environment, the Green party also celebrated some elements of the noninstitutional styles of politics as evidenced within other new social movements. They did this in a range of ways: they limited the length of office of their leaders; they rotated the Bundestag seats of their elected officials; and they donated much of the monies procured through the electoral process to NGOs and other forms of more grassroots environmental protest (Frankland 1995, 29).

The Greens first broke through at the federal level in 1983 with 5.6 percent of the vote, garnering twenty-seven deputies. Since then they have continued to poll well in German and European Parliament elections. Right throughout the 1980s they polled over five percent, which ensured them multiple representation as well as electoral funds. Despite electoral successes throughout this period, the Greens were plagued by constant internal party conflicts. The battles between the Realos and the Fundis are now the subject of environmental movement folklore and, as such, have almost become clichéd. They are significant in this context, however, because the tensions which manifested themselves were largely based on ideological/strategical differences between those who attempted to maintain the chiefly noninstitutional, *anti-party party* stance (the fundamentalists) and those who were willing to play party politics in a more traditional way (the realists). The Fundis involved themselves in extra-parliamentary politics with more radical goals, whilst the Realos emphasized reform (Frankland 1995, 32).

After blood-letting which lasted for the best part of a decade, most of the internal conflict between these two factions disintegrated with the re-unification of Germany. After an uncharacteristically abysmal showing in the first all-Germany election of 1990, the more radical, fundamental factions lost substantial power within the party, as the Realos seemed more in tune with the more pragmatic and less *post-materialist* political agenda of East Germany. This mutation into a pragmatic and more centrist party, however, "was less a result of unification than the outcome of a process already on its way in the late 1980s" (Mayer and Ely 1998, 3). As a consequence of the dominance of the realists' agenda, in 1994 the Greens bounced back, winning forty-nine seats in the Bundestag elections (Jesinghausen 1995, 108–114).

It is important to understand that the more radical, anti-institutional traits of the early Green party may have occurred due to more than one set of factors. Hirsch writes, "The new social movements' extreme 'anti-institutional' character, their strong detachment from established political institutions and forms, as well as their 'grass-roots orientation,' which valued autonomous self-organization, mass mobilization, and direct action, were not, however, a result of this political constellation alone, they were part of a legacy of the student movement's critique of parliamentarianism and the state" (Hirsch 1998, 182).

Whatever the combination of factors which gave birth to the anti-institutional characteristics of the early Green party, it is safe to say that the party rejected many of those characteristics inherited from its social-movement origins during this period of its development. Although the political party, amongst other pathways, grew from a social movement, its political form is often anathema to social movement politics, and vice versa. Parties measure their success, amongst other things, by electoral successes, coalitions, and legislation. Social movements have a longer-term time frame and are less incremental and more radical in their policy demands. Their amorphous political structures contrast dramatically with the more hierarchical mode of organization which defines most political parties. As such, during the 1990s many of the structural challenges celebrated by the early party, such as the rotation principle and the non-bureaucratic decision-making processes within party meetings, disappeared. As Mayer and Ely put it succinctly, there was a shift within the party from a movement rationality to a party rationality (1998, 7).

During this post-unification period, most of the intra-party taboos, such as those expressed in the earlier paragraph directly quoting Petra Kelly, subsided. The German Greens now looked actively to forge coalitions with other parties, to do deals with the "powers-that-be," to take their "place in the sun," as Kelly had described it. In the mid-1990s the Greens formed alliances with the Social Democrats to actually hold government in several landers (states), including Germany's largest, North Rhine-Westphalia. Of course, the ultimate access to power came in the 1998 federal election, discussed at the outset of this chapter, when the Greens formed a similar alliance with the Social Democrats to form the national government of Germany. This alliance was re-elected in the federal election of 2002, despite a substantial diminution of returns.

Although there are some activists in the Green party who would still classify themselves as Fundis or, at least, have linkages or leanings to the movement traditions of the party, these factions, though existing, are not prominent. If anything, the Realos, or party leadership, is currently being challenged from others factions espousing the position that the Realos themselves are still too caught up in the movement/party debate. For example, the New Greens have emerged in recent times as a force to be reckoned with in the party. The environmental platform includes active cooperation with industry, such as voluntary environmental codes. Many of these New Greens include younger members of the party. In 1999, the New Greens issued the following statement:

> We stand for a clear, power-conscious, pragmatic position, but also for the partial replacement of the party's membership. . . . Put an end to the tales of 1968: we understand very well that the founders have difficulties with the change from movement to a party. . . . Yes, you were for another system. Yes, you undertook the valiant but unsuccessful struggle against capital. Yes, for you the employers were part of the Evil Empire. . . . Those of us from the second generation, at least, aren't interested in how you made your peace with the market economy. The point is that you have. For us, any questioning of the system arose only for a short period, then it became clear, we are for the system, although we recognize its faults and want to put them right. (New Greens quoted in Green 2001, 12)

The transition from movement rationality to party rationality was fraught with internal paradoxes; but the metamorphosis from party rationality to government rationality may be even more difficult for the Greens to emerge from successfully. For regardless of the different stages in the lifespan of the German Greens, their past traditions still partly define them and, as such, still exist. Their decision to forge an alliance at the national level with the Social Democrat party to form government in 1998 has created new policy dilemmas to juggle with. The air raids into Bosnia detailed at this chapter's commencement are just one example of these new tensions occurring as a result of sharing government.[3]

With this transition from movement to party to government, there are obvious costs, but there are also many benefits from increased access to short-term power. To govern is to rule, to bargain with the powerful, to have access to adequate wealth, to legislate, and to implement regulations. There is far greater access, for example, to diplomacy at international levels. Much environmental problem-solving is at this level.

Not all networks of the movement, however, have made this transition. The wider movement did not simply disappear due to the success of some of their parliamentary experiments. It is true, however, that many networks within the movement did move along a path of increased institutionalization.

Institutionalization did not just occur through the life and times of the Green party; it is also evidenced in the style of politics played in green NGOs throughout the movement's lifespan. Increasingly, large NGOs received more money from the state to pursue their programs, particularly throughout the 1980s. In a quantitative study completed by Rucht and Roose of green organizations in West Berlin, this level of increased institutionalization was moderate, but lower than perhaps expected (Rucht and Roose 1999, 66–67).

Institutionalization—often hand in hand with increasing professionalism—can be measured, of course, in other ways as well. In chapter 5 different measures of institutionalization were discussed in the British movement's context. In the German movement there was an increasing "counter-expertise," including scientific expertise, germinating within movement organizations; there was increased access to mainstream media as well as the birth of new media outlets such as the *Tageszeitung* (Brand 1999, 40); and there was an ever-growing interaction between movement organizations, not just with the state or "the system," but with big business itself. In symbolic terms, green concerns had become very much part of the furniture of German, particularly West German, culture.

The move to embrace market culture has never been as smooth or as complete as that experienced in the United States (see chapter 2); but as experienced in many minority-world countries, this change has had a monumental impact on movement affairs. The German branch of Greenpeace is an excellent example of this shift toward a professional/business orientation. Originally almost totally focused on disruptive activities which attracted media attention, Greenpeace has made the transition into an organization which works closely with business, and operates almost exclusively as a business, in order to achieve its aims through market-based approaches. Brand writes on the "dialectics of institutionalization" in the German movement as follows: "Thus, marketing methods were brought into the public relations management of the big environmental organizations. A role model is the PR work of Greenpeace. . . .This change did not take place without a fierce fight. . . . This conflict lost importance as a result of the progressive cooperation between political, industrial and movement actors since the end of the 1980s. Most environmental groups were now operating with marketing strategies. People coming from the movement were partially replaced by staff qualified in marketing and management. In their election campaign in 1994 the Greens hired advertising agencies for the first time. Changes also took place within the BUND" (1999, 47–48).

Although Greenpeace had always operated in a populist and hierarchical manner, this move toward increased institutionalization and professionalism led to a splinter group—Robin Wood—breaking away from Greenpeace in 1982 over a debate about forests (Brand 1999, 45) The split between Greenpeace and Robin Wood was a cameo of the German movement as a whole. There can be no doubt that since the early to mid 1980s the movement, including local, autonomous action groups, professional NGOs, and the Green party, have all, to some extent, moved along the path of institutionalization. Critically, however, this incorporation into the system, as it were, is not uniform. There are many groups and organizations, such as Robin Wood, which have deliberately absconded from this process. Though there are tremendous pressures to formalize, or to institutionalize, these are simply pressures, not iron laws (Doyle 1989).

Let us now turn to the specifics of anti-nuclear movements, which are prime examples of social movements which include both intra-institutional and extra-institutional ecopolitics.

ANTI-NUCLEAR MOVEMENTS

Anti-nuclear movements emerged across the globe in the years subsequent to the bombing of Japan in World War II. Peace movements have, for a long time, often been one and the same with anti-nuclear movements. The nuclear clouds over Hiroshima and Nagasaki have invoked images of a nuclear holocaust for all who have lived since. During the cold war between the ex-U.S.S.R. and the United States, it seemed to many that a modern, industrial Armageddon was imminent (see box 7.1 for key nuclear protest events during this early period). In the days of the Reagan administration in the United States and the Gorbochev administration in the U.S.S.R., the doomsday clock clicked to "one minute to midnight." During this period, in surveys of teenagers in the West, one of the most commonly shared dreams of the survey participants was of global nuclear destruction.

Apart from fears of global devastation from nuclear weaponry, the anti-nuclear movement has also rallied against the production of nuclear energy. It has argued vociferously that the processes of transition from uranium ore to plutonium are inherently dangerous. There have been countless instances where nuclear *meltdowns* and other accidents have occurred at reactors which had been reported to be "fail-safe." An excellent example occurred at the Three Mile Island nuclear power plant in Harrisburg, in the United States in 1979. Radioactive gases were released, and this was followed by an evacuation of the surrounding area. An equally notorious incident occurred at the Chernobyl nuclear power plant near Kiev in the Ukraine in 1986. Over 130,000 inhabitants had to be evacuated from the region. Only the future will tell us of the final death count, though 30 died directly from the meltdown and hundreds of others were treated for severe radiation sickness (Papadakis 1998, 41). Many Europeans, downwind from the reactor explosion, were lied to by

Box 7.1

Protests against Uranium/Nuclear Energy in the Mid to Late 1970s

1974	Death of Karen Silkwood, a worker at the Kerr-McGee plutonium plant, Oklahoma, in mysterious circumstances.
1975	Mass protests against the proposal to construct a nuclear power station at Kaiseraugust, Switzerland.
1976	Mass protests against the proposals to construct nuclear power stations at Brokdorf and at Whyl, Federal Republic of Germany.
1977	Mass protests against the proposals to develop nuclear power installations at Grohnde, Kalkar, and Brokdorf in the Federal Republic of Germany and at Creys-Malville in France, and publication of an influential book by Amory Lovins, *Soft Energy Paths: Towards a Durable Peace.*
1978	Mass protests against the nuclear power reprocessing plant at Gorleben, Federal Republic of Germany;
1979	In protests against government policies on nuclear energy, around 100,000 people assemble in Hanover and 150,000 in Bonn, Federal Republic of Germany; the accident at the Three Mile Island nuclear power plant in Harrisburg, Pennsylvania; 75, 000 people gather in Washington, D.C., to take part in demonstration against nuclear power.

SOURCE: *Adapted from Papadakis 1998, xv–xvi.*

government officials, who justified their silence on the basis that they did not wish to "panic" the population. In Austria, for example, days after the event, citizens were finally told to stay indoors and close their windows. For months afterwards, fresh fruit and vegetables were off many European's menus.

There can be no doubt that there have always been enormous questions as to the economic viability of nuclear energy. By assessing it on purely economic bases, many European nations, at the beginning of the third millennium, are now questioning, and even attempting to phase out, their nuclear programs. The reasons behind advocating nuclear power, however, have not always been about the economically sustainable production of energy. Much support for the pro-nuclear lobby comes from industries devoted to the building and supply of weapons used in advanced global warfare. These industries are often inseparable from the "defense" interests of nation-states. No clearer an example need be sought that to refer to the bombing of Greenpeace's flagship, *The Rainbow Warrior,* as it stood moored in Auckland Harbor in 1984. After intensive investigations, it was revealed that this destruction of human life and property was instigated by French secret service agents working on behalf of the French government to end protests against their nuclear weapons detonations in the Pacific.

After a waning of the nuclear industry in the first world, the election of

George W. Bush as president of the United States in 2001 has reinvigorated support for the nuclear industry through such programs as the U.S. "missile defense strategy." Also, large military industrial corporations are now targeting the third world, such as India and Pakistan, in a bid to flog their wares. As mentioned at this chapter's outset, with the birth of a nuclear industry in these countries, there is also a concomitant emergence of majority-world anti-nuclear movements, for the first time (Bidwai and Vanaik 2000).

The anti-nuclear movement is very much part of the *political-ecological* tradition of environmental movements. Apart from fighting against the specifics of the nuclear industry from mining to plutonium production to nuclear waste disposal, the movement has always been at the radical vanguard of green movements across the globe. Its very raison d'etre challenges the concept of progress at all costs; it attacks the concept of short-term gains and short-term greed; it assails the concept that science and *end-of-pipe* technologies can make environmental risks simply disappear; and it objects to the overly close connections between the state and big business, often referred by movement participants as the *military-industrial complex*. Although it has often dabbled in the worlds of political parties and movement organizations, the anti-nuclear movement has continued to provide *counter-cultural* dimensions to many national environmental movements.

In the European Union there is an enormous divergence amongst member states in relation to nuclear energy (Marks and McAdam 1996, 271). They range from France, still with a commitment to, and reliance upon, nuclear energy, to the Netherlands, which is still yet to build a nuclear facility.[4] Germany lies somewhere in-between. The country possesses a number of reactors, but is currently questioning its nuclear future, attempting to phase out nuclear production over the next generation.

Two of the most forceful and sustained anti-nuclear movements have emerged in Germany and Australia. Nuclear protest began early in Germany. In 1975 protests at Whyl began as small communities were concerned about the impact of nuclear power production on their vineyards. These protests quickly became national and "escalated into a widespread antagonism toward three things: the collusion between the state government of Baden-Wurttemberg and industrial interests, the deployment of the police to solve political problems, and the dominant political parties" (Papadakis 1998, 39) Throughout the mid to late 1970s protests continued, culminating in the single biggest political rally ever held in West Germany, at Bonn, in October 1979, where 150,000 people gathered in protest over the nuclear industry. Right from the beginning, the anti-nuclear movement was at the center of the formation of Germany's modern environmental movement. Papadakis supports this contention when he writes, "During the same month, over 1,000 environmentalists met in Offenbah to discuss the possibility of establishing a new political organization that later became known as Die Grunen" (1998, 40).

At a very similar time, the Australian anti-nuclear movement was gearing up. Although there was no dramatic building program of nuclear reactors to rail against, as was the case in Germany, Australia was in the process of becoming one of the earth's largest uranium producers and exporters. In 1975, Friends of the Earth (FoE) became increasingly vocal and active in their anti-nuclear campaign (Doyle 2000, 133). In 1976 and 1977 up to fifty thousand people gathered in mass rallies in Australian cities, and in June 1997 anti-uranium protestors tried to stop the ship *ACT 6* from exporting yellowcake from the Lucas Height reactor: forty arrests ensued.[5] In a short history of the Australian peace movement, from which the anti-nuclear movement, in part, evolved, Summy and Saunders explain the reasoning behind these early mass protests: "Their objections were not confined to the link between nuclear weapons proliferation and the expansion of the nuclear power industry, but were based on a host of other factors as well. These included the environmental hazards of nuclear-waste disposal, reactor accidents, and releases of radioactivity at various stages of the nuclear fuel cycle. Other problems raised included the social and political threats to a society from terrorist use of nuclear materials, from reduction of civil liberties, and from the centralization of political and economic controls in the hands of financial bureaucratic elites" (1986, 45).

Again, at almost exactly the same time, both anti-nuclear movements made their own formal entrance into the party-political sphere. In 1983, Die Grunen won 5.6 percent of the vote; whilst in 1984, the newly formed Nuclear Disarmament party (NDP) won 6.8 percent of primary votes in the Australian federal election. In Germany, this percentage of the vote converted into twenty-seven seats in federal parliament; in Australia, a slightly higher percentage did not gain any members into the House of Representatives, and one member into the national Senate.

As this chapter has already attested to, there is no denying the relative success of the German environmental movement in attaining and maintaining access to parliamentary power. Much has been written on the subject of *political opportunity structures* to explain the German phenomenon, and some of this work obviously deserves mentioning (see Kitschelt 1986; Joppke 1992; Koopmans and Duyvendak 1995). For the purposes of this book, however, all that needs to be said is that the German *proportional representation* electoral process favors emerging and minority parties far more than the predominantly *preferential* manner of counting votes in Australia.[6] In short, proportional voting systems offer representation in direct relation to the proportion of votes cast. In the Australian context, to put it simply, only those parties which ultimately obtain an absolute majority of primary and preferential votes (50 percent plus one) in a given constituency can gain a seat in parliament. This favors big and established political parties.

There are no long-standing experiences of successful green representation in national governments in countries which do not have proportional representation, such as evidenced in the German electoral system. As argued in chapter 5, in Britain and the United States the dominance of the two major political parties is even more ironclad than in the Australian situation due to their adherence to the *first-past-the-post* electoral system, which only awards power to the parties who win a majority of primary votes in specific constituencies (Doyle and McEachern 2001, chapter 5).

There are, however, additional reasons for Australia's checkered adventures with party politics. As argued in chapter 4, wilderness movements in Australia have been far and away the dominant force within the broader environmental movement. On the contrary, in the German context, the level of power which the anti-nuclear movement exerted, particularly in the early days of the West German green movement and in the development of Die Grunen, was seminal and immense. Though there is still a certain separation in style and personnel between German anti-nuclear and "other environmental" movements, the gap between the Australian wilderness and anti-nuclear networks has always been colossal. In a quantitative study of the wilderness and anti-nuclear movements in Australia, Holloway explains the separation, "First, the historical development of the two movements is quite distinct. Secondly, the overlap is rather small—only 5% of environment groups make up the anti-nuclear movement" (1990, 37–38).

There are other hallmark similarities between German and Australian anti-nuclear activists. Both movements have always been part of the most radical wings of their broader environmental movements. They have both been profoundly committed to noninstitutional and extra-parliamentary activities. They have been fully committed to notions of grassroots and participative forms of democracy. Jo Vallentine, the NDP member elected to the Australian Senate before the party self-destructed, reminisces about this style of politics which the party was engaged in for the short period it existed in the 1980s: "People came in and offered to work and worked very successfully at the community level, it being mostly women who did the work, and often women with small children. Sometimes our office was a nightmare of kid's trolleys. But this was also a fantastic reminder of what and who we were all doing it for . . . [and] we operated a committee for the length of the campaign without any particular structure. It was non-hierarchical, whoever came along to the meetings became involved in the decision-making" (1989, 62).

In the German context, of course, an extremely powerful anti-nuclear response has been forged, for a variety of reasons, within the parliamentary

ANTI-NUCLEAR MOVEMENTS ■ 153

realm. It must be said, however, that from their inception until the present day, the dominant tradition of anti-nuclear movements, in both Germany and Australia, is one of extra-parliamentary, mass mobilizations, as distinct from appeals-to-elites tactics, which often characterize the minority-world forest and wilderness movements which were discussed in chapters 2 and 4. Let us now concentrate on one extra-parliamentary anti-nuclear campaign, relating to the storage and transport of nuclear waste in Germany.

THE BATTLES FOR GORLEBEN

In the early 1980s, in the northern German farm town of Gorleben, a huge hall was designated as an "interim" depository for high-level radioactive waste. It stood empty for twelve years until April 1995, when the first castor (a cask used for waste storage) was delivered (*Die Tageszeitung,* 24–29 April 1995). Demonstrations began several days earlier when 4,000 people gathered in the streets of Gorleben. The waste had originally made its way from the re-processing plant at La Hague in France. Germany has no such facility, nor have many other nuclear nations, for treating its own waste. Put succinctly, the reprocessing system in France takes quantities of spent fuel rods from countries with reactors and increases the mass of the waste by approximately thirty times, but simultaneously decreases the *shelf life* of the waste, so that it may be stored more *safely.* Regardless of this *reprocessing,* the waste is still re-garded by international standards as *high-level* radioactive waste.

On the Monday after these initial protests, the transport began again on German soil from a nuclear power plant in Phillipsburg in southern Germany. As soon as the transport of the waste began, protesters blocked its every move. At first they attempted to block the loading of the waste onto the train: the Deutsche Bahn AG Railway. On the following morning, a massive 2,500 people tried to prevent the conveyance of the waste after it had been unloaded from the train onto road transport. During this protest, as large as the numbers were, the ecoactivists were greatly outnumbered by approximately 7,600 policemen.

The cost of the police deployment, amongst other things, reportedly cost the German government about $18 million. The second shipment of waste, which took place a year later, cost more than $50 million, with an estimated 9,000 protestors and 15,000 police. Incredulously, a third transport was attempted in March 1997. During this movement of waste at least 20,000 protestors took to the streets, with an official figure of 30,000 police also in attendance. According to estimates, the movement of eight castors of waste cost the German government and its nuclear industry $180 million (Mariotte 1997, 3). It seemed after the third shipment that the activists had won the day, as they had deliberately set out to make transport of the nuclear waste economically nonviable. As a partial outcome of these protests, the then CDU federal government temporarily suspended further shipments.

The opposition to the shipments has been widespread on all three occasions. In personal interviews with anti-nuclear activists involved in the Gorleben protests, what emerged, perhaps unsurprisingly, was the immensely broad demographic spread of the activists. In one such interview, an activist describes the participants as follows: "I would say there is a mixture of older and younger people. Quite a lot of people in their 30s, some veterans from the 70s and 80s, and quite a few younger people. I know a couple in their 70s who usually take part in the protests. . . . In particular, among the people of Wendland, including the farmers who have really been at the forefront of the movement, you find people of all ages and classes" (Skullerud 2001).

This anecdotal evidence is further supported by other, more academic sources. Blowers and Lowry (1997) also contend that the protests included local opposition organized by the *Burgerinitiativ*, a citizen-based organization, as well as external, established green organizations at both the lander and national level, such as Greenpeace. The reasons behind the protests were, as often the case with environmental coalitions, multifarious. Local farmers and businesspeople were concerned about the health and safety risks to their produce and to their communities, whilst the established green organizations were "often dancing to a different drum, more radical and intent on the destruction of the nuclear industry" (Blowers and Lowry 1997, 51).

The first and second protests were nonviolent. Anti-nuclear participants stood or sat in front of the trucks. Regardless of this low level of actual threat to police, on both occasions police used water cannons to disperse the protesters. In cold weather, the use of water cannons can be very severe on the recipients. During the third event, although it always aspired to be nonviolent, there is some evidence as to the increasing militancy of the protesters. Some of the tactics used are very reminiscent of Britain's anti-roads campaigns (see chapter 5). One eye-witness account describes some of the alternative tactics employed:

> During the night, a group of Autonomen—radicals perhaps not organized enough to be anarchists—engage in serious street fighting near the town of Quickbon, along the only road the casks can now travel. That road hasn't been torn up, and the radicals want time to set up barricades and dig under the road. . . . Back to the present. In the center of the village, about 80 tractors—some chained together—form a barricade. A kilometer and a half down the road, there are more barricades—downed trees, dirt, concrete, and whatever the locals could find. Underneath the barricades, the road has been completely dug out—just a few centime-

ters of road and then holes several meters deep. If the 90-tonne casks try to move down this road, it will collapse. There are only farmers and workers in this village. The students and anarchists often associated with German anti-nuclear protests are elsewhere. We go to a farm which has been set up as an impromptu information center and resting station. Above us, police helicopters circled constantly, the noise of the blades now so common they're just part of the background. (Mariotte 1997, 5)

In a work by Joppke, explaining cross-national variations in anti-nuclear movements, he contends that one of the reasons why German anti-nuclear activists have often adopted more confrontational and direct-action approaches is in response to the overall stance of the German state. Joppke writes, "The totalizing ideology of the German anti-nuclear movement also stems from its direct experience of the state as a unified, repressive agent that turned nuclear construction sites into para-military fortresses of steel, concrete, and barbed wire, surveiled and persecuted movement activists, and imposed demonstration bans at its free discretion" (1992, 2).

Although an interesting point, it is not particularly exceptional to the German case. To the contrary, in most of the environmental protests/campaigns which have formed the backbone of this book (mining sites in the Philippines, big dams construction in India, road construction in the United Kingdom, wilderness destruction in the wet tropics, or forest clearance at Cove/Mallard in the United States), we have witnessed the state (oftentimes working alongside powerful industrial interests) not hesitating to use the military or the police force to uphold its progress-at-all-costs position. The German experience appears no different. Perhaps, in partial acceptance of Joppke's argument, it is the overwhelming number of police in the German situation which is mildly surprising.

What was quite astonishing (and certainly unanticipated), however, was what was to come when the Social Democrat–Green coalition was elected as the federal government in 1998. Before the election, the SDP and the Greens had promised legislation to phase out nuclear power within 100 days of forming government (Green 2001, 2). Rather than legislation, however, the Greens entered a "consensus agreement" with the SDP and the nuclear industry itself. On 14 June 2000, this agreement was signed, which specified that all nineteen reactors would serve out their average "lifespan" of thirty-two years. In reality, there is no clearly defined schedule for the end of nuclear power. This agreement created further intense dissatisfaction amongst the more traditional factions of the Green party, even more so, perhaps, than ensued after the bombing of Kosovo. The United Press International referred to this phase out agreement as "a Pyrrhic victory for the Greens" (Martin 2001). A similar judgment appeared in a 16 June Reuters report: "The sandal-wearing ecologist activists of yesteryear—now the green coalition partner in government—will be in slippers by the time the last German nuclear power plant is shut down."

A further element of the 14 June 2000 deal allowed for the continuation of the shipment of spent fuel from La Hague to Gorleben until 2005. In fairness to the Greens, there is enormous pressure on Germany to continue to take ultimate responsibility for the housing of its own nuclear waste. Critics of the government, however, believe this moral argument to be a falsehood. Rather, Cogema, the company that own the La Hague facility, has similar motives to other German nuclear corporations: "it must get rid of reprocessing wastes in order to assure the future of its operations" (Green 2001, 1).

So here was the fourth "battle for Gorleben" taking place in late March 2001. Another six castors were taken to their destination; another enormous amount of money was spent in order to protect the deadly waste. The Green party voted overwhelmingly at its 10 March 2001 party congress to oppose blockades and other direct actions at Gorleben in order to protect the *consensus with industry*. This time, there was no clearly definable *other* or *enemy* in power. Instead, it was the Greens themselves who shared government, who controlled the 20,000 strong riot police, who turned the water cannon on thousands of ecoactivists: it was Greens versus greens. Jim Green, an outspoken critic of the Greens in government, writes, "By supporting the March 26–29 shipment of high level radioactive waste from France to the German town of Gorleben, the German Greens have ditched all four elements of their original platform—environmental sustainability, disarmament, social justice and democracy. All that remains is the conservatism and opportunism implicit in their mantra 'neither left nor right but out in front'" (Green 2001, 1).

CONCLUSIONS

To accept that increased institutionalization can be equated with an end to disruptive protest—"the protest quietened down, and environmental groups concentrated their activities within established forms of interest representation" (Rucht and Roose 1999, 71)—is oversimplistic and overexaggerated. Rucht makes the following salient point: "While the trend towards institutionalization of one, probably the dominant segment of environmental groups certainly cannot be denied, we stress the fact that this trend is paralleled by a continuation and even an increase of the more radical forms of protest. Seemingly, the very fact that social movements tend to be absorbed by the system provides a motive for the radicalization of other groups, as was the case with the rise of groups such as Earth First! and the Sea Shepherd Society

Fig. 7.2. Disillusioned German Greens in Munich, protesting Joschka Fischer's involvement in the bombing of Yugoslavia, 1999. *Author's private collection.*

in the US and anti-road and animal rights groups in Great Britain" (Rucht and Roose 1999, 91).

One characteristic of the history of German environmental movement which separates it from the rest is the huge *range* of its politics. It touches every segment of the political gamut, from informal networks and groups to formal movement organizations and industry coalitions; and, finally, it actually shares national government through its formation of a green political party. No other environmental movement in the world has such a green movement, a movement with networks of influence and power weaving their way, seemingly, through all sectors and levels of society. To most green movements the world over, the very concept of actually gaining ultimate parliamentary power is a ludicrous thought. The German experiment, several steps ahead of the rest, is now also illustrating for us what happens to those more radical sectors outside of green government. Do the dwindle away, or do they flourish?

The evidence of radical protest movements continuing to exist in Germany is most purely borne out in the experience of anti-nuclear movements. The "anti-nukes" have always been part of the more radical networks of the German movement. They were an important part of the movement at its inception and, apart from a period during the 1980s, they have actually increased

Box 7.2

Native American Environment Movements:
Indigenous Anti-Nuclear Movements

Small groups, with names like Native Americans for Clean Environment (NACE), the Kaibab Earthkeepers, Dine' CARE, Native Actions, and Anishinabe Niiji, have successfully opposed huge waste dumps, multinational mining and lumber companies and the U.S. Office of the Nuclear Waste Negotiator. Often under funded (and sometimes without funding at all), these organizations wage a battle to protect the environment for future generations.

In the past few years, the U.S. federal government has begun to invest heavily in Native American environmental issues—advising tribes on options for nuclear waste storage and supporting development of new, federally funded environmental initiatives in Indian country. Millions of federal dollars are playing a major role in what may be one of the biggest territorial and environmental battles in North America.

Indian reservations, which constitute 4 percent of U.S. lands, hold vast supplies of uranium, coal, and timber. These vast, isolated lands are also attractive to industries searching for disposal sites for nuclear waste. In the past four years, more than 100 separate proposals have been made by government and industry to dump waste on Indian lands. To date, Indian communities have received sixteen of the eighteen "nuclear waste research grants" issued by the U.S. Department of Energy.

While many grassroots organizations lack financial resources, millions of dollars in federal funding have recently begun flowing into Native American communities for "environmental work," which often amounts to little more than feasibility studies for the storage of nuclear waste.

Between 1986 and 1990, The National Congress of American Indians (NCAI) received nearly $1 million in Nuclear Waste Grants to study nuclear waste storage options: more than a quarter of the group's total revenue.

The U.S. Department of Health and Human Services' Administration for Native Americans (ANA) and the Department of Commerce both fund Indian consulting firms that are actively promoting the nuclear waste industry in Indian country. A big part of this money goes to the Council of Energy Resource Tribes (CERT). In 1987, CERT received $2.5 million from federal nuclear waste contracts, constituting more than half of the organization's total income. In 1992, CERT received $1.2 million in federal grants for nuclear waste programs: 80 percent of the group's federal grants.

CERT, NCAI, and the Native American Rights Fund (NARF) have spent the last couple of years putting together a national Native American environmental organization called

the number of confrontational protests against the nuclear industry (Rucht and Roose 1999). The fact that a party which was directly born from their protest seed is now in power does not diminish the level of their protests. If anything, it has necessitated an increase.

If the militaristic stance of the Greens in relation to Bosnia and Yugoslavia seemed confusing for many of the party's traditional supporters, then the decision, in March 2000, by the SDP/Green national government to recommence the transport of nuclear waste from the reprocessing facility in La

Box 7.2

Continued

National Tribal Environmental Council (NTEC). Describing itself as "the only national tribal environmental entity," NTEC was established with a $750,000 grant from the U.S. government's ANA, a smaller grant from the EPA, and $80,000 from the Ford Foundation. However, it was NTEC's links with the nuclear industry (through founding members of CERT and NCAI) that concerned grassroots groups. "How can an organization established by CERT and NCAI have any credibility on environmental issues after their record with the nuclear waste industry?" asked Tom Goldtooth of the Indigenous Environmental Network (IEN), a coalition of approximately fifty grassroots groups.

In January, NTEC held a closed strategy meeting in Albuquerque, New Mexico, funded by the Ford Foundation, to set priorities for the organization and to "profit substantially from organizational leaders who have struggled with these issues." The meeting included tribal government representatives and the leadership of CERT, NARF, and a few other national organizations.

Responding to the exclusive nature of the meeting, IEN, NACE, the United Church of Christ's Task Force on Racial Justice, and several other groups sent protest letters to NTEC, charging that it needed to be accountable to the people who were affected by its decisions. IEN's Goldtooth dispatched a letter stating that "CERT and NARF had consistently played an active role in promoting the unsustainable development of our lands" and noting the widespread mistrust for organizations that accept federal nuclear waste money and then represent their "offspring" as environmental organizations.

Gail Small, from her reservation-based office, expressed a common concern. "Many of these organizations have little contact with the reservations. There are a lot of Indian people (who are) lawyers, doctors, and teachers. We can do it ourselves. What we really need is money, not more national organizations in Washington, Albuquerque or Boulder with big federal money and no accountability to the communities. . . . If ANA has $750,000 it wants to give to Indian country to do environmental work, that should go to tribal governments and communities to (help them to) establish their own environmental codes. The work is really on the reservations—that's where the accountability is," Small said.

SOURCE: *Adapted from http://www.indians.org/library/nate.html; LaDuke 1994. (Winona LaDuke is an Anishinabe Indian and the campaign director of the White Earth Land Recovery Program, the program officer for the Seventh Generation Fund Environmental Program, a Greenpeace/U.S. board member, and a frequent writer on native environmental issues.)*

Hague, France, to Gorleben in Germany was simply overwhelming. Indeed, initially, some defended the Green's decision to bomb Bosnia as it was publicized that this was a trade-off with the SDP, which would see nuclear energy phased out in Germany. Others explained it as less of a trade-off with the SPD, but rather reflecting the particularities of the German Left. Whatever the rationale, with the reintroduction of nuclear transport there has never been a greater gulf between the grassroots "movement" component and the highly professionalized parliamentary wing of the greens. This gap between the two is now producing conflicts within the green movement, conflicts which may be larger than any which have preceded them. These two very distinct tiers of the movement have contrary approaches to resolving the issue of Germany's nuclear future.

At the broader level of anti-nuclear movements across the globe, it is extremely interesting to see anti-nuclear movements emerging for the first time in the majority world. As aforesaid, these movements also share an active disdain for the buildup and utilization of nuclear weapons. More salient than this, however, is the reframing of nuclear issues as environmental justice concerns by indigenous communities living in both the North and the South. Native Americans in the United States and Australian Aboriginal communities are now facing proposals which will see the establishment of extensive systems of nuclear waste dumps on land which they now inhabit as "reservations" or "missions." Box 7.2 outlines the growing Native American environmental movement opposed to this additional form of "white settlement."

This lack of transnational connection and protest in relation to anti-nuclear movements is most apparent. Rucht and Roose contend, "To our surprise, transnational and international mobilisation of protests within German territory did not increase over time as the widely discussed trend towards globalization might suggest. When we compare the 1980s with the first half of the 1990s the proportion of such protests actually declined for both environmental protests . . . and anti-nuclear protests" (Rucht and Roose 1999, 72). A partial explanation for this apparent and relative lack of transnational activism in relation to nuclear issues is that anti-nuclear activists have been very much focused at the nation-state level of politics. It is in nation-state arenas where such issues as energy production and utilization have traditionally been contested. Another reason may be that movements in the South have not been involved in the nuclear phenomenon until quite recently. In recent times, it is these majority-world movements which have often been the driving force behind building transnational green linkages. Now that the South is establishing its own nuclear programs, a transnational campaigning trend may develop in anti-nuclear movements.

CHAPTER 8

CONCLUSIONS TO ENVIRONMENTAL MOVEMENTS

Environmental movements are a globalizing force. First, the symbol "environment" has become almost universally recognizable: it is an extremely powerful global symbol. No doubt, the rise of the English language as *the* new global lingual code is partly responsible for the global currency which the symbol enjoys. Similar, although not exact, concepts in different cultures have had their edges bashed off them to fit within the rubric of this dominant word, this universal symbol. Of at least equal importance, however, is the political structure of the social phenomena which sells, which fights for this meaning system amongst others: new social movements (NSMs). Whilst accepting that the medium and the message are often one and the same, for the purposes of analysis, let us now briefly separate these two words—"environment" and "movement"—in a closer bid to understand the extent of their global currency.

ENVIRONMENT AS A GLOBAL SYMBOL

So environmental politics is not just about "goodies" versus "baddies." This symbol environment has such power that numerous cultures, and the powerful and powerless within them, invoke its name for disparate purposes (Doyle and McEachern 1998, 4).

In a book written with Doug McEachern, we attempted to document the diversity of green political responses as they have emerged around the globe over the past generation (Doyle and McEachern 1998, 2001). It was a difficult task, as the diversity of interpretations of the "environment" or "green" symbols is staggering. The utter heterogeneity of the symbol is perfectly suited to the equally amorphous and ambiguous forms of politics played by the noninstitutionalized parts of new social movements (NSMs). Indeed, this is the true power of the symbol: its ability to cross borders without the need to accurately define its presence, without its need to create rigid categories of enemies and allies.

Why is it that the environment symbol is invoked for such disparate reasons, sometimes being interpreted in exactly the opposite ways in different situations? For example, in the 1980s, Die Grunen was challenging the excesses of free-market and "democratic" economic/political systems in what was then West Germany. During this very same time frame (what would later be known as the Velvet Revolution), on the other side of the Berlin Wall, the East German environmental movement was advocating the antithesis, championing free-market economic and democratic principles as part of its green platform.

The environment flag, then, means many different things to different people, in different *environmental movements,* in different time and space continuums. It is not necessarily that the environment symbol is a charlatan. Rather, it is a symbol almost as broad as nature itself. It is perfectly chosen for the infinity of possible responses which gather under and around it. Just when its appears that a safe net of definition can be caste over it, it wriggles out of the corner and takes on a new guise, in a separate context.

Murray Edelman, in his yet to be matched work on the symbolic usage's of politics, defines a powerful symbol as something which will attract as broad a constituency of support as possible (1972). "Environment" matches this description beautifully. Consequently, there are many paradoxical and ambiguous positions within environmentalism as an ideology. Despite my assertion at this book's outset, whether there is one movement of this name across the globe or whether there are many is very open to conjecture. Regardless of the outcome of this debate, however, there can be no doubt that environmental movements are an increasingly global phenomenon.

Environment is at once a symbol for liberation and repression. Too often, environmentalists assume that they are on the "side of right" simply by being on the "side of the planet." One particularly repressive idea system to emerge from minority-world environmentalism is the concept of *sustainable development.* This concept emerged from the public relations industry, working for big business interests, leading up to the time of the Rio Earth Summit in the 1992 (Doyle 1998). Sustainable developers, with their supporting mantras of free-market environmentalism and U.S.-style pluralist democratic systems, sell the concept of the "win/win" situation: all environmental problems can be resolved through efficiency/effectiveness equations (best practice manage-

Box 8.1

Anti-globalization Movements (AGM)

The current anti-globalization movement has roots in environmental and human-rights movements based on the principles of nonviolent direct action. It shares a structure based on small autonomous groups, a practice of decision-making by consensus, and a style of protest that revolves around mass civil disobedience.

The most dramatic moment of the anti-globalization movement in the United States was the mobilization against the World Trade Organization in Seattle in late November and early December of 1999. In the series of demonstrations that took place over the course of several days, the young, radical activists who engaged in civil disobedience were greatly outnumbered by trade unionists and members of mostly liberal environmental organizations. But it was young anarchists who blockaded the meetings of the WTO, fought the police, "liberated" the streets of Seattle, and whose militancy brought the attention of the media to a mobilization that would otherwise have gone relatively unnoticed outside of the left. The alliance that formed in Seattle between anarchists, feminists, trade unionists, and environmentalists was loose and has remained so at subsequent anti-globalization protests across the globe, most particularly in the minority world.

SOURCE: *Adapted from Epstein 2001.*

ment), and the fears of the modern-day limits-to-growth theorists of the 1960s and '70s are ill-founded. The sustainable development rhetoric continues: In fact, business is good for the environment, and the environment is good for business. The sustainable development ideological package is currently being widely criticized for its detrimental effects on the economies and ecologies of the majority world in the interests of a global, largely minority-world elite. The environment, caste in this vein, is construed by some as a symbol of darkness, a form of ecological imperialism instituted by the minority world over the majority.

On the other hand, it could be argued, that the environment symbol is one of freedom and liberation. It is often argued that it has emerged through necessity as a counterforce to the largely ungoverned rampages of transnational corporations saddled up to their ideology of global free markets. In very recent times, these movements have been involved in direct clashes with police and the military at predominantly Northern forums in Seattle, Prague, Melbourne, Zurich, and Genoa, challenging the economic and cultural forces of U.S-style, transnational corporation-dominated globalization (See box 8.1 for a brief outline of the anti-globalization movement).

It is important to note, also, that not all movements characterized as part of the anti-globalization push can necessarily be referred to as environmental movements. For example, at the S11 Protest in Melbourne against the World Economic Forum there were three clear blocs which formed the protest: black (indigenous peoples), red (labor) and green (environmentalists). At the S26 protest in Prague against the International Monetary Fund/World Bank, the colors were different again: yellow (Zapatistas), blue (anarchist), and pink (socialist) (Chesters 2001). These groupings are also supplemented by church and human rights groups, feminists, and many others. Obviously, the decision to label such protests as exclusively environmental or otherwise is a political decision with political ramifications.

Environmental movements are interconnected with anti-globalization movements, as component parts, sharing networks. From this perspective, environmental movements can be seen as a liberationist force, railing against the extremes of a unifying global ideology based on the god of the Western marketplace. In this complexion, the environment is also a symbol of light. Part of this counter-ideology which does abide within the green is the promotion of the importance of place and community. "Place" in this vein is something which exists outside of cyberspace, in that it has real biophysical existence. Part of this place—at least in the experience of the majority world—includes people who, living within a community, have a key role in governing themselves and often have a sacred connection to the place and people in question. Often the forces of market globalization (which are neither necessarily unified nor coherent) denigrate the movement's position as a "tribalist" one. The concepts of place and community are, needless to elaborate upon, anathema to global market players, as they may pose collective opposition to the liquid flow of trade between individuals of *no fixed address:* the market as a global river.

Paradoxically, however, this position within some green movements in defense of more local communities attached to place is, at the same time, a global one. Globalization has, on the one hand, created the "necessity of" counter-response, and, at the same time, it has created a vehicle where environmentalism can also become a globalzing force, also crossing nation-state/ethnic/religious boundaries with relative ease. In some ways environmental movements are vigorous endorsers and promoters of globalization, regardless of whether they are movements of the light or dark variety (many environmental movements, such as the *anti-golf movement,* organize and, importantly, identify themselves in a global manner: see box 8.2). Even the progressive environmental justice movements, by projecting themselves as "the other" to the operations of global capital, are often interpreting all conflict, all important political allegiances, in a global light: between two great globalizing forces which subsume and make meaningless all subalternate identities. In this manner, environmental movements which support the struggles of the powerless against the excesses of global development recast the identity and the boundaries of these communities in a way which can only be understood as "the global other," only existing in terms of what is *not* the North/the West/the minority world. It is in this fashion that the lives of the powerless are forever caste as existing in a globalized shadow, rather than living in the light of their own local community's making.

Whilst accepting the liberating and empowering elements of some of these green movements, this cross-boundary movement can be as invasive of local communities as global capitalism. Local narratives can be understood, but also, ultimately they are colonized by these cross-boundary "green traders," a different collection of elites, to pursue their own narratives, their own pursuit of power. In her intriguing study of tribal conflicts over development in India's Narmada Valley (see chapter 6), Amita Baviskar writes of the environmentalists' reframing of the lives and interests of the *adivasi* (the indigenous peoples of the valley): "The privileging of elite consciousness which divides the world into development and resistance does endow the struggles over land, forest and river with legitimacy in the eyes of environmentalists elsewhere. And, by linking local struggles to a global context, such appropriation *is* strategically important. . . . But, however noble the cause, appropriation leads to the meditation of the adivasi consciousness by that of the scholar. The discourse of the general theory of development does not allow people to speak for themselves; it tends to be deaf to people's own understanding of their predicament" (1995, 241).

Regardless of very recent trends which suggest an increasing interplay between different cultures'/countries' environmental movements, the empirical reality is very different. In fact, it is still their profound differences in ideology and focus, rather than their similarities, which define the green movement experience across the globe, rather than cross-boundary, shared political activities/identities. As argued earlier, many of these differences can be characterized by the geopolitical categories generated by the differences between majority and minority worlds.

NEW SOCIAL MOVEMENTS

To study environmental movements is to enter into the engine room of politics itself: social movements. It is within social movements that living politics begins: new forms of political action are actually born or reinvented here. They are, on the whole, the most alive, unstructured forms of politics; they are more open to new ideas and long-term visions of what the earth and its people could be, rather than experienced within more institutionalized forms of politics. Unfortunately, when politics is usually studied in primary and secondary schools across the globe, it is usually only the latter, more inert forms of politics which are taught and discussed, as if the earth's citizens can only cope with styles of politics which are already in their coffin, formalized into a shape which can be more readily controlled and understood. This explains the over-

Box 8.2

Global Anti-Golf Movement

The Global Anti-Golf Movement (GAGM) was launched on World No-Golf Day (29 April 1993) following a three-day conference on Golf Course and Resort Development in the Asia-Pacific Region in Penang, Malaysia, from 26 to 28 April 1993. The three sponsoring organizations are the Japan-based Global Network for Anti-Golf Course Action (GNAGA), the Thailand-based Asian Tourism Network (ANTENNA), and the Malaysia-based Asia-Pacific Peoples Environmental Network (APPEN). Delegates from Hawaii, Hong Kong, India, Indonesia, Japan, Malaysia, the Philippines, and Thailand were also present.

Below is the statement of the movement:

1. Golf courses and golf tourism are part of a development package which includes infrastructure (multi-purpose dams, airports, ports, roads, bridges), mass tourism, expensive housing, entertainment facilities, export-oriented agriculture (flowers, exotic fruits, and vegetables), and industrial parks/zones.

2. At the heart of the golf industry is a multi-billion-dollar industry involving transnational corporations, including agribusiness, construction firms, consultancies, golf equipment manufacturers, airlines, hotel chains, real estate companies, advertising and public relations firms, as well as financial institutions. The transformation of golf memberships into a saleable commodity has resulted in widespread speculation and dubious practices. In many countries golf course/resort development (including time-sharing resorts) is in reality often a hit-and-run business. The speculative nature of memberships and associated real property transactions also makes the industry very high risk. In the wake of the current slowdown in the Japanese economy, many golf course and resort companies have become bankrupt, with investors and banks bearing the losses. The bulk of the foreign exchange earned from golf courses and golf tourism does not stay in the local economy. The benefits which do remain are reaped by a few business people and their patrons.

3. The green golf package can be compared to the Green Revolution package in agriculture. Golf courses are, in fact, another form of monoculture, where exotic soil and grass,

propensity for understanding environmental politics through the study of administrative systems, corporate structures, political parties, and other government perspectives.

In some ways the entire form of new social movements challenges the power of nation-states in just as dramatic a mode as does the plutocracy of transnational corporations, but in very different ways, and for very separate reasons. Although many social movement organizations, such as NGOs, are also under siege alongside the state to adopt market-based operational structures and agendas, NSMs, as a whole, are one structural political entity which seems to have escaped relatively freely from the homogenizing global corporate form. Their deliberate informality, transience, and translucence have also enabled them to largely escape from the cost-benefit equations of corpora-

Box 8.2

Continued

chemical fertilizers, pesticides, fungicides, and weedicides, as well as machinery, are all imported to substitute for natural ecosystems. These landscaped foreign systems create stress on local water supplies and soil, at the same time being highly vulnerable to disease and pest attacks. Just as the Green Revolution is collapsing in country after country, the Golf Green is also fraught with ecological problems. The environmental impacts include water depletion and toxic contamination of the soil, underground water, surface water, and the air. This, in turn, leads to health problems for local communities, populations downstream, and even golfers, caddies, and chemical sprayers in golf courses. The construction of golf courses in scenic natural sites, such as forest areas and coral islands, also results in the destruction of biodiversity.

4. In addition to environmental damage, golf course and resort development often creates skewed land use, displacing local communities or depriving them of water and other resources. In a number of countries, the victims of such projects are subject to police or military intimidation when they protest against the destruction caused by golf courses.

5. The golf industry aggressively promotes an elitist and exclusive resort lifestyle and notion of leisure. This globalization of lifestyle is also a form of exploitation, the victims being the wealthy urban population, who are encouraged to spend their surplus dreams and illusions, at the expense of the environment and other members of society. Golf course and golf tourism development violate human rights in every sense of the word.

6. In the face of growing criticism of the adverse environmental impacts of golf courses, the industry is promoting the notion of "pesticide-free," "environmentally-friendly," or "sensitive" golf courses. No such course exists to date, and the creation and maintenance of the "perfect green" comprising exotic grass inevitably requires intensive use of chemicals.

SOURCE: *Adapted from http://multinationalmonitor.org/hyper/issues/1993/11/mm1193_13.html.*

tions. As their very structure operates largely within the black economy and polity of informal relations, the traditional sticks and carrots of both nation-states and corporations have not been wielded as effectively as they have been upon other social units, such as families, communities, and other subcultures.

The political form of new social movements seems most suited to cross boundaries. They can be understood as *palimpsests,* often boundless, amorphous, "post-structuralist," anarchistic, ambiguous, many-faceted, and lacking the defined edges of more institutionalized political bodies. For example, whereas governments of nation-states appear increasingly inadequate in monitoring and tracing the activities of transnational corporations, NSMs, due to their jelly-like structurelessness, seem more capable of *border osmosis,* of oozing through largely noninstitutionalized pores in the fabric of frontiers, tracking and contesting the rapidly expanding power of transnational capital. Due to their decentralized and amorphous forms, they have been particularly adept at utilizing recent developments in information technology. Klein writes,

> Despite this common ground, these campaigns have not coalesced into a single movement. Rather, they are intricately and tightly linked to one another, much as "hotlinks" connect their websites on the Internet. This analogy is more than coincidental and is in fact key to understanding the changing nature of political organizing. Although many have observed that the recent mass protests would have been impossible without the Internet, what has been overlooked is how the communications technology that facilitates these campaigns is shaping the movement in its own image. Thanks to the Net, mobilizations are able to unfold with sparse bureaucracy and minimal hierarchy; forced consensus and labored manifesto are fading into the background, replaced instead by a culture of constant, loosely structured and sometimes compulsive information-swapping. (2000, 88)

The following quotations are taken from two separate articles: the first, by P. P. Karan, refers to a common trait of three Indian environmental movements: Chipko, Silent Valley, and the Save the Narmada movements (the latter being a specific case study in chapter 6). The second quotation was written by Cassandra Pybus with direct reference to the Save the Franklin campaign in Australia (an anti-dam protest movement: also see chapter 6). "They cut across social and cultural cleavages that might have been expected to be divisive. They unite people who differ by sex, age, religion, ethnicity, caste, class, and region by stressing shared interests in saving the environment. . . . The integrative nature of the movement cuts across ancient and powerful ethnic barriers" (Karan 1994. 8). "The Franklin dispute was a trauma for Tasmania. It was a time of extreme volatility where allegiances to political positions became emotionally-charged articles of faith. Families were ruptured by conflict; no-one was able to stay aloof. The scars of that time have cut deep into the political psyche and have been a long time healing. Perhaps nowhere is that more evident than in the Labor Party, which was torn apart by conflict and indecision" (Pybus 1990, 18).

Both quotations are interchangeable, because, regardless of global or cultural context, one of the key defining characteristics of these struggles is their *new social movement* form. This structural form defies and, for the period of specific struggle, overrides barriers and borders, such as class, religions, established political parties, and even families, which were previously regarded as inviolate and impermeable. Environmental movements, then, rally and protest on a contextual basis. Strange bedfellows appear from the center as well as from the extremes of the traditional left-right political continuum in multifarious situations. Not only this, these NSMs strike new identities, some for a fleeting moment, others more lasting. Obviously, this NSM characteristic to drift through barriers or to violently disperse them has positive and negative ramifications. In the examples given above, in both India and Australia, in the majority and the minority worlds, the ability of environmental movements to do so has, on the one hand, created tremendously broad coalitions of support which have been utilized, on occasions, to empower the powerless. Alternatively, this ability to spread tentacles of influence with insufficient regard for tradition has created confusion, tensions, and, sometimes, violence amongst human collective forms of all denominations.

The ability of these movements to cut across powerful preestablished borders of identity was amply demonstrated to me whilst on fieldwork in the Philippines in 1998 (see chapter 3). As part of an International Fact-Finding Mission into the operations of transnational mining companies operating on the island of Mindanao, I witnessed the coming together of Muslim and Christian forces in an environmental campaign against one particular mining company. Previously, and since this time, militia on both sides of this religious fence have often been locked into a form of bloody and vicious civil war.

Whilst this is the most striking example of environmental movements drifting like ether through barriers hitherto perceived as impassable, other examples are numerous in nature, also demonstrating this characteristic of environmental movements. On this occasion, it is not the boundary around a religious collectivity which is challenged, but one which is class based. Baviskar writes of the Narmada campaign as follows: "The issue of land has united two disparate constituencies. Class conflict is temporarily submerged in the alliance between the adivasis of the hills and their traditional foes, the Patidars. The cause of displacement by the dam is more important than anything else; energies are concentrated on co-operation towards fighting the Project" (1995, 220).

In some ways symbols such as environment championed by these NSMs have no "center" as could be defined by past categories of politics. This lack of current definition could be assumed as being obvious, as the past categories are based on outdated, "modern" understandings of history, on lines drawn not just in the temporal sands of the present, but in the blood and stone of centuries. The lines of opposition which rally around environment in different cultures at different times may often be instantaneous; but they are real: present for the spark of conflict, the instant of new allegiance. That some of these networks may dissipate so quickly afterwards may be construed by more formal political analysis as a weakness. But, of course, it is also the major source of strength—the ability to don the coat of many colors, to rally and gather, often against an enemy which is equally dispersed. This is the polity of post-modernity, the politics of "no fixed address" (Doyle 1998), politics without history.

Obviously, as time goes by, shared interactions galvanize into partly or wholly shared identities. Indeed, the work of eminent social movement theorist Mario Diana sees this identity-building function of social movements as one of this political form's key defining features. Diani states, "We can define the second component of the concept of social movement as follows—'The boundaries of a social movement network are defined by the specific collective identity shared by the actors involved in the interaction'" (1992, 9).

In the case of environmental movements studied in this book, this shared identity, if and when it ever happens, is a long way off from fully emerging. There is an emerging body of evidence that globalization will enlarge the level of interactivity between environmental movements of different ilk. As already touched upon, campaign structures are changing to make full use of the Internet. For example, at the recent climate-change conference in The Hague, an international green campaign was run almost exclusively in cyberspace. There can be no doubt that this interactivity has multiplied since the first emergence of the above mentioned Franklin and Narmada campaigns. The Narmada movement, typifying many other environmental struggles in the majority world, began as a fight for the rights of people's livelihoods against the mega-development of the state and transnational capital. Later it began to adopt the "environment" label and discussion of a "green agenda" emerged. There can be no doubt that the latter type of arguments came from Northern environmental movements, and that these movements, in a sense, sought to co-opt Southern struggles into a global frame which would strengthen the Northern resistance against a Northern "enemy." In this sense, there are substantial elements of ecological imperialism here, with the more "dangerous" arguments of the South being omitted or side-lined. Krishna comments on this changing agenda in the Indian context as follows: "Liberal opinion, and both national and international NGOs, empathized with the motif of trees. They also related much more easily to the broad issue of conservation than to the specific politico-economic questions of employment, labor conditions, and local industry. . . . [It] has transformed outraged response into a meditation on ecology" (1996, 157).

But, as so happens with social movements, it is not so simple. There is also dramatic evidence that in more recent times Southern movements are increasingly driving the global green movement agenda, with many Northern NGO players taking a subservient role, for now. For the flow of history is a mirror opposite in the green movements of the minority world. Like the Franklin, many began as post-materialist movements, interested in trees, parks, and threatened species, but are gradually coming to terms with the fact that people are also part of the environmental equation: they are not separate from nature. As a consequence, we have seen the beginnings of environmental justice and democracy movements evolving in the North for the first time.

This has occurred due largely to the amplified power of Southern movements in recent times. Princen and Finger, in their study of environmental NGOs across the globe, support this argument when they write, "Just as Northern NGOs are becoming more institutionalized, Southern NGOs are building organizational skills and financial independence and, as a result, increasingly demand greater autonomy and less dependence on Northern supporters. . . . As Southern NGOs are becoming more independent and setting the international agenda, Northern NGOs are looking to the South for ideas, as well as to establish their own international credibility" (1994, 8).

It would be vacuous, however, to suggest that power moves both ways, like the tide, and that in the end some form of global balance will be struck by this increased interplay between social movements of the majority and minority worlds. As there is no such thing as a free market, or a free lunch, there is also no such thing as a free political space. The amorphousness and structurelessness of new social movements (alongside their cyberspace equivalent in the supposedly equally structurelessness Internet) will ultimately deliver results to the more powerful players.

Within the "new world order" there has been a move toward promoting both global and local meaning systems over those of the nation-state. This is certainly a good description of the current period. Local identity systems, based on sacred senses of place and community, are currently very visible in their opposition to global capitalism; and this explains, in many ways, the multitude of very different movements, gathering under both the umbrella of environment and other social causes. But this "glocalization" (Newman 2000) may be just a transition phase. Paradoxically, the championing of the "local" by an increasingly global movement of resistance, which includes environmental movements, may ultimately decimate this well-documented local diversity of experience in favor of more homogenous, simplistic dichotomies and dualisms utilizing Western capitalism as the base point upon which everything else is measured. In this manner, environmentalism, as "the other," with its ambiguous but increasingly shared strands of support and meaning, may also be acting as a globalizing catalyst, leading to the creation of a diaspora of vast proportions—a globe crawling with environmental refugees—condemning the majority world to a place which is at once beyond boundaries and, at the same time, within a prison cell of global poverty and ecological degradation.

But the future, of course, is not a time or place within fixed, defined boundaries. This book is more of a celebration of differences than similarities: more evidence of the fact that there are many environmental movements across the earth, rather than one. Environmental movements across the globe must persist in this salutation of diversity and resist the all-powerful but understandable urges to overly homogenize opposition, using the justification of global resistance and, in doing so, creating *one* environmental movement. A more creative and longer-lasting solidarity—capable not only of resistance to "Earth as corporation," but of creation of resilient societal alternatives—will emerge from a continued respect and reverence for diverse localized experiences found within a multitude of ecological communities, both human and nonhuman.

NOTES

Chapter 1: Introduction to Environmental Movements

1. Whether or not environmental movements or new social movements in general are united by common goals is a hotly contested debate which will be addressed in the final chapter of this book. At this stage, it is necessary to say that the author believes that the diversity of goals within environmental movements is far more apparent than the possibility of a shared single goal existing. Rather, environmental movements are simply broad constellations of networks based on loose notions of shared identity. The boundaries which separate environmental movements from other movements and other parts of society are ever-changing and undergoing constant redefinition by innumerable actors. In this book, environmental movements simply include all those participants who consider themselves part of them.

Chapter 2: Forest Movements

1. In 1995 and 1996 the author was a visiting professor at two American universities: Clark University, Massachusetts, and the University of Montana. The research embarked upon in this chapter was initiated during this period.

2. Although I am fully aware that the United States is not synonymous with all of the American continent, sometimes I use the word "America" to denote this limited definition.

3. I have written on this subject in detail in Doyle 1998a.

4. In chapter 8, the extent to which various types of environmental movements are transnational will be investigated.

5. U.S. NGOs are buying "wilderness" areas in the South by paying off the debts of poor nations to creditors on a one-in-ten ratio. This means every ten dollars of debt only costs one American dollar. Whilst there are obvious gains for wilderness protection here, in the cases of Bolivia, Costa Rica, Brazil, Ecuador, and even Poland, the human rights implications are unclear. Is a minority-world-defined wilderness area something which is actually attractive to a forest dweller or a subsistence farmer?

Chapter 3: Movements against Mining

1. The author draws on his own fieldwork to provide the primary evidence for this chapter. He was the chair of the Public Inquiry into Uranium in Australia. In addition, as president of the

Conservation Council of South Australia (CCSA) he represented environmental concerns at the Earth Charter meeting in February 1999; and he was on the Olympic Dam Community Consultative Committee, which is the WMC's roundtable forum which monitors the mine's performance at Roxby Downs in Australia. Also, he has undertaken fieldwork in the Philippines aimed at comprehending the different forms of environmental protest pursued there. He was a member of the International Fact-Finding Mission into Western Mining's operations in Mindanao (Southern Philippines) in November 1998, organized by the Filipino activist community opposed to the Tampakan mine. The IFFM conducted a series of extensive interviews with a range of different stakeholders.

2. This first-person account is a much smaller version than one which first appeared in the preface of Doyle 2000.

3. The author has been involved in two main periods of fieldwork in the Philippines relating to this project, in 1998 and 2001.

Chapter 4: Wilderness Movements

1. This discussion of wilderness as a dominant concept within the environmental movement in Australia first appeared, in somewhat expanded form, in Doyle 2000.

2. These five stages, which break down the Wet Tropics campaign, were first published in Doyle 2000a.

3. According to many interviews I conducted with people who lived in the area, advice from organizational environmental activists (when they did arrive) was largely ignored. Among these interviewees was Hans Niewenhasen, on whose property the protesters camped.

4. The fight for the Franklin River took place in southwest Tasmania in 1983 (see chapter 6 re anti-dam movements). Again nonviolent-action tactics were employed by protesters in the temperate rainforest. The Franklin campaign was so powerful that it has been credited with changing the national government in 1983. Eventually a decision to save the Franklin River was taken by the High Court—the utmost adversarial body in Australia—in a case fought by the newly elected federal Labor government against the conservative state government of Tasmania.

5. For a full analysis of this final period in the Wet Tropics campaign, read Doyle 1989, 28–47.

Chapter 5: Anti-roads Movements

1. In 1992 I was a visiting scholar in the Department of Economics and Government at the University of Northumbria. It was during this period that my research on environmental movements in Britain commenced.

2. For a solid treatment of these issues see Baker, Milton, and Yearly 1994.

3. It is recognized that Britain is not really a country, but a grouping of nations which includes England, Scotland, Wales, and Northern Ireland. Most of this chapter, however, will concentrate on the English movement.

4. This project, entitled the Transformation of Environmental Activism, was coordinated by Christopher Rootes of the University of Kent. Its description reads thus: "The project aims to examine the various forms of environmental activism, changes in their relative incidence over the past decade and movement organizations (EMOs) and their relationships with other actors within and outside the wider environmental movement from one EU member state to another, changes in environmental movements, to advance explanations for the patterns of variation, and to examine their implications for policymaking at the European level" (EC contract no. ENV4-CT97-0514).

5. Thanks are due to Brian Doherty of the University of Keele, who served as a visiting scholar at my university in the first half of 2003. His insights into British anti-roads campaigns, and European movements in general, were invaluable.

6. For excellent coverage and analysis of the Manchester airport campaign, see Griggs, Howarth, and Jacobs 1998.

7. As various campaigns of the anti-roads movement continued, there was some evidence that British police began to use more violence than in the beginning. In 1998, for example, in a protest against Greenfield housing developments in Bangor, Wales, police officers used pressure points behind the ears of activists to force them to remove themselves from lock-ons at the site. Activists claimed this technique to be "torture": "It felt like I had a broken bone beneath my ears and I was deaf in my right ear," said Kevin, one of the protests. Eight campaigners were admitted to a local hospital. (Warwick 1998, 13)

8. The campaign to stop the Cape Tribulation Road from being built through the Daintree Rainforest in North Queensland in the early 1980s was not defined by Australian activists as an "anti-roads movement." Instead, the activists saw it as a wilderness campaign.

9. The Hastings bypass was eventually shelved, though new roads were being built elsewhere (much less so, however, than in the early 1990s).

Chapter 6: River Movements

1. This research was first embarked upon in the first half of 2000, when the author was scholar-in-residence in the Center for the Study of Geopolitics at the University of Panjab, India. A second period of fieldwork in the drought-stricken areas of northern and central India was undertaken in the latter part of 2002.

2. For a thorough and thoughtful analysis of the politics of mega-dams, read McCully 1998. In addition, as aforementioned, one of the earliest and most ground-breaking popular critiques of mega-dams emerged out of the journal *The Ecologist*, edited by Edward Goldsmith in London, in the mid 1980s; see, for example, Goldsmith and Hildyard 1984—many arguments against the Aswan and other dams made within this special edition of *The Ecologist* are still used today by anti-dam movements around the world.

3. For full accounts of the Franklin Dam campaign and its movements, see Green 1981; the Wilderness Society 1983; Connolly 1981; Thompson 1984.

4. There are many different terms in different cultures for the equivalent of non-governmental organizations. In the United States, for example, these groups are often referred to as civil society. In India and other parts of the majority world, these NGOs are sometimes also referred to as citizen-based organizations (CBOs). In Europe, the term environmental movement organizations (EMOs) is also used. In this light, NGOs are seen as much larger, more institutionalized, and often international organizations.

Chapter 7: Anti-nuclear Movements

1. Finland, Italy, France, and Belgium have all had green party members within a national government.

2. In 1998 the author attended the European Community Political Research Conference at Mannheim in Germany. It was during this time that the bombing of Yugoslavia commenced.

3. In 1996, before the Greens shared power in the national government, Joschka Fischer, then a Green member of parliament, voted in favor of sending troops to Bosnia as part of the Dayton Accord to protect the Bosnian Muslims. Obviously, this was a clear and early indication of the party leadership's later stance toward the NATO bombing of Bosnia. Even in 1996, this led

to a split within the party between those who advocated pacifism and those who argued for "the prevention of genocide" (*New Perspectives Quarterly* 1996, 52–53).

4. See Marks and McAdam (1996) for a close investigation as to why European anti-nuclear movements have comparatively failed in getting the European Union to control nuclear policy for the region. One reason which is posited relates to the forms of organization of the anti-nuclear movements. The article reads, "In combination, then, the relative youth of the movement and its philosophic commitment to non-traditional organizational forms has prevented any real institutionalization of the movement at the national level. Instead, the national movements have tended to remain loose networks of adherents rather than enduring coalitions of formal movement organizations" (Marks and McAdam 1996, 272).

5. Until this time of writing, Australia still only has one nuclear reactor, at Lucas Heights, though there is currently much pressure to upgrade this facility.

6. For a discussion of how electoral systems impact upon the green vote, see Doyle and McEachern 2001, chapter 5.

REFERENCES

Alliance for Genuine Development (1997) pamphlet, unpub., General Santos City, Philippines.

Agnew, J. 1998. *Geopolitics: Re-visioning world politics.* Routledge: London and New York.

———. 1999. Mapping political power beyond state boundaries: Territory, identity, and movement in world politics. *Millennium: Journal of International Studies* 28, no. 3: 499–521.

Ahmad, A. 1982. Class and colony in Mindanao. *Southeast Asia Chronicle* 82.

Allworth, D. 1984. Discussion notes, tropical rainforest campaign, 20 June.

Almeda, C. 1998. Globalization and mining. Paper presented at the International Conference on Mining Transnational Corporations, Manila, Philippines, November 14–16.

Alston, D. 1992. Transforming a movement: People of color unite at summit against environmental racism. *Sojourner* 21: 30–31. See *http://www.ejrc.cau.edu/ejinthe21century.htm.*

Amin, A. 1994. *Post-Fordism: A reader.* Oxford, U.K.: Blackwell.

Amin, S. 1993. Social movements at the periphery. In *New social movements in the south,* ed. P. Wignaraja, 76–100. New Delhi: Vistaar Publications.

Anderson, R. 1988. *The power and the word: Language, power, and change.* London: Paladin Grafton Books.

Armed Propaganda Team. 1998. Mindanao, personal communication.

Arvanitakis, J., and S. Healy. 2000. S11 protests mark the birth of the third wave environmentalism. *Ecopolitics* 1, no. 1: 24–29.

Aylen, B. 2001. A critique of the Adelaide JAG/ENuFF group. Paper presented in Department of Geographical and Environmental Studies, University of Adelaide, October.

Bahuguna, V. 1990 *"The Chipko movement" in a space within the struggle.* New Delhi: Kali for Women.

Baker, S., K. Milton, and S. Yearly, eds. 1994. *Protecting the periphery: Environmental policy in peripheral regions of the European Union.* Frank Cass: London.

Banuri, T., and F. Apffel Marglin. 1993. *Who will save the forests?* London: Zed Books.

Baviskar, A. 1995. *In the belly of the river: Tribal conflicts over the development in the Narmada Valley.* Delhi: Oxford University Press.

Bell, S. 1995. The environment—a fly in the ointment. *Chain Reaction* 73–74: 30–33.

Bidwai, P., and A. Vanaik. 2000. *New nukes: India, Pakistan, and global nuclear disarmament.* Oxford, U.K.: Signal Books.

Blowers, A., and D. Lowry. 1997. Nuclear conflict in Germany: The wider context. *Environmental Politics* 6, no. 3: 148–155.

Bonefeld, W., and J. Holloway. 1991. Introduction: Post-Fordism and social form. In *Post-Fordism and social form: A Marxist debate on the Post-Fordist state*, ed. W. Bonefeld and J. Holloway. London: Macmillan.

Brand, K.-W. 1999. Dialtectics of institutionalism: The transformation of the environmental movement in Germany. *Environmental Politics* 8, no. 1: 35–58.

Brecher, J., T. Costello, and B. Smith. 2000. *Globalization from below: The power of solidarity.* Cambrige, Mass.: South End Press.

Broad, R. 1994. The poor and the environment: Friends or foe. *World Development* 22, no. 6: 811–822.

Broad, R., and J. Cavanagh. 1993. *Plundering paradise: The struggle for the environment in the Philippines.* Berkeley: University of California Press.

Bullard, R. 1990. *Dumping on Dixie.* Boulder, Colo.: Western Press.

Bullard, R. D. 1993a. Race and environmental justice in the United States. *Yale Journal of International Law* 18 (winter): 319–335.

———. 1993b. The threat of environmental racism. *Natural Resources and Environment* 7 (winter): 23–26, 55–56. See http://www.ejrc.cau.edu/ejinthe21century.htm.

Cairns and Far North Queensland Environment Centre (CAFNEC). 1984. Cape Tribulation to Bloomfield Rd. blockade information sheet for site occupiers and support personnel, January, 2.

Calman, L. J. 1992. *Toward empowerment.* Boulder, Colo.: Westview Press.

Chatterjee, P., and M. Finger. 1994. *The earth brokers: Power, politics, and world development.* London: Routledge.

Chesters, G. 2001. The rebel colours of SA26: Social movement framework during the Prague IMF/WB protests. Paper presented to the ECPR Summer Conference, University of Kent, September.

Clarke, P. 1991. Adelaide as an aboriginal landscape. *Aboriginal History* 15, no. 1–2: 54–72.

Cockburn, A. 1995a. Wilderness Society new shame. *The Nation* 260, no. 7 (20 February): 227–228.

Cockburn, A. 1995b. Wilderness Society: The saga of shame continues. *The Nation* (6 March): 300.

Cohen, I., and J. Seed. 1984. In defense of Daintree. World Rainforest Report no.2, August newsletter produced by the Rainforest Information Centre.

Connelly, J., and G. Smith. 1999. *Politics and the environment: From theory to practice.* London and New York: Routledge.

Connolly, B. 1981. *The fight for the Franklin.* Sydney: Cassell.

Cooke, F. 1999. *The challenge of sustainable forests: Forest resource policy in Malaysia.* Honolulu: University of Hawaii Press.

Corpez, O. 1966. *The Philippines.* Englewood Cliffs, N.J.: Prentice Hall.

Coumans, C. 1995. Ideology, social movement organization, patronage, and resistance in the struggle of Marinduquenos against Marcopper. *Pilipinas* 24 (spring): 37–74.

Cove/Mallard Coalition. 1994. Cove Mallard: A first! Victory? www.wildrockies.org/cove/newnewz/1024new.

Della Porta, D., and D. Rucht. 2002. The dynamics of environmental campaigns. *Mobilization: Special Issue Comparative Environmental Campaigns* 7, no. 1 (February), ed. D. Della Porta and D. Rucht, San Diego State University, California.

Diani, M. 1992. The concept of a social movement. *Sociological Review* 40, no. 1: 1–25.

Diani, M., and P. Donati. 1999. Organizational change in Western European environmental groups: A framework for analysis. *Environmental Politics* 8, no. 1: 13–34.

Dobson, A. 1991. *The green reader.* London: Andre Deutsch.

Doherty, B. 2000. Manufactured vulnerability: Protest camp tactics. In *Direct action in British environmentalism,* ed. B. Doherty, M. Paterson, and B. Seel, 62–78. London: Routledge.

———. 2002a. Anti-roads movement. In *International encyclopedia of environmental politics,* ed. J. Barry and E. G. Frankland. London and New York: Routledge.

———. 2002b. *Ideas and actions in the green movement.* London: Routledge.

Doherty, B., A. Plows, and D. Wall. 2001. Comparing radical environmental activism in Manchester, Oxford, and North Wales. Paper for the workshop on Local Environmental Activism, European Consortium for Political Research Joint Sessions, Grenoble, 6–11 April.

Doherty, B., M. Paterson, and B. Seel, eds. 2000. *Direct action in British environmentalism.* London and New York: Routledge.

Dowie, M. 1994. The selling (out) of the greens. *The Nation,* 18 April, 514–518.

———. 1995a. *Losing ground: American environmentalism at the close of the twentieth century.* Cambridge, Mass., and London: MIT Press.

———. 1995b. The fourth wave: An opinion by Mark Dowie. *Mother Jones,* March/April, 34–36.

Doyle, T. 1989. Oligarchy in the conservation movement: Iron law or aluminium tendency? *Regional Journal of Social Issues* (summer): 24–28.

———. 1994. Direct action in environmental conflict in Australia: A re-examination of non-violent action. *Regional Journal of Social Issues* 28: 1–13

———. 1998. Sustainable development and Agenda 21: The secular bible of global free markets and pluralist democracy. *Third World Quarterly* 19, no. 4: 771–786.

———. 1999. Roundtable decision-making in arid lands under conservative governments: The emergence of wise use. In *Environmental Policy 2,* ed. K. Walker and K. Crowley, 122–141. Sydney: University of New South Wales Press.

———. 2000a. The campaign to save the wet tropics. In *Securing the wet tropics,* ed. G. Mc Donald and M. Lane, 103–116. Sydney: Federation Press.

———. 2000b. *Green power: The environment movement in Australia.* Sydney: UNSW Press.

———. 2002. Environmental campaigns against mining in Australia and the Philippines. *Mobilization: An International Journal* 7, no. 1: 29–42.

———. 2004a. An agenda for environmental security in the Indian Ocean region. In *Geopolitical orientations and security in the Indian Ocean,* ed. D. Rumley and S. Chaturvedi, 154–171. New Delhi: South Asian Pubs.

———. 2004b. Dam disputes in Australia and India: Appreciating differences in struggles for sustainable development. In *India and Australia: Issues and opportunities,* ed. D. Gopal and D. Rumley, 365–384. New Delhi: Authors Press.

Doyle, T., and A. Kellow. 1995. *Environmental politics and policy-making in Australia.* Sydney: Macmillan.

Doyle, T. (Chair, The Public Inquiry into Uranium), and D. Matthews (Coordinator, Nuclear Issues Coalition). 1998. Playing green politics outside the state: The public inquiry into uranium. Paper presented at the Ecopolitics XI Conference, University of Melbourne.

Doyle, T., and D. McEachern. 1998. *Environment and politics.* London and New York: Routledge.

———. 2001. *Environment and politics.* 2nd ed. London and New York: Routledge.

Eckersley, R. 1992. *Environment and political theory: Toward an ecocentric approach.* London: UCL Press.

Edelman, M. 1972. *The symbolic uses of politics.* Urbana: University of Illinois Press.

Epstein, B. 2001. Anarchism and the Anti-Globalization Movement. *Monthly Review* 53, no. 4 (September): 1.

Fox, W. 1990. *Toward a transpersonal ecology: Developing new foundations for environmentalism.* Boston, Mass.: Shambala.

Frankland, E. 1995. Germany: The rise and fall and recovery of Die Grunen. In *The green challenge,* ed. D. Richardson and C. Rootes. London and New York: Routledge.

Friends of the Earth. 2001. Press release 19 March. Hastings Alliance launched.

Fuchs, D., and D. Rucht. 1994. Support for new social movements in five Western European countries. In *A new Europe? Social change and political transformation,* ed. C. Rootes and H. Davis, 86–111. London: UCL Press.

Gundjehmi Aboriginal Corporation (GAC). 1999. Jabiluka: A briefing paper, Jabiru, NT 0886.

Goldsmith, E., and N. Hildyard. 1984. The politics of damming. *The Ecologist* 14, no. 5–6: 221–231.

Grainger, A. 1980. A hymn to the forest. Personal manuscript.

Gray, D. 1984. Quoted in the *Sydney Morning Herald,* 7 January 1984.

Greater Daintree National Park newsletter. 1984. No. 4: 3.

Green, J. 2001. Germany: Greens betray anti-nuclear movement. *Green Left Weekly* 444 (April): online at *www.geocities.com/jimgreen3/germangreens.*

Green, R. 1981. *The battle for the Franklin.* Sydney: Fontana.

———. 1984. Greenies act on Joh's land. *Sydney Morning Herald,* 7 January: 26.

Green, J. 2001. Germany:Greens betray anti-nuclear movement. *Green Left Weekly* 444 (April).

Griggs, S., and D. Howarth. 1999. New social movements and the politics of environmental protest: The campaign against Manchester Airport's second runway. Paper presented to the 1999 ECPR Joint Sessions of Workshops, March, Mannheim, Germany.

Griggs, S., D. Howarth, and B. Jacobs. 1998. Second runway at Manchester. *Parliamentary Affairs* 51, no. 3: 358.

Hay, P., and M. Haward. 1988. Comparative green politics: Beyond the European context? *Political Studies* 36: 433–448.

Hemstreet, L., and J. Kreilick. 1995. Defending the last big wild. www.wildrockies.org/care??/about/Defending.

Henry, D. 1984. Letter to A. Keto, 13 March.

Hill, R. 1984. Quoted in *Sydney Morning Herald,* 1 July, 26.

Hirsch, J. 1991. Fordism and Post-Fordism: The present social crisis and its consequences. In *Post-Fordism and social form: A Marxist debate on the Post-Fordist state,* ed. W. Bonefeld and J. Holloway. London: Macmillan.

———. 1998. A party is not a movement and vice versa. In *The German Greens: Paradox between movement and party,* ed. M. Mayer and J. Ely, 180–190. Philadelphia: Temple University Press.

Holloway, G. 1990. The organizational structure of the wilderness conservation and anti-nuclear movements in Australia. Ph.D. thesis, Department of Sociology, University of Tasmania.

Hrichak, M. (2001) *Strength lies in quiet work: forging coalitions and change in the Philippines, The World and I,* June, no. 6, pp. 208–209.

Hutchings, V. 1994. Support your local village green. *New Statesman and Society* 7, no. 293 (March 11): 20–22.

Hutton, D., and L. Connors. 1999. *The history of the Australian environmental movement.* Sydney: Cambridge University Press.

International Fact Finding Mission (IFFM). 1999. Uniting Church of the Philippines and BAYAN, November, concerning operation of Western Mining Corporation in Mindanao.

Indigenus Pilipinas. 2000. WMC to quit the Philippines: Celebration and protest. Press release, Sydney, 19 May.

Inez Ainger, K. 1999. The meek fight for their inheritance. *Guardian Weekly,* 21 February: 23.

Inglehart, R. 1997. *The silent revolution.* New Haven, Conn.: Princeton University Press.

International Union for the Conservation of Nature and Natural Resources for the World Heritage Committee. 1984. The world's greatest natural areas: An indicative inventory of natural sites of World Heritage quality. Report from Switzerland.

Jesinghausen, M. 1995. General election to the German Bundestag on 16 October 1994: Green pragmatists in Conservative embrace or a new era for Green party democracy. *Environmental Politics* 4, no. 1 (spring): 108–114.

Johnston, H., E. Larana, and J. Garfield, eds. 1995. New social movements: From ideology to identity. *Social Forces* 73, no. 4 (June): 163–165.

Johnstone, E. 1985. *The Australian,* 11 March: 1–2.

Joppke, C. 1992. Explaining cross-national variations of two anti-nuclear movements: A political process perspective. *Sociology* 26, no. 2: 311–321.

Kalland, A., and G. Persoon, eds. 1997. *Environmental movements in Asia.* Richmond: Curzon.

Karan, P. P. 1994. Environmental movements in India. *Geographical Review* 84, no 1 (January): 32–42.

Kelly, P. 2000. Global is good, lie e-business: The human face of the Davos Economic Forum, *The Australian,* 2 February: 13.

Kerin, R. 1998. Correspondence with T. Doyle, 24 April 1998: 1.

Keto, A. 1984. Report to her network members, RCSQ report, 12 September: 1–2.

Kitschelt, H. P. 1986. Political opportunity structures and political protest: Anti-nuclear movements in four democracies. *British Journal of Political Science* 16: 57–85.

Klein, A. 2000 Political participation and protest mobilization in the era of globalization. *Forschungsjournal Neue SozialeBewegungen* 13, no. 4 (December): 88–90.

Koopmans, R., and J. W. Duyvendak. 1995. The political construction of the nuclear energy issue and its impact on the mobilization of anti-nuclear movements in Western Europe. *Social Problems* 42, no. 2 (May): 235–251.

Krishna, S. 1996. *Environmental politics: People's lives and development choices.* New Dehi: Sage.

LaDuke, Winona. 1994. Native Environmentalism. *Cultural Survival Quarterly* 17, no. 4.

Lamb, R. 1996. *Promising the Earth.* London and New York: Routledge.

Lane, M. 1997. The importance of planning context: The wet tropics case. *Environmental and Planning Law Journal* (October): 368–377.

Langton, M. 1998. *Burning questions: Emerging environment issues for indigenous peoples in northern Australia.* Darwin, Northern Territory: Centre for Indigenous, National, and Cultural Resource Management.

Legge, K. 1985. Backlash fear stopped Daintree action. *The Age,* 4 April.

Lester, J. (1998) Looking backward to see ahead: the evolution of environmental politics and policy, 1890–1998, *Forum for Applied Research and Public Policy,* winter, v. 13, 14, pp. 30–37.

Liane. 1984. Comments on the Rainforest Conservation Society's submission to the Australian Heritage Commission. Quoted in RCSQ Newsletter, no. 14 (October).

Lindblom, C. 1977. *Politics and markets: The world's political-economic system.* New York: Basic Books.

Lisle, I. 1985. Coordinator of QCC retail outlet, personal communication, 3 November.

Lowe, P., and J. Goyder. 1983. *Environmental groups in politics.* London and Boston: Allen and Unwin.

Lowe, P., and S. Ward, eds. 1998. *British environmental policy and Europe.* London: Routledge.

Mariotte, M. 1997. The siege of Gorleben. *The Third Opinion: Australia's Independent Quarterly Energy Journal* (autumn): 3–6.

Marks, G., and D. McAdam. 1996. Social movements and the changing structure of political opportunity in the European Union. *Western European Politics* 19, no. 2 (April): 249–278.

Martin, B. 1984. Environmentalism and electoralism. *The Ecologist* 14, no. 3: 110–118.

Martin, T. 2001. Not easy being green. *Europe* 403 (February): 22–24.

May, R. 1987. A perspective from Mindanao. In *The Philippines under Aquino,* ed. P. Krinks. Canberra: Australian Development Studies Network.

———. 1989. The Moro movement in the southern Philippines. In *Politics of the future,* ed. C. Jennett and R. Stewart, 321–339. Melbourne: Macmillan.

Mayer, M., and J. Ely, eds. 1998. *The German Greens: Paradox between movement and party.* Philadelphia: Temple University Press.

McCully, P. 1998. *Silenced rivers: The ecology and politics of large dams.* Hyderabad, New Delhi: Orient Longman Limited.

Mehta, G. 1993. *A river sutra.* London: Minerva.

Menotti, V. 1999. Forest destruction and globalization. *The Ecologist* 29, no. 2 (May/June): 180–181.

Mineral Policy Institute et al. 2002. *Moving mountains.* Sydney: MPI Press.

Minerals Policy Institute. 1998. *Glossy reports, grim reality: Examining the gap between a mining company's social and environmental record and its public relations campaigns.* Sydney: MPI Press.

Mittleman, J. 2000. *The globalization syndrome: Transformation and resistance.* Princeton, N.J.: Princeton University Press.

Moody, R. 1996. Mining the world: The global reach of Rio Tinto Zinc. *The Ecologist* 26, no. 2 (March/April): 46–52.

Moyo, S., P. O'Keefe, and N. Middleton. 1993. *The tears of the crocodile: From Rio to reality in the developing world.* London: Pluto Press.

Mudd, G. 2000. Personal correspondence to D. Noonan, Australian Conservation Foundation, 3 May.

Newman, P. 2000. Theoretical and methodological issues relating to boundaries. Paper presented at Rethinking Boundaries: Geopolitics, Identities, and Sustainability Conference, University of Panjab, India, 20–24 February.

Newman, P., and J. Kenworthy. 1992. *Winning back the cities.* Sydney: Australian Consumers Association and Pluto Press.

Noonan, C. 1999. Out of sight, out of mind. *Habitat.* February special supplement. Melbourne, Australia.

Oko, D. 1996. War and peace in the woods. *Missoula Independent,* 18–24 April, 11.

Orzanski, R. 2000. Personal communication, 11 November.

Paige, S. 1998. The "greening" of government (environmental movement gains power in the U.S.). *Insight on the News.*

Papadakis, E. 1998. *Historical dictionary of the green movement.* Lanham, Md.: Scarecrow Press.

Pichardo, N. 1997. New social movements: A critical review. *Annual Review of Sociology* 23: 411–431.

Plane, T. 2001. City dry zone a simplistic, racist response to problem. *City Messenger* (Adelaide), 4 April: 4.

Prince, J., and K. Denison. 1992. Launching a new business ethic: The environment as a standard operating procedure. *Industrial Management* 34, no. 6: 11E.

Princen, T., and M. Finger. 1994. *Environmental NGOs in world politics: Linking the local to the global.* London and New York: Routledge.

Pybus, C. 1990. *The rest of the world is watching.* Sydney: Pan Macmillan.

Queensland Conservation Council (QCC). 1986. Conservation policy, Brisbane, July.

Quantum Market Research. 1984. Greater Daintree National Park: Developing and promotional strategy. *Qualitative Research Report* (May): 1.

Rawcliffe, P. 1995. Making inroads: Transport policy and the British environmental movement. *Environment* 37, no. 3: 16–32.

———. 1998. *Environmental pressure groups in transition.* London and New York: Routledge.

RCSQ. 1984. Study of the conservation significance of the wet tropics of north-east Queensland. Prepared for the Australian Heritage Commission

Richards, L. 1997. *Western mining in the Philippines.* Sydney: Indigenous Filipinos Press.

Richardson, D., and C. Rootes, eds. 1995. *The Green challenge: The development of Green parties in Europe.* London and New York: Routledge.

Roberts, G. K. 1999. Developments in the German Green party. *Environmental Politics* 8, no. 3: 147–152.

Rohde, M. 1999. A comparative analysis of the anti-roads movement of Britain with similar movements in South East Asia. Paper presented in the Department of Geographical and Environmental Studies at the University of Adelaide.

Rohrshneider, R. 1991. Public opinion toward environmental groups in western Europe: One movement or two? *Social Science Quarterly* 72, no. 2: 251–266.

Rootes, C. 1995. Environmental consciousness, institutional structures, and political competition in the formation and development of green parties. In *The green challenge: The development of green politics in Europe,* ed. D. Richardson and C. Rootes. London and New York: Routledge.

———. 1999. *Environmental movements.* London: Frank Cass.

———. 2000. Environmental protest in Britain, 1988–1997. In *Direct action in British environmentalism,* ed. B. Doherty, M. Paterson, and B. Seel. London and New York: Routledge.

Rootes, C., and A. Miller. 2000. The British environmental movement: Organizational field and network of organizations. Paper presented to the workshop Environmental Organizations in Comparative Perspective, ECPR Joint Sessions, Copenhagen, 14–19 April.

Rootes, C., B. Seel, and D. Adams. 2000. The old and the new: British environmental organizations from conservatism to radical ecologism. Paper presented to the workshop Environmental Organizations in Comparative Perspective, ECPR Joint Sessions, Copenhagen, 14–19 April.

Routledge, P. 1993. *Terrains of resistance: Nonviolent social movements and the contestation of place in India.* Westport, Conn.: Praeger Publishers.

Roy, A. 1999. *The greater common good.* Bombay: India Book Distributors.

Rucht, D. 1999. The profile of recent environmental protest in Germany. Paper presented at the European Consortium of Political Research, Mannheim University, 27–31 March.

Rucht, D., and J. Roose. 1999. The German environmental movement at a crossroads. *Environmental Politics* 8, no. 1: 59–80.

Rudig, W. 1992. *Green politics two.* Edinburgh: Edinburgh University Press.

Rutten, R. 2000. High-cost activism and the worker household: Interests, commitment, and the costs of revolutionary activism in a Philippine plantation region. *Theory and Society* 29: 215–252.

Select Panel of the Public Inquiry into Uranium. 1997. *The report of the public enquiry into uranium.* Adelaide: CCSA, November: 1–40.

Sheth, P. 1997. *Environmentalism: Politics, ecology, and development.* Jaipur, New Delhi: Ravat Publications.

Shiva, V. 1989. *Staying alive: Women, ecology, and development.* London: Zed Books.

———. 1991. *Ecology and the politics of survival: Conflicts over natural resources in India.* Tokyo: United Nations University Press.

———. 1992. The green movement in Asia. *Research in Social Movements, Conflicts and Change,* supplement 2: 195-215.

Shripad. 2000. Interview at NBA headquarters, Vadadora, Gujarat, 24 March.

Simms, M. 1989. Democracy, freedom, and the women's movement in the Philippines. In *Politics of the future,* ed. C. Jennett and R. Stewart, 340–354. Melbourne: Macmillan.

Simpson, A. 1998. Buddhist responses to globalization; Thailand and ecology: The Yadana gas pipeline. Paper presented at the Sixth World Wilderness Congress, Bangalore, India, 24–29 October.

Singh, A. M., and N. Burra. 1993. *Women and wasteland development in India.* New Delhi and London: Sage Publications.

Singh, J. 2000. Transboundary conservation in the African context: A threat to sovereignty? Paper presented at Rethinking Boundaries: Geopolitics, Identities, and Sustainability Conference, University of Panjab, India, 20–24 February.

Sison, J., and J. De Lima. 1998. *Philippine economy and politics.* Manilla: Aklatng Bayan Publishing House.

Skullerud, J. 2001. Personal correspondence with the author, 12, 15 June.

Snow, D., ed. 1992. *Inside the environmental movement: Meeting the leadership challenge.* Washington, D.C., and Covelo, Calif.: Island Press.

Stannard, M. 1985. Personal communication, 2 May.

Stern, B. 1997. The next last stand: A brief history of Cove/Mallard, 4 October. *www.wild rockies.org/care/about/Next_to_last_stand.*

Summy, R., and M. Saunders. 1986. *A history of the peace movement in Australia.* Armidale, N.S.W.: University of New England.

Sustran Network. 2000. *Moving towards a better urban transport.* A report from the Sustran Network, Bangkok, Thailand.

Swain, A. 1997. Democratic consolidation? Environmental movements in India. *Asian Survey* 37 (September).

Swami, P. 1994. Narmada Diary. *Frontline,* India, 30 December: 116.

Szabo, M. 1994. Greens, cabbies, and anti-communists: Collective action during the regime transition in Hungary. In *New social movements: From ideology to identity,* ed. E. Larana et al. Philadelphia: Temple University Press.

Taylor, B. 1991. The religion and politics of Earth First! *The Ecologist* 21, no. 6: 258–266.

Thakkar, H. 2000. Centre for Water Policy, New Delhi, interview, 17 March.

Thompson, P. 1984. *Bob Brown of the Franklin River.* Sydney and London: Allen and Unwin.

Tighe, P. 1992. Hydroindustrialization and conservation policy in Tasmania. In *Australian environmental policy,* ed. K. Walker, 124–155. Sydney: University of New South Wales Press.

———. 1986. Even high court justices have environmental values. Paper presented at the Conference of the Australasian Political Studies Association, Brisbane.

Townsville Bulletin. 1985. Editorial, plan gives best of both worlds, 11 March.

Toyne, P., and R. Johnston. 1991. Reconciliation or the new dispossession. *Habitat Australia* (Australian Conservation Foundation) 19, no. 3 (June).

Truelove, C. 1985. CTCC, personal interview, 7 May.

United Press International. 2000. Germany to shut nuclear plants, 16 June.

———. 2001. German nuclear waste shipment arrives, 29 March.

Vallentine, J. 1989. Defending the fragile planet: The role of the peace activist. In *Politics of the future: The role of social movements,* ed. C. Jennett and R. Stewart, 56–75. South Melbourne: Macmillan.

Van der Heijden, H. 1997. Political opportunity structures and the institutionalization of the environmental movement. *Environmental Politics* 6, no. 4: 25–50.

Van Houtum, H. 2000. European geographical theories on borders in the European Union. Paper presented at Rethinking Boundaries: Geopolitics, Identities, and Sustainability Conference, University of Panjab, India, 20–24 February.

Wall, D. 1999. *Earth First! and the anti-roads movement.* London and New York: Routledge.

Warwick, H. 1998. Point of order. *Guardian Weekly,* 18 April: 13.

Washington, H. 1984. Letter to A. Keto, 15 November.

Waud, P. 1984. Daintree campaign report, Brisbane, 20 March: 3.

Welsh, I. 2001. Re-framing social movements: Margins, meanings, and governance. Paper presented to the ECPR, Environmental Politics Steam, University of Kent, September.

White, S. 1991. *Political theory and postmodernism.* Cambridge, U.K.: Cambridge University Press.

Wilderness Action Group. 1984. *The Trials of Tribulation.* Kajola: Mossman.

Wilderness Society. 1983. *The Franklin blockade.* Hobart: Wilderness Society.

Wilderness Society. 1985. Rainforest rescue, campaign pamphlet, Brisbane, 27 November.

Williams, E. 1998. Tampakan: Another Bougainville in the making. Foreign Correspondent, Australian Broadcasting Commission, Sydney, October.

World Commission on Dams. 2000. Final report, Netherlands, November.

World Information Service on Energy. 1995. First castor in Gorleben stored (online at www .antenna.nl/wise/432/4266).

———. 1996. Second (and last?) castor to Gorleben (online at *www.antenna.nl/wise/452/4476*).

INDEX

ABOUT THE AUTHOR

Timothy Doyle is Reader in Politics in the School of History and Politics at the University of Adelaide, where he teaches and researches politics and environmental studies. He is also a dedicated environmental and human rights activist.